GENDER, LINEAGE, AND ETHNICITY
IN SOUTHERN AFRICA

Women and men harvesting and bagging maize
on agricultural cooperative in Zimbabwe.

*Susan Lastarré C.
January 1999*

Gender, Lineage, and Ethnicity in Southern Africa

Jean Davison

WestviewPress
A Division of HarperCollinsPublishers

Published in 1997 in the United States of America by Westview Press, 5500 Central Avenue, Boulder, Colorado 80301-2877, and in the United Kingdom by Westview Press, 12 Hid's Copse Road, Cumnor Hill, Oxford OX2 9JJ.

Library of Congress Cataloging-in-Publication Data
Davison, Jean, 1937–
    Gender, lineage, and ethnicity in southern Africa / Jean Davison.
        p.   cm.
    Includes bibliographical references and index.
    ISBN 0-8133-2759-8. — 0-8133-2760-1 (pbk)
        1. Ethnicity—Zambezi River Region.   2. Clans—Zambezi River
Region.   3. Matrilineal kinship—Zambezi River Region.
4. Patrilineal kinship—Zambezi River Region.   5. Sex role—Zambezi
River Region.   6. Zambezi River Region—Ethnic relations.
7. Zambezi River Region—Social life and customs.   I. Title.
GN657.Z32D38   1997
305.8´009679—dc20   96-30267
                                                                                            CIP

The paper used in this publication meets the requirements of the American National Standard for Permanence of Paper for Printed Library Materials Z39.48-1984.

10   9   8   7   6   5   4   3   2   1

gender
ethnicity
Africa

land rights

Contents

Figures and Tables

Figures

Tables

Preface

This is a book about the confluence of gender, lineage ideology, and ethnicity in central southern Africa—a region that encompasses the length of the Zambezi River and its tributaries. The intertwining of gender and lineage over time within specific ethnic contexts is a primary concern. Gender is both the catalyst and the conveyor of lineage and descent differences in the region. The way that matriliny and patriliny and their attendant residence practices influence women's and men's access to and control over productive resources is at the base of this study.

Two sets of voices inform the inquiry: first, the perspectives of those most involved—the people whose daily lives are affected and those who have become the articulators of a particular state's needs; second, the interpretations of others, including missionaries, colonial administrators and, later, development practitioners.

Discussing the interrelationships of gender, lineage, and ethnicity without linking them to issues of underdevelopment through colonial capitalism and development in the postindependence period serves little purpose. Therefore, my ultimate concern is how attention to matrilineal and patrilineal ideologies as lived can further our knowledge of rural women's and men's needs, interests, and priorities and how this knowledge can in turn further development as empowerment rather than welfare and dependency.

The idea for this book came while I was running along a winding road through a rural village in Malawi early one morning; people were already in their fields, hoeing, removing rocks, and burning brush. Because I had come from an immersion in rural East Africa that spanned, off and on, twenty years, my lens was decidedly patrilineal. I expected to see women helping one another in their fields. I did not—women worked alone, with older children, or with their husbands. This initial brush with matrilineal southern Malawi led to questions about how matriliny influences gender relations of production. I had three years of running every morning to make observations, carry out a small survey on labor allocation, and share my findings with Malawians at the University of Malawi, where I was teaching sociology and coordinating a master's degree program. A return visit in 1994 enabled me to witness Malawi's transition to democracy and to relate what I was witnessing to my observations about the gendered state in the region.

In the meantime I had made one visit to Mozambique in 1986 and another to Zimbabwe the same year. I managed to visit Mozambique again in 1992 and Zimbabwe several times, collecting data and evidence on the difference that lineage makes in the way gender is structured and restructured in various groups in these two countries. Much of my material on Zambia comes through the other two countries and through the Zambian Association for Research and Development (ZARD). In the process of data collection, three women in Mozambique were particularly helpful and deserve thanks—Anastacia Guimaraes of the Organization of Mozambican Women (OMM), Teresina de Silvia of the Ministry of Health, and Mrs. C. Moiyane, formerly deputy minister of foreign affairs. In Zimbabwe, Grace Chimonyo, who works with a seed company that supplies women farmers; Bertha Msora of Ranche House College; and Rudo Gaidzanwa of the Sociology Department, University of Zimbabwe, were helpful. In Malawi, among those professional colleagues who helped to push my thinking were Professor Kings Phiri, head of the History Department, and Professor J.A.K. Kandawire, former head of the Sociology Department. In Zambia, my initial contact with Maud Mutemba was helpful.

The manuscript for this book was written while I was a visiting scholar at the Institute for Research on Women and Gender at Stanford University between September 1992 and December 1993. I am grateful to the staff and other visiting scholars, particularly Bernice Lott, Mary Felstiner, and Yung-hee Kwon, for their support and comradeship during my residence. The eclectic environment of the institute encourages the exchange of interdisciplinary ideas and methods and furthered my work. I am especially indebted to Iris Litt, the institute's director, for her interest in my research activities in Africa and her personal support; to Sherri Matteo for her suggestions; to Sally Schroeder, Gini Gould, and Lorraine Macchello for expediting all the tiny details of my stay; and to Pam Mosher, who processed the references.

Many thanks.

Jean Davison

1

Introduction:
Lineage, Descent,
and Ethnicity

Who gets access to land and labor in Africa is an emotive issue. Lineage ideologies with their accompanying descent patterns historically were used to justify the transfer of land from one generation to the next. At the heart of lineage is gender. In the majority of African societies men inherit, develop—often with the assistance of wives—and pass on land to their sons because these societies ascribe to patrilineal ideology. In the minority of societies that ascribe to matriliny, women inherit, develop, and bequeath land to their daughters and granddaughters. A few societies are bilineal: Lineage is traced through both sides, and daughters and sons benefit equally from inheritance. The amount and quality of land inherited varies depending on the size of the family, its class and economic resources, and the political environment.

Who has control over labor likewise varies. It is more often the case that males control female labor, but where matrilineal groups practice uxorilocal residence such that a husband moves to his wife's village at the time of marriage, women have rights to male labor. This gendered scenario was persistently contested by the colonial establishment.

Though lineage ideologies are often linked to ethnicity, in reality they hurdle historically constructed ethnic boundaries. In some cases a single group may include members that embrace opposing lineage ideologies, as in the case of the Tumbuka of Malawi, some of whom were patrilineal and others matrilineal in the early twentieth century. Lineage affiliation influ-

FIGURE 1.1   The central southern Africa region.   SOURCE: *Africa Report*
March–April 1989.

ences women's and men's opportunities for development differently depending on the lineage ideology that their group ascribes to at a particular
point in time. Characteristically, women in groups that are predominantly
matrilineal have been shortchanged by Western-initiated development programs.

In this book I look at how lineage ideologies are constructed and how
they change, including the way that lineage and the production of ethnicities became confounded under colonial rule. The book contributes to studies of gender by critically examining the way lineage ideologies construct
and deconstruct gender relations in various groups over time. I limit the
discussion to one geographical region where matrilineal and patrilineal ideologies coexist—the greater Zambezi River region of southern Africa. I
argue that lineage ideology continues to hold currency in this region,

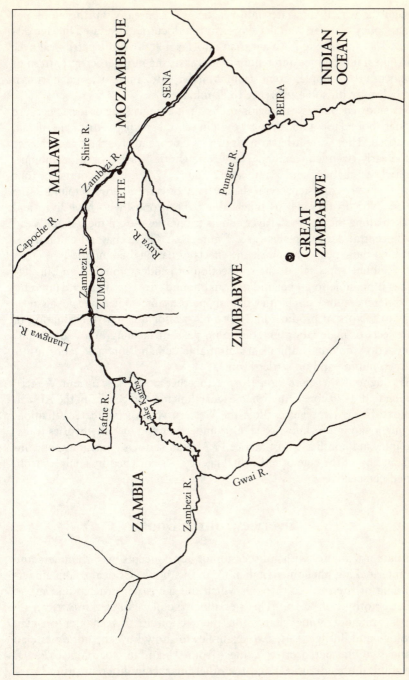

FIGURE 1.2   The Zambezi River region and tributaries.

though the way it translates into practice varies greatly. Furthermore, national policy planners and development interlocutors have used lineage differences as a wedge to push agrarian reforms that advocate patrilineal over matrilineal inheritance and tenure practices as the more efficient pattern of production.[1] Examples come from Malawi, Mozambique, and northern Zimbabwe, with some reference to Zambia.

My study encompasses a region rather than a single state or locale because the state boundaries that currently exist in central southern Africa are spatial, not social. They were arbitrarily drawn by Europeans for their convenience in the early twentieth century. These state entities, including Mozambique, Malawi, Zimbabwe, and Zambia (see Figure 1.1), are not consistent (nor were they ever consistent) with the diversity of cultural groups found in the region. Nor do they tell us much about the peoples who have lived and worked along the Zambezi River and its tributaries—from the Indian Ocean to the central African plateau (see Figure 1.2). The social and cultural ties that bind these people minimize the effects of national boundaries.

A regional approach to the transection of gender, ethnicity, and lineage makes it possible to go beyond national boundaries to investigate interethnic differences and similarities that shape peasant women and men's relations to factors of production. It also allows for qualitative evaluation of the effects of male labor emigration on peasant farming in a region characterized by colonial capitalism's insatiable demand for male labor (especially in mining and on settler farms).

Throughout the discussion I bring together both African and Western scholars' ideas to conceptualize lineage, ethnicity, and gender in the African context. In my experience, often the Western voice gets greater attention, leaving a gap in our knowledge. Our understanding of how theories translate into and conflict with practice in African settings—including our understanding of the role of individual agency—is enriched by analyses from varied perspectives.

Overview of the Book

I initiate my inquiry with a discussion of key concepts used to understand the interlocking phenomena taken up in this book. Critical to our understanding of the process through which lineage is constructed and modified are notions of "clan." Theories about the place of clan in African societies are undergoing change. In the section in this chapter on clan ideology and lineage, I use two examples to show how the notion of clan changes. One perspective comes from Ugandan sociologist E. D. Mwamula-Lubandi (1992) and the other, markedly different, from historian David Newberry (1991). The fact that "clan," an organizing principle in many African societies, structures and maintains a particular set of social relationships at the same time that it is constantly being redefined and modified illustrates the tensions, ambiguities, and adaptive potential of such a concept. Encompassed within the clan ideal are assumptions about lineage as it pertains to the evocation of genealogies, descent, and practices of inheritance. These lineage ideologies have historically served to legitimate the socioeconomic and political authority of either patriclans or matriclans in southern Africa.

The second term taken up in this chapter is ethnicity, a concept that has been troubling anthropologists and sociologists for a long time and over which there is little agreement (Comaroff 1987a; Keefe 1989; Fox 1990). How ethnicity relates to African societies depends on one's understanding of ethnicity. A Euramerican concept, ethnicity has multiple and multidimensional meanings. It is not bounded or exclusionary except in its most reactionary political form. It acts as both process and structure depending on whether we are referring to the way in which a group comes to understand itself as a collectivity different from others (process) or as a set of relationships that is structurally ordered through social norms that are adhered to in varying degrees (structure) (Comaroff 1987a). In its most basic form, ethnicity is the cultural production of a collective public image (Fox 1990:4). It is an image that results from either external or internal production—"how people conceive of themselves or are conceived of by others, and how people live out and live with these conceptions" (Fox 1990:3). In colonial constructions of ethnicity, lineage and ethnicity converged.

Lineage, in its gendered form, affects women and men differently. The way that groups have ordered lineage and inheritance determines, in part, the position of women in these societies at any one time. Women in some matrilineal societies have had significant roles as sociopolitical leaders (Colson 1951; Ntara 1973; Mandala 1990), spiritual facilitators (Rangeley 1952; Ntara 1973; Schoffeleers 1980; Milimo 1986), and joint household heads (Hirschmann and Vaughan 1984; Mandala 1990; Davison 1992).[2] Women in matrilineal groups in Malawi, for instance, were in some cases village heads, clan leaders, or war leaders (Ntara 1973; Phiri, Vaughan, and Makuluni 1977; Mandala 1990). They continue to take on roles as village heads or clan leaders. These are options that have been less available to women in most patrilineal societies.

Implicated in lineage, then, is the construction of gender. In many African societies gender, as socially constructed, developed over a life span through a series of stages. It was, and still is, shaped either by initiation into adulthood or by parenthood. In matrilineal groups the initiation of pubescent girls was the critical ritual. In patrilineal groups, it was the initiation of boys. Childhood was viewed as an ambiguous period that became more en-gendered with time, as Chapter 2 illustrates. Although some attenuated form of initiation is practiced in many rural areas in the region, the tenets of Christianity and formal education have precluded initiations in others. Such rituals have largely disappeared in urban areas. Parenthood has become the dividing line between ambiguous childhood and gendered adult status.

Historically, females and males lived and often worked in distinct spatial arenas, carrying out different tasks. This arrangement has been described as complementary by some African scholars (e.g., Muchena 1979; Afonja 1986) and referred to as a "dual" or "parallel" sex/gender system by others (e.g., Okonjo 1976; Poewe 1981; Amadiume 1987). Yet in some parts of southern Africa where the basic unit of production in precapitalist times was the matrilineal hearthhold, women and men worked jointly in agricultural production (Mutemba 1982; Milimo 1986; Mandala 1990). In some places they still do. Gender relations of production have varied depending on the group, its lineage ideology, and the political-economic circumstances of the moment. Equally important, the gender roles defined by a society are not unequivocal. Males and females may assume the roles of the other gender in certain circumstances (Edgerton 1971; Oboler 1985; Amadiume 1987).

The way that gender intertwines with lineage influences the relationship between women and the means of production. This relationship also is contingent on periodic shifts generated by intercultural contact at many levels: precolonial contact between differing social groups in various relations of power; the trauma-ridden encounter between colonials and indigenous groups; and the postliberation struggles between politicized ethnic groups or nationalities for control over future development.

Examining the historical roots of shifting gender relations of production in groups ascribing to either matrilineal or patrilineal ideologies provides a context for understanding why women and men have experienced labor alienation differently. In Mozambique, matrilineal groups have predominated in the north (Niassa, Nampula, Tete, and Zambezia Provinces) and patrilineal have dominated in the south (Dos Santos 1940; Newitt 1973; Ferreira 1975). The effects of the Arab slave trade and Portuguese colonial capitalism on gender relations in preexisting patrilineal and matrilineal societies are taken up in Chapter 3. Prior to colonization, horticulturalists practiced extensive methods of agriculture that included shifting cultivation and fallowing. For households with sufficient resources, family labor was supplemented by slave labor (Weinrich 1982; White 1987; Mandala 1990). Slaves were procured through the spoils of war or the destitution of impoverished households. Arab traders and their coastal Swahili agents gave a new twist to the alienation of labor when they began trading in slaves for export to the Arabian peninsula and beyond. In collusion with indigenous leaders who sought trade goods and ammunition, the Arab traders took by force or through exchange Africans from weakened societies and then sold them into bondage.[3] Women as well as men were part of this captured potential labor force (Wright 1993).

In Malawi and eastern Zambia (formerly Nyasaland and Northern Rhodesia, respectively), matrilineal groups in many places were the norm prior to and at the time of British colonial penetration (Richards 1950; Colson 1962; Ntara 1973; Milimo 1986; Skjønsberg 1989; Mandala 1990). When the matrilineal (and variously matrilocal) practices of these groups became known to the androcentric, patrilineal Victorian male missionaries, settlers, and colonial administrators, the latter set about to modify these practices to ones more consistent with their own. It was a process that did not occur all at once but slowly and unevenly over time, as Chapter 4 makes clear. The reaction from local matrilineal groups was mixed. The extent to which virilocality became the practice rather than the exception and men acted to gain more control over family resources varied by ethnic group and within such groups.

In many rural areas in eastern and northern Zambia, matrilineal ideology persisted but virilocal residence and male control of resources became more pervasive with the penetration of capitalism (Richards 1982; Milimo 1986; Poewe 1981; Stromgaard 1985). However, in some parts of Northern Province, matriliny identified with uxorilocal residence practices has persisted in areas where agriculture has become only partially commoditized and most crops continue to be produced largely for family consumption. This pattern also remains dominant in rural areas of central and southern Malawi, where the intensification of postindependence capitalist production has affected the export-driven plantation sector to a much greater extent than it has affected the larger peasant sector; the latter is only partially tied to the market economy (Chisala and Mthindi 1989).

Zimbabwe (formerly Southern Rhodesia) has a smattering of matrilineal groups, such as the Gwembe (Zambezi Valley) Tonga, on its northern border. The Gwembe Tonga are related to the adjacent Plateau Tonga on Zambia's southern border. By and large, the current ethnic groups identified in Zimbabwe ascribe to patriliny, as do many of their neighbors to the south in Botswana, South Africa, Lesotho, and Swaziland. The major groups in Zimbabwe are the Shona-speaking population (including Manyika, Zezuru, Korekore, Kalanga) and the less populous Ndebele, Venda, and Shangaan in southern Zimbabwe. The patrilineal groups in Zimbabwe and matrilineal groups in Malawi and eastern Zambia provide a chance to weigh qualitatively the effects of British colonialism on groups with different lineage ideologies.

The experience of women and men under British colonial capitalism differed, as Chapter 4 illustrates. In nearly all cases, women's socioeconomic status dropped. The experience of men varied. Some gained from land acquisition, education, and training; others were forced to sell their labor locally or abroad. The effects of men's emigration on their families varied. In matrilineal families where women held land and recruited and allocated labor for agricultural production, men's roles were peripheralized.

With increased missionization and settlement in the latter part of the nineteenth century in the British colonies and even earlier in Portuguese East Africa, women and men began losing ground to Europeans bent on claiming the most fertile land for mission stations and agricultural "development." As the various Christian denominations carved out physical spheres of influence, land thought to be "idle," which in reality fell under the control of particular dominant clans, was taken for mission stations (Newitt 1973; White 1987; Hara 1991). The process of land alienation accelerated with the arrival of European settlers and Afrikaners from South Africa who were wedded to the notion of enhancing their economic status by growing cash-value crops for export. What the settlers lacked, however, was labor to work the vast tracts of land they possessed.

Even as the slave trade was being abolished, a new form of labor alienation arose. With the entrenchment of colonial regimes from Portuguese East Africa to the Rhodesias, local colonial administrators were advised by their superiors in Europe of the need to raise revenue locally to support their growing semiautonomous colonial infrastructures. The pivotal strategy for meeting these revenue demands was a hut tax—the burden to fall on indigenous Africans in each colony. The tax was designed to support services that primarily benefited colonial administrators, missionaries, and settler producers while solving the problem of labor shortages in the colonies (Mondlane 1983; Mutemba 1982; Isaacman and Isaacman 1983; Gaidzanwa 1988; Mandala 1990).

African families were forced to pay the tax either by indenturing their male family members to work as contract labor (e.g., *chibalo* in Mozambique) or by raising the cash payment through the alienated labor of male family members (e.g., *thangata* in Malawi). As a result, women in these families either carried a double work burden or solicited male labor from outside the family. At the same time, women who controlled land either directly or indirectly found themselves with a dwindling, less fertile land base on which to raise food crops for their families. Women in patrilineal and matrilineal groups were affected by these events in different ways, as Chapter 4 illustrates. However, the increased pressure for male labor in mining operations and on settler farms led to a pervasive pattern of male emigration that affected women in both matrilineal and patrilineal groups.

Even though the dominant actors affecting gender relations of production in agriculture have changed from colonial administrators to national administrators, the processes that initiated and perpetuated male bias have remained fairly entrenched, as Chapter 5 suggests. In Malawi and Zambia,

Western-educated (male) elites took the reins of government, and women were virtually ignored in the quest for nation building and economic development even though women in both countries continued to hold key roles in development as agricultural producers.

In Mozambique, women participated in defense forces with men in the liberation struggle that resulted in independence in 1975. Part of the promise of socialist transformation initiated by the Front for the Liberation of Mozambique (FRELIMO) was gender equity; women were to have a major role in decisionmaking at all levels. The extent to which this strategy succeeded is analyzed using a case study of an agricultural cooperative in Sofala. The case is compared with the experience of a similar cooperative in "socialist" Zimbabwe in the mid-1980s.

Like women in Mozambique, Zimbabwean women played an active role in their liberation struggle. Given that role, Zimbabwe's women were determined to be included in the fruits of liberation. The new nationalist state complied, rhetorically, by recognizing women's central role in development and the need to improve women's status. In practice, however, the state has dragged its heels in enforcing laws that were designed to give women greater equality with men.

Women's specific access to and control over various forms of labor has not been adequately assessed within the context of differences in lineage and marriage patterns. Governments and donors have failed to acknowledge intragender differences in access to and control over land in matrilineal and patrilineal societies, differences that in turn affect the gendered control of crops grown for food as distinguished from crops grown for cash. These issues are taken up in Chapter 6 with examples from Zambia and Malawi. In that chapter I also compare state-sponsored cooperatives in Mozambique and Zimbabwe to assess the extent to which gender equity was achieved in the decade after independence.

The processes through which states in the region have perpetuated gender bias have been unwittingly encouraged by development donor agencies; they have assumed, until very recently, that neither ethnic differences nor gender affect the outcome of development. The role of the international community (bilateral and multilateral donors) in defining women's place in development varies according to the constellation of agencies that operates within a particular state. I use Malawi as a case study to examine how donors have negotiated with the state to craft policies that advance girls' and women's opportunities for advancement. I use Zimbabwe to examine donor agencies' reliance on nongovernmental organizations for collaboration; these organizations, rather than the state, have been the major actors for addressing gender inequities in that country. The extent to which development agencies have addressed women's strategic needs for greater empowerment is central. In view of the assumptions made by development agencies regarding matriliny, Chapter 6 concludes with a plea for the right of people in matrilineal societies in the region to be heard and their preferences for matrilineal production and inheritance respected as an alternative to patrilineal production.

Theories of Clan

The problem with theorizing about African realities is that we run into the barriers of Western theory as authority based on our own cultural experience. In recent efforts to deconstruct some of these theories, an effort has been made to reevaluate African realities as lived historically and currently (e.g., Feierman 1990; Werbner 1991; Skjønsberg 1989). However, within Africa, scholars' ability to be involved in the deconstruction process and in building new theories based on concepts that come from their particular experiences is constrained by several factors. These include the limitations that African university researchers face in terms of scarce financial and other resources and in accessing international publishing houses and journals. The ongoing debates over ethnicity and lineage ideology would benefit from increased African input.

We need new concepts that better describe what we see. As Barnett and Silverman have suggested, the assumption of Western scholars that "a language of description and analysis exists which can make sense out of other peoples' social formations through using the same terms as one uses for one's own [society]" creates liabilities of interpretation (1979:6). We homologize African social experience in terms of our own. To use Barnett and Silverman's phrase, we create "categories of convenience" to help us make sense of the particularities that exist within a global framework (1979:8). Ideological constructs such as clan and lineage are "categories of convenience" used to describe and explain variations in African social relationships. But ideologies have their ambiguities, as others have pointed out (see Hogan 1980; Marks 1986; Amadiume 1987; Mannathoko 1992; Ekejiuba 1995).

In linking clan with ideology, I use two dimensions of ideology that apply while acknowledging that ambiguities do occur. The first is ideology as lived and the second is ideology as a legitimating power. I am particularly interested in the way that various ideological constructions—of clan, of lineage, of ethnicity—"articulate with one another" in the process of everyday living (Barnett and Silverman 1979:15). At the same time, I recognize, as Bloch has pointed out, that "by reference to a transcendental order, which is defined as an ultimate ideal," ideology becomes a legitimating force (1987:335). Clan and lineage ideologies, despite their ambiguities, act as legitimating social forces, as will become clear shortly.

Two theories of clan inform my discussion. One is the notion of clan as a solidarity unit with specific functions (Mwamula-Lubandi 1992). The other is the notion of clan making as a process affected by larger historical processes (Newberry 1991). The first theory, generated within Africa, seeks to explain the significance of clan as a social unit appropriate for motivating rural development. The second, generated externally, seeks to explain how the ideal of clan has changed over time as a result of historical events and how it continues to change with new inputs.

Clan as Solidarity Unit

In describing what he refers to as *group imago*, Ugandan sociologist E. D. Mwamula-Lubandi theorizes that a group or organization visualizes its existence through a dynamic set of relationships among its members (1992:25). Critical to these relationships are bonds of clan. Clan refers to a common descent group through which organizing relations are identified and maintained (18). But clan also has symbolic capital in the form of ancestral names, totems, and "other clan-formation criteria" that reinforce one another to keep "the essence of clan identity alive and operating" (20).

A Zimbabwean woman who aided guerrilla fighters in the war for liberation gave details about her background that illustrate the importance of clan as a factor of social organization: "My father was born in Wedza in Ruzane's kraal—Ruzane himself is of Rozwi origin but my father is of the Mbire clan, of the house of Choto" (Mushore in Staunton 1990). A Kenyan schoolgirl was more explicit: "My clan refers to where my father came from. Even my oldest sister is called Wanjiku, which means 'of the Unjiku Clan.' My sister is named for my father's clan. The clan is still important to the Agikuyu, and sometimes, when something has to be decided—for example, about land or even *ruracio* (bridewealth)—the members will call a meeting" (Davison 1989:189).

Networks of relations are the tapestry through which clan and lineage are sustained in African societies. Every member of a group theoretically is expected to know basic information about his or her heritage (Mwamula-Lubandi 1992). Clan may act as a means of identifying where people come from and to whom they are related by tracing back to common ancestors—what Werbner, with reference to the Kalanga of Zimbabwe, calls "starting from the root" (1991:83). In some cases clan names come from the group's progenitors and in others they are derived from particular characteristics associated with a group's common history.

Malawian historian Samuel J. Ntara (1973) maintains that clan names of the Chewa arose as a result of distinguishing characteristics or as nicknames given by others to particular women or men who were the progenitors. According to Chewa oral history, two of the original Chewa clans, the

Phiri and the Banda, took their names from a set of circumstances related to an early migration. Phiri (meaning "hill") referred to those people who slept on top of a hill during a migration in search of food; Banda ("those who tread grass under their feet") referred to those who slept at the foot of the hill (Ntara 1973:7).

The significance of clan varies by group. Mitchell (1956) claims that before Europeans came into southern Malawi, each member of the Yao took the clan name of his or her mother but that the Yao had only a "vague tradition" of a common clan ancestress. Clan names were not commonly invoked at the time of Mitchell's research in the late 1940s, and he hypothesizes that many of the names were borrowed from the Chewa with whom they intermixed (1956:70). It was membership in a clan that brought affinity and forged obligations and responsibilities among the Yao in the 1940s.

Though the basic relational unit in African societies is the family, as Mwamula-Lubandi argues, the basic "solidarity" unit is the clan. "Clan-based life styles and the clan itself have roots in being used as categories of perceptible things with real existence in clan-based societies" (Mwamula-Lubandi 1992:3).

In Mwamula-Lubandi's schema, the clan has three major dimensions, although in my opinion its functions reach beyond those he has outlined. The first is connected with the organization and implementation of initiation rites and the related formalization of age sets where they exist; the second is the control over rites of birth and death; and the third is control over medico-religious practices such as rain-calling and the rituals associated with the installation of a new leader that link him or her to past leaders and thus legitimate his or her position (Mwamula-Lubandi 1992).

Historically, among some groups both boys and girls were initiated at the same time before the community (Hobley 1910; Wilson 1957; Kenyatta 1968). In others, the genders were separated, and those observing and participating in the ritual event were the same sex as the initiate (Richards 1982; Turner 1962; La Fontaine 1977). Although modified because of pressure from missionaries, these rituals persisted through the colonial period. In urban southern Africa initiation rites no longer are practiced, but they continue to persist in attenuated form in many rural areas. They symbolize for those who participate in them what it means to be part of a particular clan and ethnic group (Banda 1984; Kapakasa 1990; Makambera 1992).

A similar observation can be made for birth and death rites with relation to their significance and practice. Among many groups, funeral and burial rites, especially, continue to be clan affairs in terms of the scheduling, organization, and significance for the participants. Clan elders are central to the planning of such events.

Clan leaders, who are responsible for moral guidance, may be either female or male (Colson 1951; Phiri, Vaughan, and Makuluni 1977; Mandala 1990). Even though colonial administrators supported the authority of male leaders and discouraged females from being leaders, women have emerged as clan leaders in some areas of postcolonial Malawi and northern Mozambique. Clan leaders with unusual spiritual powers historically acted as rain-callers (Rangeley 1952; Linden 1974; Ntara 1973; Schoffeleers 1984; Feierman 1990). Ntara (1973) describes several cases of historically powerful women in Chewa society, including the rainmaker Makewana (in Chichewa "the mother of the children"). According to oral accounts, Makewana could speak directly with the Creator rather than through ancestors and was perceived as something of an oracle or "spirit (possessed)" woman (Rangeley 1952; Ntara 1973). Critical to her people's survival, her knowledge of weather patterns and her powerful abilities as a rain-caller gave her great prestige as a leader (Ntara 1973:41).

In parts of southern Tanzania, Malawi, and Zimbabwe clan elders with similar special abilities continue to act as intermediaries with the ancestors to "call down rain" or "heal the earth" (Weinrich 1982; Feierman 1990; Chimombo 1994). During the droughts of 1991 and 1992, rain-callers who had powerful reputations for carrying out successful rain-calling ceremonies were recruited by their communities to perform these rituals.

Clan elders of both sexes earn a highly respected position, reinforcing the value placed on gerontocracy in African societies. That position allows them to monitor group behavior. Clan imperatives have moral value, acting as social controls.

Historically, if certain individuals within a clan deviated from normative clan behavior, cleavage occurred. The deviant left or was ordered out of the group and gathered followers to form a new group. Environmental factors (e.g., lack of rain, insufficient food crops due to poor soil conditions) and political disputes between competing leaders were the primary causes of fissioning. Illicit sexual relations also could lead to cleavage. If a potential junior leader knew that his wife was having relations with a rival or senior clan leader, he left the group (Ntara 1973).

Clan elders historically were responsible for settling marital disputes and property disputes, especially over land. They continue to have authority through customary courts in southern African states such as Malawi, Swaziland, and Mozambique. Mwamula-Lubanda illustrates with cases from Uganda, Tanzania, and Mozambique the way that certain aspects of clan authority—those connected with the management of economic activities—were incorporated into national development plans after independence (1992:142–146). He argues that the clan, as a basis for group solidarity, has been underutilized as a motivational force in achieving rural participatory development goals in Africa. In the development context, he believes, clan has the potential for becoming an agent of change.

Clan as Changing Cultural Phenomenon

Clan not only provides a mechanism for social change but is itself affected by larger, often externally generated shifts in political and social relationships. When placed within an ongoing social process of historical change, clan as process enables us to account for how clans (and lineages) are created and their diversity over time (see Comaroff 1987b; Vail 1989).

Historian David Newberry views clan as a changing cultural phenomenon. He argues that no "clear and consistent definition of clan" is possible because as a cultural unit clan is a historically derived construction. He posits that "clan identities and the actions based on them [are] individual social constructs, each formed under its own specific conditions and fully capable of changing, rather than . . . primordial givens" (1991:5). This deconstructive, relativist perspective reminds us that what we know about clan as a concept characterizing African societies prior to colonial penetration is speculative at best and is often based on oral narratives that themselves are subject to modification. Whereas we can accept that a current formulation, such as that proposed by Mwamula-Lubandi (1992), may be possible, we must treat with caution formulations of clan described for societies that predated European and Arab contact. Similarly, colonial ethnographers' descriptions of "clan identities" must be critically evaluated within the context of the colonial asymmetrical relations in which the ethnographers worked and viewed Africans as "others" (Mitchell 1956; Harries 1989; Feierman 1990).

Due to the retrospective nature of historical investigations, Newberry (1991) prefers to examine clan ideology as it evolved and changed among a particular group bounded by space and time—the clans on Ijwi Island in Lake Kivu, Rwanda, between 1780 and 1840. Newberry maintains that the changing nature of clan identity in this period was influenced by shifting local and regional social processes. It is the "external components of clan identity" (a clan's relations with others) to which Newberry turns rather than the "internal constituents of clan identity [genealogies, land use, religious functions]" (1991:6).

Among the Ijwi, Newberry maintains, the clan was the "largest social identity group," but within the clan there were "different levels of social identity and different types of groups." For example, among one of the largest clans, the Balenga, there were several subgroups differentiated by regional and historical differences. For some of these subgroups, there was no local territorial focus, claim to a common historical origin, clan head, or corporate function; for other groups some of these characteristics were present (Newberry 1991:5). Even the internal constituents of clan varied for the Ijwi.

Newberry describes new clan identities on Ijwi Island coalescing at "precisely the time when political competition was most intense" (1991:4). Clan identities were consolidated within the concept of "kingship," but kingship itself had meaning only within the broader preexisting clan structure: "The meaning of royal rituals goes beyond the ceremonies themselves. . . . They validated clan identities in a society which held no other corporate expression of clan membership [except, to some degree, in *bukumbi*, or joking] relations" (212).

The notion that clan is invented and reinvented by the vagaries of social and political circumstances comes very close to the way ethnicity as a sociocultural construction based in changing political power relationships is currently perceived (Comaroff 1987; Vail and White 1989; Harries 1989; Ranger 1989a; Roberts 1989; Fox 1990). That clan is perceived as a changing cultural phenomenon subject to the influence of historical political factors and, at the same time, is viewed as an organizing principle—the largest solidarity unit—testifies to its historical adaptability.

Whereas in many rural areas clan or, alternatively, lineage is a sociopolitical reference point for village organization, in urban areas the significance of clan has waned. For the minority of educated urban dwellers for whom clan identity is less important and cash more available, urban institutions such as professional and recreational clubs have become surrogates for the solidarity that was formerly provided by clan membership (Mwamula-Lubandi 1992:20). From my own observations, among urban Africans clan affiliation and club affiliation are not mutually exclusive but reflect different dimensions of their daily lives. That clan ideology can be modified and re-created in new social situations is one of its strengths.

Lineage and Descent Groups

Clan encompasses a set of subrelationships that often have more meaning than clan identity in the daily lives of Africans. Clan ideology includes both a theory of lineage embodied in descent groups and the practice of property inheritance attached to such groups. Marital residence patterns are often linked to lineage ideologies. Structurally, clan is perceived to be the broadest social category with descent groups a subcategory, but this can change with sociopolitical circumstances, as Newberry (1991) illustrates.

The anthropologist working in Africa historically perceived clan and lineage as bounded social units. Basehart, for example, working among the postcolonial, matrilineal Ashanti, maintained that clan was the widest and most diffused expression of "matrilineal relatedness" and that all seven to eight Ashanti clans were found in each territorial domain (1962:283). The notion that clans were bounded units reflected the structural concerns of British anthropologists in the 1960s (e.g., Schneider 1962). However, this concept of clan has more recently been challenged based on evidence that such social "units" were historically permeable and have changed with opportunities and wider influences (e.g., Comaroff 1987a; Newberry 1991).

In southern Africa the ideal of clan has given way to smaller, identifiable networks of relationships based on ascriptive descent ties. S. J. Ntara, although noting that "nobody in Malawi is without a clan name," observes of the Chewa that by the 1940s, "lineages within a clan" rather than the clan had become the salient factor in sociopolitical groups (1973:8). Audrey Richards (1950) found a similar phenomenon among the Bemba, Bisa, and Lamba peoples in what was then Northern Rhodesia (now Zambia). In the same period, Colson (1951, 1962) pointed out that for the Plateau Tonga, the *mukowa*, the matrilineal group, was the smallest group through which members traced descent through females but that the exact genealogical ties were irrelevant because it was the corporate aspects of the *mukowa*—in terms of inheritance, succession, and the provision and sharing of bridewealth—that were critical to the Tonga (Colson 1962:41). Holleman noted a similar tendency among the Shona-speaking groups in Southern Rhodesia—lineage and descent had become the salient factors in clan ideology (1951:382).

In his analysis of African "systems of kinship," the anthropologist Radcliffe-Brown argued not only that the normative descent pattern among Africans was unilineal but that lineage ideology had a bearing on marital residence patterns. He observed, based on his fieldwork in eastern Africa, that "a patrilineal extended family is formed by a custom whereby sons remain in their father's family group, bringing their wives to live with them" (Radcliffe-Brown and Fortes 1950:5), whereas the reverse is true for a matrilineal extended family, "a domestic group consisting of a man and his wife with their daughters and the husbands and children of the latter" (6). What Radcliffe-Brown's description reveals—in addition to androcentricity in his description of the matrilineal "family"—is that he believed marital residence patterns were dependent on lineage ideology. This is not necessarily the case.

Marital residence among the matrilineal Tonga, for example, has been virilocal since at least the 1940s. Colson (1951) points out that among the Plateau Tonga, a woman left her natal home to go live in her husband's village upon marriage. Nor is matrilineality always linked to matrilocality or uxorilocality in late-twentieth-century southern Africa (Phiri 1977; Wright 1983; Davison 1993; Moore and Vaughan 1994). As Aberle has observed, matrilocality is not a necessary condition for matriliny (1962:660).

I prefer to take the question of marital residence out of a discussion of lineage and descent because marital residence patterns vary greatly and do not necessarily conform to lineage ideology. Marital residence is conditioned by many other variables, both social and economic, that influence where a couple resides, as will become clear in Chapter 2.

Lineage Ideologies: Matriliny and Patriliny

Collier and Yanagisako (1987), in looking at the intersection of gender and kinship, stress that in analyses where gender is central, we must begin with "social wholes" rather than functional domains. Because gender is central to lineage ideologies in southern Africa, using an approach that targets social wholes, however ambiguous, may be the best approach. Collier and Yanagisako offer three analytical trajectories that have utility for an analysis of lineage and gender: explanations of cultural meanings attached to ideologies in which gender is implicated, the construction of models of the dialectic relationship between practice and ideology, and a historical analysis of continuity and change (1987; see the introduction). I begin with cultural meanings attached to lineage and the dialectic relation between lineage ideology and practice.

"In the African way of living it makes a great deal of difference if we are dealing with matrilineal or patrilineal social formations, even if these do not exist in absolute forms," contends Mwamula-Lubandi (1992:27). Mwamula-Lubandi seems to be arguing that Africans in general attach value to the concept of lineage, much as North Americans attach value to the concept of democracy. Further, he suggests that differences in lineage ideology are dependent on gender; the distinction between patrilineal and matrilineal descent is a difference to which Africans attach critical meaning. At the same time, he acknowledges the dialectic between practice and ideology; gendered lineage ideologies exist, but the way they get translated into practice is a negotiated process that at times bends or even contradicts the theory.

The anthropologist Audrey Richards, who worked in Zambia from the 1920s through the 1940s, was one of the first external observers to recognize that matriliny and patriliny do not exist in "absolute forms" but rather in negotiated forms depending on class, family circumstances, and individual proclivities that converge with lineage (Richards 1950:207, n. 2). She also realized that lineages change over time. More recently, Bridget O'Laughlin (1995) has observed that a dialectic relation exists between what patrilineal elders in southern Mozambican villages relate as the lineage ideal—including the importance of knowing particular patrilineages—and what is practiced in a village at various levels. She contends (1995:71) that in Mozambique, "lineages tend to be shallow, each extended family is potentially a new lineage segment, long ancestral lines are identified with political power, social ties of kinship are forged bilaterally, [and] people are often tied to more than one descent group." Yet it is the cultural meaning that a particular group or individual attaches to lineage that gives it value. For Mwamula-Lubamba (1992) and other Africans, the distinction between matriliny and patriliny is real even though neither lineage ideal is fully achieved. That much is known about patriliny in Mozambique and far less about matriliny (see Pitcher 1993; Sheldon 1994) is indicative of the value that colonial powers and the state attached to the former.

Of the two lineage ideologies, patriliny predominates in Africa. Even so, throughout recorded time, evidence of matrilineal descent groups exists—from the Senegal coast in western Africa to central, eastern, and southern Africa. Although most groups in southern Africa have been classified as patrilineal, clustered within precolonial central southern Africa were a significant number of groups that were identified by colonial ethnographers as "matrilineal." Included in this category are the Bemba, Bisa, Bima, Plateau and Gwembe Tonga, Lakeside Tonga, Chewa, Yao, Tumbuka, Mang'anja, Ndau, and Kaonde.

The degree to which matriliny is still ascribed to and practiced varies. Periodically it has been pronounced doomed when, in reality, it has continued to flourish in various quarters (see Colson 1970; Douglas 1969). Its vulnerability is partly linked to the extent to which colonial capitalism or independent capitalism has penetrated a particular area and the way it has interacted with local social formations. In urban areas matriliny has less currency than it does in rural areas. Urban residents from groups that ascribe to matrilineal descent ideologies often intermarry with those ascribing to patrilineal descent, confounding ideologies of descent that may no longer serve a purpose.

It is noteworthy that because matriliny is less prevalent in Africa, was unknown in Europe, and was practiced in North America only by certain Native American groups (e.g., the Cherokee, Iroquois, Crow, Hopi), matrilineal practices are much less understood. Mitchell, who worked in Malawi, amplified the problems of investigating matrilineal groups early on when he observed that "the modern confusion about clan-names is no doubt partly due to the emphasis placed on patrilineal descent by the purveyors of White culture, the Administrators and the Missionaries, and also by the same emphasis in Islamic trade" (1956:72). Aberle (1962) observes that matriliny is scattered throughout the world and that it is found at all levels of social and political development. Yet the marginalization of matriliny is still with us. It continues to be viewed as an aberration even by Western-educated African male scholars from matrilineal groups who find themselves in the position of having to defend a "different" social order.

Matriliny intrigues the female Western observer. Scholarly attempts have been made to account for the appearance of matrilineal ideology, its practice and continuance (Richards 1950; Colson 1951; Gough 1962; Douglas 1969; Schlegel 1972; Sacks 1979; Poewe 1981). In most of these accounts, matriliny is viewed as a counterpoint to patriliny or as some "primordial" form of social organization that has largely died out or been subsumed within patrilineal capitalist relations of production. However, evidence from Poewe (1981), Stromgaard (1985), Skjønsberg (1989), Moore and Vaughan (1994), Crehan (1994), and Munalula and Mwenda (1995) on Zambia; from my own work and that of Peters (1994) on Malawi; and from Hafkin (1973), Arnfred (1988), and Pitcher (1993, 1995) on northern Mozambique suggests that matriliny persists in rural central southern Africa. As Aberle (1962:659) maintains, it is adaptable and yet resilient, having spread to groups where it did not previously exist. Rather than being studied as a counterpoint to patriliny, it needs to be studied in its own right.

Descent and Inheritance

Descent often is paired with inheritance practices. Among patrilineal groups, land is passed down from father to sons. Occasionally a father will give his daughter a piece of land to till, but it rarely becomes heritable in her name. Among most matrilineal groups, either a mother's brother or her daughters inherit the land she has acquired and tilled during her lifetime. Her movable property is inherited by her immediate descent group. Except in avuncular relationships, men do not generally inherit land. However, there are exceptions. If a man has proved himself to be an exceptional farmer, he may be allowed to keep a piece of land on the death of his wife. Also, many men have an avuncular role to play in their descent group and through this avenue gain access to land and movable property.

The practice of matrilineal inheritance differs from patrilineal inheritance in the advantages that women gain. In the latter, women gain access to land usually as wives. If a woman becomes a widow or divorces, she may lose access to the land her husband allotted her. Usually she returns to her natal home with or without children unless as a widow she marries her deceased husband's brother. For women in matrilineal groups, security of land tenure is not an issue. Women often, but not always, remain in their natal homes, where they exercise and maintain control over a particular parcel of land that they in turn pass down to their daughters or granddaughters. Even when they marry virilocally, they retain rights to a piece of land in their natal home. Notwithstanding, where land has been privatized and commoditized, it may be purchased by either males or females provided they have the cash or credit to buy it. In many rural areas of central southern Africa, however, land is communally held and therefore may not be sold.

The allocation and control of resources varies in matrilineal and patrilineal descent groups; women in matrilineal groups have more direct control over land and other productive resources than women in patrilineal groups. However, differences exist among matrilineal groups. Women in matrilineal groups in northern Mozambique and southern Malawi have tended to retain relative control over land even though there is less of it. Matrilineal groups in Zambia have historically been more affected by capitalist relations of production; women there have often lost control over productive resources (see Milimo 1986; Poewe 1981). Even though matriliny is associated with particular ethnic groups in southern Africa, it is not dependent on ethnicity. For example, the majority of the population in central and southern Malawi, composed of many groups, is predominantly matrilineal—68 percent (Pryor 1990:25).

Alternatively, matrilineal and patrilineal descent may occasionally exist within a single ethnic group; the Tumbuka in northern Malawi recognize both, although Nyirenda (1931) suggests that this group was formerly matrilineal. To understand how lineage and descent interface with ethnicity, we need to explore how ethnicity became a product of social formation in African societies.

Ethnicity and African Social Formation

Ethnicity is a politically subjective and conceptually evasive term in any geographical context. It is the conundrum of our times. Certainly, this is the case in Africa. For example, the Eritreans, who have identified themselves as a distinct ethnic group with a common language (Tigrinya) and common history (Aksum), fought long and hard to become a nation independent of Ethiopia. Several states in southern Africa, including Botswana, Lesotho, and Swaziland, grew out of a single ethnic group's demand for nationhood. And within several African nations ethnicity has been a factor contributing to contests of power that sometimes led to bloodshed and even ethnic genocide.

The term "ethnic group" is often used by Europeans and Westerners and Western-educated Africans to refer to a group that differentiates itself or is differentiated by others based on certain characteristics of language, belief, and behavior. Although every ethnic group has its own political identity, ethnicity is a negotiated concept. It differs from the pejorative term "tribe," derived from the colonial vernacular. The latter grew out of a superordinate-subordinate relationship between colonials and colonized that left little room for negotiation.

In many regions in Africa, cultural groups that transcend national boundaries ignore them, as with the Maasai in eastern Africa, the Mandinka in western Africa, and the Yao in southern Africa. The border between Mozambique and Malawi is indiscernible in places, and Yao kin travel back and forth for trade, visits, and security depending on the political winds.

In other situations, cultural groups form self-consciously defined and socially recognized "ethnic groups" within existing nation-states. The Shona of Zimbabwe are an example. In some cases they form political parties or interest groups competing for political capital (see Vail 1989; Ranger 1989a). Vail suggests that "ethnicity became the home of the opposition in [postindependent] states where class consciousness was largely undeveloped" (1989:2). That lack of class consciousness gives birth to politicized ethnic identity, however, is not borne out by Zimbabwe's experience; class awareness had already developed in urban locations prior to independence and grew along with intensification of ethnic identity in the postindependence era. Likewise in South Africa, class consciousness and ethnic consciousness coexist and sometimes coalesce, as in the case of the Zulu miners who protested their working conditions as a distinct ethnic group within an exploited underclass.

In precolonial southern Africa, some scholars have argued, preexisting groups did not have a sense of ethnic identity (Vail 1972; Vail and White 1989; Beach 1980; Ranger 1989a). Other scholars have argued that for specific groups an ethnic self-awareness existed (Mainga 1973; Papstein 1989; Newberry 1995). As African peoples in the Zambezi region left no written records, it may be left to historical imagination whether various groups in the region acknowledged some form of ethnic identity. Portuguese records provide us with names of groups and individuals that identified themselves with a particular chieftaincy or ruling lineage elite, such as the Rozwi, Manyika, and Mavari. A common language, lineage ties, and shared cosmology were the major cultural markers of these hierarchical societies, although Ranger (1989a:121) argues that for the Manyika in eastern Zimbabwe, "most people did not think of themselves as related in any way to the Manyika chief." It is difficult to know what the Manyika thought in the seventeenth century; as they left no written records, much is left to "historical imagination" (Comaroff and Comaroff 1992). Portuguese records describing the precolonial Manyika are somewhat ambiguous. It appears, however, that for the peoples of the Zambezi region, social obligations between patrons and clients, rather than spatial ties, defined their identities.

Papstein (1989:372–373), in describing the peoples of the upper Zambezi region, contends that "ethnic differentiation based on differences of langugage or dialect, historical traditions, differences in cosmology did exist. . . . The Luvale-, Lunda-, Luchazi-, and Mbunda-speaking peoples of the upper Zambezi area certainly had a developed ethnic self-awareness prior to either their contact with mercantile capital through participation in the trans-Atlantic slave trade . . . or their experience as colonized peoples between 1906 and 1964."

Papstein views ethnic awareness in the region as growing out of "a long-term historical process in which the particularism of early Bantu-speaking segmentary lineages evolved into a view of an enlarged social field with loyalties defined in terms of similar languages and culture and with primary and social economic allegiances" to lineages and clans (1989:372). The same matrilineal clans could be found in all the groups of the Upper Zambezi. Papstein (374) argues that what changed with British occupation was the institutionalization of "tribal" designations where once ethnicity based on affinities of language, lineage, and clan had existed.

In some cases, especially where the groups were widely dispersed, they may not have ascribed to a particular ethnic identity. In other cases, ethnic identities were likely to have arisen as the product of asymmetrical or symmetrical relations (Holleman 1951; Ntara 1973; Newberry 1995). In the latter cases, some ethnic identities arose as the result of symmetrical relations of reciprocity, for example, in trade; in others they were based on asymmetrical relations of conquest and often enslavement.

Comaroff (1987a) argues that prior to European conquest, indigenous groups that subjectively differentiated themselves from other groups based on language, common history, and custom can be divided into two categories—those whose interrelations were characterized by relative equality, which he refers to as "totemic groups," and those characterized by unequal relations, referred to as "ethnic groups" (Comaroff 1987a: 306–311). For Comaroff, then, unequal relations of power are the defining feature of ethnicity.

Ethnicity at any one time in precolonial history was likely to have been purposely ambiguous and at times contradictory. It had both exclusive and inclusive dimensions where asymmetrical relations between groups existed (Newberry 1995). Newberry (1995) shows how this double meaning of ethnicity can be applied to explain how royal lineages in Rwanda grew to view themselves as distinctive from others; these "others"—often subjugated groups—came to view themselves both as having a separate identity and as sharing many of the cultural features of the dominant group. I find Newberry's analysis useful in weighing how precolonial ethnicities in the Zambezi region might have developed. And here I part company with Beach (1980), Vail (1989), and Ranger (1989a) because I believe it plausible, based on Arab and Portuguese descriptions, that ethnic identities did exist in the pre-British colonial period. On the one hand, ethnicity might serve to define politically exclusive groups such as the royal dynasties of the

Rozwi of Zimbabwe or the Lunda of Zambia, each of whose members shared a specific elite history and culture. In this exclusive meaning, ethnic identity, growing out of lineage ideology, was used to maintain sociopolitical distance from other cultural groups that were subjugated. On the other hand, ethnicity might also be used in a culturally inclusive sense to include all those sharing the same broad category of languages and the same cosmology and customs.

First with Arab trading and later with Portuguese trading in the sixteenth century, asymmetrical relations between groups based on trade and slavery contributed to the formation of ethnic identities. The Yao of Mozambique, for example, were feared by the Chewa and Lakeside Tonga of Malawi because as contract traders for the Swahili, they carried guns and often traded in slaves as well as other goods (Ntara 1973; Nyirenda 1931; Dorward n.d.). That some indigenous groups had more power and authority than others was recognized by Arab traders and the first European explorers. However, the more powerful were not necessarily the groups that were later recognized by the colonial states.

Colonial Constructions of Ethnicity

Ethnicity as contrived by colonial administrators in consultation with hired European ethnographers took on a "tribal" dimension for purposes of indirect rule and tax collection. Unlike ethnicity, which is often negotiated, "tribe" was a concept imposed on the less powerful by the colonial holders of power. And even though it was a term that grew out of unequal racist relations, it became so psychologically internalized—a form of false consciousness—that in postindependent Africa, ethnocentrism often was equated with "tribalism." It is only within the past two decades that the term "ethnic group" has gained currency among Africans. This section takes up the role of the colonial powers in circumscribing and defining ethnicity.

The current thinking of many historians is that "ethnicity" is attributable to the historically politicized relationships that arose between colonizers and colonized (e.g., Vail 1989; Harries 1989; Ranger 1989a; Feierman 1990; Moore and Vaughan 1994). Vail (1972, 1989), as mentioned earlier, has posited that prior to colonial penetration, many groups were not conscious of being specifically distinguishable "ethnic" groups, a historical interpretation that closely resembles Comaroff's notion of totemic groups. Vail argues that a sense of ethnic identity in southern Africa did not arise until the twentieth century, a thesis that depends on one's definition of "ethnicity," or ethnic identity.

Vail bases his definition of ethnicity largely on relations of power deriving from missionization and colonial rule. To wit, "In those societies where missionaries did not work, or where African intellectuals emerged only at a late period or not at all, the development of ethnic ideologies was either stalled or never occurred" (1989:12). He does not describe examples where missionaries did not work and thus where the rise of ethnic identity was forestalled but rather concentrates on the process through which ethnization occurred, using the Tumbuka of northern Malawi as an example (Vail 1972). He relates that the Tumbuka were not unified by a sense of group identity prior to British colonization but lived in scattered groups and clans, a situation corroborated by the Tumbuka oral historian L.S.N. Hara (1991). For Vail, a key indicator of ethnicity appears to be geographical location and historical circumstances.

Vail and White (1989) show how the Tumbuka began in the early part of the twentieth century to coalesce as an ethnic group with the production of their written history under the auspices of missionaries at Livingstonia. Thus mission-educated African intellectuals who wrote down the histories of their cultural groups, such as Saulos Nyirenda and Andrew Nkhonjera for the Tumbuka and Samuel J. Ntara for the Chewa, contributed significantly to the production of an ethnic consciousness among these groups. That the missionaries took the Tumbuka under their wing legitimated their political position against their historical enemy, the Ngoni, who were entrenched with the colonial government (Vail and White 1989:160). Consequently, ethnicity became a legitimating force that provided a window of opportunity for the Tumbuka and helped to level the colonial playing field for one group of missionaries.

That colonial rule legitimated the ethnic identity of particular groups is demonstrated by the way British colonial administrators favored the Yao over the Anguru (later Lomwe) in southern Malawi. Both groups had originally come from Mozambique, the Yao arriving first. The Yao, who began migrating into southern Malawi in the nineteenth century, conquered the preexisting Mang'anja to become chiefs. Later, when the Anguru arrived, they were included in the network of chieftaincies crafted by the Yao (Mitchell 1956; Rangeley 1963; Phiri, Vaughan, and Makuluni 1977). The Yao were granted political legitimacy by the British colonial administration based on their trading skills and the abilities of their chiefs to maintain order—a major concern of those interested in nurturing indirect rule. In contrast, the more recently arrived Anguru were viewed by the colonial state as "troublemakers" because they were identified with a particular Christian sect whose leader was responsible for the first attempted rebellion against the British in Nyasaland in 1915 (Vail and White 1989:170–72). The colonial powers contributed to an escalation in asymmetrical relations between groups, which in turn intensified the significance of ethnic identity. Similarly, Ranger (1989a:125–37) points to the roles of the American Methodist Episcopal Christian mission (AMEC), the Anglicans, and the Catholic missionaries in codifying various forms of the Manyika and Zezuru languages and in educating Manyika youth, which led by the 1930s to the development of a Manyika ethnic identity that was recognizable among migrant Manyika workers in Salisbury. This identity was later subsumed within the larger Shona identity—not without conflict and protestation.

In northeastern Zambia, a different set of circumstances arose. Prior to British occupation, the militant Bemba elite, descended from a royal matriline, had built a series of fortified villages to protect Bemba communities from marauding slave raiders, from competing forces in the region such as the Ngoni, and possibly from one another in the case of disputing chieftaincies (Werbner 1967). With the imposition of Pax Britannica, such armed forts were no longer necessary, and Bemba-speaking peasants rapidly dispersed to take up once again the practice of *citemene*, a specific form of cut-and-burn cultivation that required periodically shifting from one place to another (Richards 1939; Berry 1993). As Berry (1993:37) points out, the British South Africa Company (BSAC) was not comfortable with this human dispersion, preferring the neat and tidy village model they were accustomed to in order to impose their own form of indirect control through selected Bemba chiefs. As a result the BSAC tried to ban the practice of *citemene* in 1907 with little success, a strategy that the colonial state later pursued with more vigor.

It is interesting with regard to the evolution of Bemba ethnicity that in the century prior to colonial occupation some form of elite Bemba identity existed that was based on descent, language, and military might. Although scholars disagree as to its significance (e.g., Richards 1940; Werbner 1967), a network of chiefs who identified themselves as Bemba and who were linked in various ways to a paramount chief did exist prior to colonial occupation. It may be that Bemba identity in the nineteenth century assumed a militant posture to ensure group survival at a time when the Bemba elite were being threatened—a not uncommon response under such circumstances. That the Bemba began to scatter once their perceived enemies were removed during the colonial period (Epstein 1975; Berry 1993) reflects their need for economic survival based on an extensive system of agriculture rather than the disintegration of social ties. The BSAC and later the colonial state, in the interests of indirect rule, sought to circumscribe the Bemba spatially and politically. In 1929, four out of some thirty recognized Bemba chiefs in Northern Province were designated official "native authorities" responsible for controlling the Bemba-speaking population within circumscribed settlements (Berry 1993:37). The ambiguous Bemba were being redefined.

Moore and Vaughan (1994) argue that the colonial state defined Bemba ethnicity from the 1930s onward in terms of *citemene,* a factor that for the colonials symbolized the Bemba political economy. Thus the authors' understanding of ethnization under colonial rule is linked to economic conditions, including gender relations of power and production, rather than to missionization, as in the case of Vail and White's (1989) historical analysis of Tumbuka ethnicity and Ranger's (1989a) analysis of Manyika identity. *Citemene* became the linchpin in colonial constructions of Bemba ethnicity, according to Moore and Vaughan.

In a reinterpretation of Audrey Richards's early work on the Bemba (1939, 1940), Moore and Vaughan (1994) acknowledge that the Bemba were an aristocratic group, as described by Richards (1940), but further posit that their "ethnicity" became intertwined culturally with *citemene,* which in turn depended on men to fell trees for the cultivation of millet. Linking *citemene* to a particular ethnic group, even though other groups in Northern Province practiced the same system, made it easier for the colonial administration to target this group for "modernizing" agricultural interventions designed to increase production. Thus ethnic identity became tied to a particular farming system for better or worse.[4]

In Zimbabwe, ethnic productions also were being initiated with the assistance of colonial ethnographers. One such ethnographer, J. F. Holleman, illustrates how a particular ethnic group was created. After describing how the once dominant Rozwi "clan/tribe" became fragmented when its power was broken up by Swasi, Ndebele, and later the Europeans in Mashonaland, Holleman explains, "In describing the general pattern common to all the communities in central Mashonaland, the usefully inclusive but foreign [Ndebele?] term 'Shona' will be used, because there seems to exist no indigenous term which could be used *conveniently* as a common denominator" (my emphasis) (1951:355–356).

For the convenience of the colonials, several Shona-speaking groups, including the Rozwi, were subsumed under the general term Shona. This Shona group later consolidated its ethnic power to contest Rhodesian rule at the expense of another, less populous ethnic group, the Ndebele. Ranger (1989a) ably shows how the quest for ethnic power by the Manyika Shona in the mid-twentieth century through ZANU-PF (Zimbabwe African National Union–Patriotic Front) led to their entrenchment in Zimbabwe's first national government.

It is debatable, however, that ethnic groups arose merely in response to colonial capitalism. Evidence exists for various regions in Africa suggesting that prior to colonial penetration, Africans perceived themselves as being distinct groups that vied for control of people and resources (Holleman 1951; Ntara 1973; Mainga 1973; Mudenge 1988; Mandala 1990; Newberry 1995).

Toward a Definition

Ethnicity is a Western concept; it derives from the experience of social formations and reformations in Europe and the Americas. It may or may not be a concept that adequately explains the human variation that characterizes Africa. Whether it has emic validity for Africa has yet to be discussed by Africans; most analyses have come from Western pens.

Ethnicity is no longer thought of merely in terms of bounded entities (see Ranger 1989a; Feierman 1990; Young 1993). Rather, ethnicity includes both group identity and the process through which it comes about, and the changes that it is subject to over time. As a concept it is open to many interpretations given specific realities. In its functionalist sociological form it comes closest to defining an entity—a group of people bonded by language, history, social norms, values, and behavior. But we know that not all people within a group ascribe equally to a group's ideal or practice its perceived ideology. In its anthropological form, ethnicity currently is defined as the cultural production of a public identity (Fox 1990:4). Hence the emphasis is on process and agency. In its historical form it is a product of change—an identity either externally or internally generated and based in historical political processes. From a political perspective, ethnicity is viewed in terms of competing ethnonationalist forces that challenged nation building in the immediate postcolonial period in Africa and that continue to contest the nationalist interests of politically insecure states in the late twentieth century (Young 1993:14–15).

In all these meanings, ethnicity shares certain characteristics with nationalism and racial identity. Basotho ethnicity, for example, includes a common, culturally produced history, language, and economy that became the basis for Lesotho's nationalism at a particular moment in history. A similar case can be made for Swaziland and, to some degree, for Botswana.

Racial identity is often, but not always, linked with ethnicity in southern Africa. In South Africa under apartheid and in the former Southern Rhodesia, racial identity was used as the basis for a degrading, racist class system that legitimated white hegemony for decades. But Afrikaners viewed race and ethnicity as indivisible. For Afrikaners, language and culture converged with race in their self-identity based on an ideology of superiority (Gilomee 1989; Butler 1989). Despite the demise of the formal apartheid system, racial identity continues to be a basis for differentiating people and, often, their opportunities.

For others in South Africa, ethnicity does not include racial identity. For example, Zulu and Xhosa perceive themselves to have differences that have little to do with race and more to do with past history and present political contingencies. In southern Zimbabwe, the Shona-speaking Kalanga perceive themselves as different from the neighboring Ndebele. Even though racially the two groups are the same in language, customs, and lineage beliefs, they differ in ways that affect intergroup relations. A Kalanga woman's comments are illustrative. In referring to a relative who took a Ndebele wife, she says, "Most of them [family members] say it should be said it is Dzilo's mother who came first [was the first wife]. But in those days they did that [made Buka's mother junior] because she was a Mlilo [Ndebele by descent], and so they sent her back, and said they would not have a Mlilo senior wife. They wanted one who was a Kalanga" (Werbner 1991:69).

Thus the speaker equated ethnicity with exclusivity as a way of differentiating "us" from "them." Taking a principal wife from an ethnic group different from one's own caused trouble among co-wives and led to disharmony in this instance. At the same time, the woman hints that such distinctions between ethnic groups, which were amplified by the colonial state, no longer matter.

Despite the colonial state's role in circumscribing ethnicities, Africans, as much as Americans or Europeans, recognize customs and "traditions" that distinguish one group from another, and these are often used as a rationale for a particular type of political or social behavior. The simplest answer to the question What is ethnicity in an African context? is perhaps: It is a response to social difference—the "we-they" subjectivity. These differences exist either within the consciousness of others or in the consciousness of the individuals who create the group's identity. In other words, ethnicity may be etically constructed from the outside, as when one group labels another based on certain traits or behavior, or it may be emically constructed from within, as in the Basotho case. In many cases ethnicity arises in response to a combination of emic and etic forces that serve to define difference.

What distinguishes one group from another changes over time, but a common history (including that which arose from the colonial experience) and language and common cultural values and customs are the major aspects that Africans point to. Often one or more of these ethnic attributes are used to justify a particular course of action or a group's social or political position.

Ethnicity as It Relates to Clan and Lineage

In addition to language and history, a significant cultural feature often linked to ethnicity by Africans is the way clan and lineage are ordered and the impact of these on inheritance. Clan ideology may be invoked by kin to gain control over heritable goods and land. In cases where wife and husband come from different ethnic groups, a life crisis such as the death of a spouse may prompt tensions among family members representing the two ethnic groups, as happened in the case regarding the death of Kenyan lawyer S. M. Otieno (Stamp 1991).

In the Otieno case, Otieno's Luo clan members went before the customary court against his Gikuyu widow for control of the deceased man's body. They wanted him to be buried in his home village in Western Kenya rather than in Nairobi, as Otieno and his wife had planned. The clan also sued for control of his property. The customary court legitimated the clan's right to the deceased husband's body for burial, thus reinforcing clan "tradition." However, the widow contested the clan's right to her husband's property in the statutory court system. She won her case, preventing the Luo clan members from gaining access to her deceased husband's material property. I observed a similar case in Malawi, where clan members of one ethnic group used clan ideology to justify gaining access to most of a deceased male relative's movable property, thus preventing the widow and her children, who were from a clan in another ethnic group, from inheriting the property.

The previously cited clan contests over competing claims have a gender dimension. Even though in the Kenyan case both ethnic groups ascribed to patrilineal descent and in the Malawian case both ethnic groups practiced matrilineal descent, it was the deceased husband's male clan elders who used ethnic differences as a rationale to preempt any rights the widow and her children might have had to her husband's property. In Kenya the widow was successful in protecting her inheritance rights to her husband's property in the Westernized court system even though she lost control to burial rights in the customary court. In Malawi, the widow was partially successful in protecting her right to some of her husband's movable property through the customary court system. Ethnicity and clan ideology are often perceived as being linked in African societies, and at times clan or lineage becomes the surrogate for ethnic identity to represent cultural differences. However, the Kenyan and Malawian cases also have a gender dimension. In both cases, wives were pitted against their deceased husbands' relatives.

In this chapter I have identified the continuing salience of lineage as it relates to ethnicity and gender in Africa. It is important to recognize not only that notions of clan and lineage have historical roots and often current functions depending on the degree to which a group ascribes to its ideology but also that the particular structure of clan and lineage varies from one setting to the next and changes with time and circumstances. Likewise, ethnicity is subject to both historical production and current manipulation. Though problematic, it remains a useful concept to describe cultural groups that identify themselves as distinct from other groups in Africa.

In the next chapter I take up gender, showing how it becomes defined in African societies and the role of ethnicity and lineage ideology in that formation.

Notes

1. See Okoth-Ogendo's (1993) discussion of this point. He points out that colonial agricultural officers often discounted matrineal landholding patterns and relations of production without examining their underlying rationale or the ways they benefited indigenous farming systems.

2. I use the term "matrilineal societies" and "patrilineal societies or groups" to indicate that the majority of people within that particular society or group ascribed at a particular point in time to matrilineal ideology in the first instance or to patrilineal ideology in the second instance. These "ideologies" were ascribed to in practice to varying degrees. However, colonial historians and anthropologists glossed the terms "matrilineal" and "patrilineal" to cover societies or groups, and I have referred to them in this way where historians and anthropologists have described them this way. Lineage, after all, is a Western term that is used to make sense of what the European or Western observer sees, but it does not always fully describe the reality.

3. Throughout southern Africa, interclan and interethnic rivalries over land and control of people during the period between the sixteenth and the mid-nineteenth centuries, and the effect of Arab and Portuguese trading on preexisting power arrangements, caused former leaders to lose their authority and clans to fragment and disperse, many in weakened conditions.

4. Thankdekile Mvusi (1995) critiques Moore and Vaughan's (1994) analysis of Audrey Richards's work on the Bemba as "a colonial discourse about a colonial discourse" because in both cases Bemba peasants are treated as "objects" of study—actors whose voices are muted or largely missing. Even though Bemba were interviewed in both cases, we learn very little about how they interpret *citemene*, their roles in production, and their perceptions of the ways these roles shifted during the 1930s and 1940s as a result of rural-urban labor migration. Nor do we learn much about the cultural meanings these peasants, past and present, attach to matrilineal ideology and its implications for rural production. Rather, Moore and Vaughan (1994) criticize Audrey Richards's understanding and interpretations of matriliny, which were far more flexible than Moore and Vaughan would have us believe, as indicated in an earlier section (see, e.g., Richards 1950:207).

2

Gender: Where Ethnicity, Clan, and Lineage Meet

Tracing the way gender is structured and restructured throughout a life span indicates something about the way women's and men's roles and experience shift with time. Central to the gender-structuring process is lineage ideology, which involves some key questions: Does matriliny, in contrast to patriliny, structure gender relations in a way that affects women's and men's understanding of themselves? Does lineage dictate different roles for men and women regarding control over productive and reproductive resources? How does lineage ideology influence women's power and development? Can we expect women in matrilineal groups to respond to Western-initiated development schemes in the same way that women in patrilineal groups respond to such schemes? Gender is at the heart of debates over lineage ideology. As lineage often is linked to ethnic identity, rightly or wrongly, the latter is implicated.

I begin this chapter with an overview of gender as a social construct and then discuss challenges to Eurocentric notions of gender by Afro-American and other women of color that have relevancy for this study. In that discussion, I draw on the work of Mohanty (1992, 1993a), Collins (1993), and Gaidzanwa (1992) as illustrative of the critiques. I then turn to the work of three African feminists who have contributed to building an alternative set of gender theories to explain gender realities in specific African societies. Each example has some relevancy for my central concern—the way gender, lineage, and ethnicity intertwine. A discussion of the ways that gender is constructed within African contexts follows, using a life-cycle model. This model focuses particularly on critical transitions in the gender-structuring process where lineage plays a central role, including initiation, marriage (with its attendant residence patterns), parenting, and elderhood. It demonstrates that the cultural meanings attached to each transition have shifted over time in response to changing sociopolitical and economic conditions.

Gender as a Social Construct

Concentrating on gender means examining the sociocultural factors involved in constructions of female and male and their relationship to one another. A biological determinist stance is concerned with sexual difference as determined by chromosomes, hormones, and anatomy. Once we change our perceptual lens to look at the way that being "male" or "female" is constructed within societies, we see that even a phenomenon such as sexuality derives much of its meaning from a particular context.

Sexuality is the direction in which the sex drive is ordered and shaped; culture intervenes in this process. What may be considered provocative in one culture may not be provocative in another. For some societies clothing is an extension of sexuality; in others it is used to mask sexuality. Moreover, perceptions of sexuality differ by gender. We cannot make global assumptions about the way sexuality is ordered—it has varied historically and continues to vary (see Foucault 1980). Judith Butler (1990:6) pinpoints the critical role of culture in our notions of sexuality and gender when she observes, "If gender is the cultural meanings that the sexed body assumes, then a gender cannot be said to follow from a sex in any one way." When societies permit greater diversity of expression, gender takes on new and multiple meanings.

With this new perceptual lens, we can look at the ways in which particular sex categories are created, sustained, and changed over time. In this context, gender refers to the socially derived network of beliefs, attitudes, customs, behaviors, and activities that differentiate sex categories in a specific society. No two societies construct gender in quite the same way. Minimally, societies recognize two genders—female and male. Each has attached to it a set of ever-changing, socially defined characteristics that includes sexual orientation, procreative values and behaviors, and the social scripts through which individuals and groups interact and provide for their economic and social survival.

Gender is a comparative, relational concept. Looking at only males or only females in any particular society excludes one-half of the human experience. Merging them into a single aggregate category masks gender differences, usually to the detriment of females. For example, women's use-value labor, including their so-called family labor, is not included in national estimates of labor force participation, thus preventing an assessment of women's contribution to economic development.

Related to gender are other intertwined modalities. Critical to gender structuring are social variables such as race, ethnicity, class, religion, and age, among many. Regional variations also impinge on inter- and intragender identities (Meena 1992; Gaidzanwa 1992; Mannathoko 1992). Each of these modalities, singly or in combination, interacts dialectically with gender in a given society at a specific point in time, altering the way women and men are perceived and perceive themselves.

Challenges to Eurocentric Models

Constructions of gender depend heavily on positionality. Patricia Hill Collins (1993) argues that the production of knowledge and knowledge claims about gender, as well as other phenomena, are forced to submit to a Eurocentric validation process that disadvantages those outside the majority culture. A world of difference exists between black feminist standpoints and those of white males. The latter dominate what Collins (1993:93) refers to as the "knowledge validation procedure." That white males control the knowledge validation process leaves African American and other Third World feminists with little support for their views of the world. Because their standpoints differ from the patriarchal Eurocentric standpoints, Third World feminist views have been discounted and, at times, even ostracized (see also Minh-ha 1989; Narayan 1989). Included among black feminists are African feminists who have their own particular Afrocentric viewpoints on gender.

At the risk of essentializing an Afrocentric standpoint, Collins (1993:95) maintains that Afrocentric feminists have certain values in common. Foremost among these are social connectedness (rather than individualism and separation) and a worldview that is holistic and seeks harmony. This view of the world is at odds with the Eurocentric notion of competition and individual achievement. In sum, Collins critiques Eurocentric scholars for not honoring competing claims of knowledge that arise from other cultural experiences.

Attacking Eurocentric feminist constructions of gender from another angle, Chandra Mohanty (1992, 1993a, 1993b) criticizes Western feminists for essentializing women's experience regardless of race, class, or nationality. Mohanty (1992) faults Western feminists for universalizing women's oppression. She argues that liberal Western feminists psychologize complex and often contradictory historical and cultural realities that mark differences among women. Differences—particularly among women—need to be engaged rather than transcended. She aims her attack at three lines of Western liberal feminist discourse that globalize women as victims (1993b). The first discourse includes Fran Hosken and her colleagues who, in launching a campaign against "female genital mutilation" in the 1980s, globalized women, especially African women, as victims of male violence. Hosken failed to acknowledge women's agency, differences in ages, cultural practices, and the fact that such rites do not occur everywhere in Africa; in fact, there are a sizable number of societies that do not include and have never included any form of female genital surgery with girls' initiations, and in other areas such practices have long been abandoned (see Davison 1989, 1996a, for a similar critique). Mohanty (1993b) also rightly critiques Cutrufelli's (1983) work *Women of Africa: Roots of Oppression,* as painting a generic picture of African women as dependents and victims of the colonial process without taking into consideration differences in race, class, nationality, and region, including rural-urban distinctions that differently influence African women's experiences. Finally, she critiques liberal Women in Development (WID) theorists for their economic reductionism (1993b:63–66) and the contradictions that exist due to women's location and circumstances. In objectifying women as victims, we lose sight of individual agency and regional, national, and historical particularities.

Mohanty (1993a:7) observes that "women of color" and "third world women" form a viable opposition to Western liberal feminism, an opposition that comes out of a "common context of struggle." The contexts for this struggle are colonialism and imperialism. In her assessment of colonial states and imperial cultures (1993a:15), she argues that three factors arising from colonial-imperialist ideologies have adversely affected Third World women: (1) the ideology of white masculinity as the norm; (2) the effects of colonial institutions and policies in transforming indigenous patriarchies and consolidating middle-class cultures globally; and (3) the rise of feminist politics and consciousness in colonial contexts and against the backdrop of national liberation movements. Mohanty's critique of white masculinity and its hegemonic aspects resonates with Patricia Collins's critique discussed earlier. Her criticism of masculinist colonial institutions and policies and the rise of feminist politics in colonial contexts reflects the concerns of African feminists such as Amadiume (1987), Gaidzanwa (1988, 1992), Mannathoko (1992), Meena (1992), and Ekejiuba (1995). In the next section, I use Rudo Gaidzanwa's (1992) work as an example of feminist critiques coming out of southern Africa.

Feminists in southern Africa come from various schools of thought depending on their national and cultural orientations. Zimbabwean feminist Rudo Gaidzanwa (1985, 1988, 1992) is not only involved in critiquing what exists but is grappling with alternatives. Her work demonstrates that historical, regional, and national circumstances influence the construction of gender. Gaidzanwa (1992:92) makes a point similar to Mohanty's, sharply criticizing what she refers to as liberal "bourgeois theories of gender" that emerged in Europe during struggles against monarchies, church, and state in the eighteenth century and later influenced Britain's conquest of southern Africa. She maintains that "colonial gender politics in Southern Africa closely mirror[ed] that of Britain in that suffrage was extended first to those who were privileged on the basis of sex, namely, white men, then a few men of the labouring classes or races, then white women and lastly black women" (1992:100). Thus ethnicity and class are primary factors in shaping gender.

Using Zimbabwe as an example, Gaidzanwa (1992) argues that colonization was resisted by both the Shona and the Ndebele. In precolonial Shona society women with special talents—such as the spirit medium Nehanda Nyakasikana—played leading roles. These opportunities were curtailed under British colonial occupation. It is notable that Gaidzanwa singles out Zimbabwe's two major ethnic groups for discussion. Her analysis reveals ambiguities: On the one hand, there were opportunities in Shona society for exceptional women to lead; on the other hand, patrilineal ideology prevented Shona women from achieving autonomy. Noting that both the Shona and the Ndebele are patrilineal groups, she observes, "As such, they shared some common ideas about the need to control the conditions under which women interacted with strangers, particularly males" (1992:109). She points out that the anticolonist struggle that emerged in the latter part of the twentieth century was led by Zimbabwean males who were educated in Western, British institutions, where patriarchal perceptions of gender were standard. She indicates that there were continuities between colonial and colonized men's ideas in terms of the need to subordinate women. As a result, women's involvement in the liberation armies was resisted initially because the male leaders of the movement perceived women's roles as confined to cooking, cleaning, and supplying male freedom fighters (1992:110). In Gaidzanwa's Afrocentrist view, Zimbabwean women's subordination differs from Western feminist notions of subordination because Zimbabwean women's subordination was shaped by colonial patriarchy and then was reinforced by colonized men's patriarchy. Thus the structural relations between men and women differ for this southern African country and, therefore, cannot be compared with Western feminist notions of gender.

Of the three critiques discussed in this section, Collins's work represents an Afrocentric feminist critique, but one that reflects a middle-class African American experience. Mohanty's work is mainly a critique of liberal feminism and the essentialization of women as a global category; she argues for a politics of positionality that acknowledges intragender differences and builds on them. She does not offer an alternative to existing feminist theories coming out of Third World experience. Rather, her position mirrors that of the DAWN group (Development Alternatives for Women Network) and multicultural, socialist feminists. African critiques of Western feminism abound, but African feminist theories of gender are more elusive. Where they exist, they vary depending on the time period in which a person is writing, the society from which she or he originates, and the global gender issues that are emerging. Here I limit the discussion to two theories of gender advanced by African feminists that have utility for an analysis of gender in southern African societies. The theories come from the fieldwork of Kamene Okonjo (1976) and Ifi Amadiume (1987), carried out at different times in Igbo communities in Nigeria, and from Fatima Mernissi (1987), whose work is based in Muslim Moroccan society.

The Production of Gender Theories

In analyzing gender within African societies, scholars—including African scholars—most often have depended on Western theoretical models (see, e.g., Van Allen 1976; Awe 1977; Meillassoux 1981; Obbo 1980; Bryson 1981; Mutemba 1982; Guyer 1984; Afonja 1986; Davison 1988a; Gaidzanwa 1988). Rarer are the scholars who have developed alternative gender theories birthed in the African experience. Kamene Okonjo's theory of the dual-sex political system in Igbo society (1976) has applicability beyond the Igbo context. Amadiume (1987), although agreeing that a dual-sex system exists in Igbo society, contends that it is mediated by instances where females assume roles normatively associated with males and vice versa. She looks at contradictions in the dual-sex system. Fatima Mernissi's analysis of gender relations in Moroccan society in *Beyond the Veil: Male-Female Dynamics in Modern Muslim Society* (1987) is most applicable to societies that have a significant Muslim population, as do Mozambique and Malawi. I begin with Okonjo's dual-sex system.

The Dual-Sex System

Okonjo's earliest work came out at the same time that the liberal feminist notion of separate gendered spheres divided into private (female) and public (male) domains was gaining a following in the West (see Rosaldo 1974), along with the notion of women's global subordination (e.g., Sacks 1979). Okonjo (1976) challenged the global applicability of a single-sex social system in which patriarchy subordinates women. She argued that in precolonial Igbo society a dual-sex system existed with separate, parallel political roles for men and women accompanied by a gendered system of checks and balances (1976:48). Both sets of political roles (women's and men's) were clearly in the Nigerian public domain. This was not the masculinized public domain of dichotomized models analyzed cross-culturally by early feminist anthropologists (e.g., Rosaldo 1974; Sanday 1974). Rather, Okonjo's dual-sex system was based on complementarity within the particular experience of one ethnic group in Nigeria, the Igbo. This gender system was destabilized by colonial occupation.

Okonjo argued that women and men of high rank had comparable and complementary positions in the Igbo political system. The authority of the Igbo Omu arose not from her role as a wife of the Obi, her male counterpart, but as the mother of the community, a powerful role in itself. In the capacity of Omu she was charged with the responsibility for women's affairs and had far-reaching authority, including the management and operation of the women's market (1976:48–51). She and the *ilongo,* her council of women elders, had the power to challenge male authority should women's interests be forgotten. The complementary political roles of men and women in Igbo society ensured a gender balance. It is the kind of balance that Simi Afonja (1986) alludes to in her work on precolonial and current Yoruba political economies. Noting that Western studies of Yoruba women's economic activities fail to show how trade is integrated with other areas of production and reproduction (1986:123), Afonja argues that the gender division of labor was historically based on a complementarity that was in turn based on reciprocity, an arrangement little understood by those colonial capitalists who set about to change it (1986:126).

Okonjo's gender analysis of Igbo society likewise illustrated that the authority of women in positions of power was undermined by colonial-capitalist administrators who recognized only the male half of the preexisting dual-sex political system. She argued that some of the most positive aspects of this precolonial dual-sex system were being reintegrated into late-twentieth-century Nigerian society. The usefulness of Okonjo's work lies in her Afrocentric standpoint. By demonstrating that historically a unitary gender political system controlled by adult males did not exist in places such as southern Nigeria, she provoked Western feminists to reevaluate their essentialist conclusions about the subordination of women.

Okonjo's dual-sex political model became relevant for other scholars looking at the influence of British colonial capitalism on preexisting groups in Africa, including those working in central southern Africa. For instance, Poewe (1981:22) implicitly draws on Okonjo's work in constructing what she refers to as "sexual parallelism," a model she applies to gender relations among the matrilineal Luapula in Zambia. She further demonstrates how the gender balance that preexisted colonial occupation in Luapula was preempted by the colonial-capitalist patriarchy, including Christian masculinist mores.

Ifi Amadiume, writing a decade after Okonjo, argued that Okonjo's analysis of Igbo society oversimplified the dual-sex system in that the nature of the dual-sex system allowed for exceptions. Amadiume accepts the notion of a dual-sex system as an organizing principle in Igbo communities

(1987:27, 57, 152). But she objects to collapsing Igbo women into a single gender category and holds Okonjo's understanding of patrilineal sociopolitical lineage organization responsible. In Amadiume's study of the Nnobi Igbo, she demonstrates that within the Nnobi patrilineal system, women held different and contrasting positions in their roles as daughters and as wives. Lineage daughters held greater power, especially in monitoring the behavior of wives, who married into their husbands' homes, and in orchestrating funerals, which were lineage affairs. She points out that as daughters and as wives, women occasionally might assume roles recognized as being male.

In cases where there were no sons, a lineage daughter might be given the involuntary title of *nhayikwa*, or male daughter. Often this title went to first daughters. Amadiume relates that one woman she interviewed, Nwajiuba, was called from her marital home to her father's home when he was terminally ill. She remained in his house and assumed the status of a son; thus on his death she was entitled to inherit his patrilineal lands. Amadiume notes that girls and women who became *nhayikwa* and those who were incorporated into the lineage of the Obi felt uneasy about having a status usually enjoyed by men. She also makes clear that such was the exception rather than the rule (1987:34).

The other situation where a female could assume a male role was in woman-to-woman marriage (*igba ohu*). Usually older women, especially those with status, became female husbands. There were two possible scenarios in such cases. A female husband might give her wife to a male husband from somewhere else and become the mother of the wife. More characteristically, an *igba ohu*'s wife, or wives, might stay with her and bear children in her name. Although childless women often assumed the role of an *igba ohu,* in a society where wealth historically was counted in wives and children, any wife of means might acquire younger wives to assist her with daily work and bear children in her name. Amadiume notes that the widow of a deceased big man became the husband of twenty-four wives! The practice of female husbanding, or woman-to-woman marriage, is not specific to the Igbo. It has occurred in other societies throughout Africa, including southern Africa (see, e.g., Gluckman 1950; Krige 1974; Oboler 1985).

Women in Igbo society fulfilled roles additional to the political ones described by Okonjo (1976). Due to the centrality of the goddess Idemili in Igbo cosmology, any woman with particular attributes associated with this goddess, especially industriousness and hospitality (the pot of plenty), was singled out to become an Ekwe. These women were viewed as economically powerful and clever and wielded great authority over other women. Symbolic of an Ekwe's status was her dependence on other women to carry headloads for her. All Ekwe belonged to what Amadiume refers to as an "exclusive club" (1987:44). The tie with Idemili was strong, and her influence as goddess was so critical that no one in Igbo society dared enter her shrine except the shrine priest, a "female man" who was her consort and who tied his wrapper in the style of women to symbolize his role. Hence women as goddesses and as producers and reproducers held significant roles in this predominantly patrilineal society. Moreover, even though Igbo society was characterized by gender parallelism, there was room for flexibility in gender classification. This flexibility "allowed the incorporation of certain categories of women into the male category, giving them positions of authority in the power structure" (Amadiume 1987:51).

Like Okonjo, Amadiume shows how the dual-sex political system of the Igbo, and particularly women's institutions, titles, and worship of the goddess Idemili, were undermined by a European single-sex, Christian, capitalist system. The result was a dialectic process of change, one that resonates with the southern African experience. Amadiume's contribution also includes an analysis of the postindependence erosion of women's authority with the advent of electoral politics. She makes the point that women, through their gender-specific organizations, had a shared sense of political consciousness that also gave them a sense of self-worth. In turn, their self-esteem was reinforced by women's solidarity. This sense of solidarity was undermined as women's groups came under the authority of a male-dominated civilian government. The once powerful Igbo women's groups became marginalized politically in Nnobi.

What I find missing from both Okonjo and Amadiume's gender analyses of the Igbo is attention to class differences among women. Amadiume hints at class when she notes the difference in ages between female leaders such as the Ekwe and their followers. She also hints at the asymmetrical relation between female husbands and their chosen wives. Women with extraordinary talents were targeted for titles, but what about the ordinary peasant woman or the woman who became enslaved? Were they as eligible to become Ekwe? Were they members of the *ilongo*? Did they have options for assuming male roles to the same degree that the daughter of a landowner or the wife of a headman had? I am left with such questions.

Sexual Space in Muslim Societies

For African societies where Islam is a major dimension of the society, Fatima Mernissi's model of sexual-space boundaries has a certain salience. Mernissi suggests that contrary to Western assumptions, "Islam does not advance the thesis of women's inherent inferiority. Quite the contrary, it affirms the potential equality between the sexes" (1987:19). Like Okonjo and Amadiume, Mernissi questions Eurocentric notions of women's global subordination.

In Moroccan Muslim society women are viewed as having power, sexual, creative power that has the potential for creating life or for provoking chaos, the latter referred to as *fitna* (Mernissi 1987:31). *Fitna* has the additional meaning of a femme fatale, one who makes men lose their self-control. Women's unruly sexuality is controlled through the Qu'ranic ideal of *umma*, the communal family of which Allah is the head, as men are the heads of their families. The sacredness of family is central to Islam. Men are responsible for their spiritual journey on this earth and for the well-being of family. In order to prevent men from becoming distracted on their journey by women's power, women are kept away from men—spatially—so that their creative energy is used within the family, serving its interests. Spatial boundaries take the form of women's segregation and seclusion through purdah and veiling in public.

Interestingly, Islam recognizes the existence of matrilineal forms of descent among Arabs and north Africans prior to the arrival of Muhammud (Mernissi 1987:73–74; Callaway 1987:8). However, that the children belonged to the mother's clan in *sadiqa* (friend of the woman) marriages was contradictory to the concept of *umma*. Therefore, Muslim men's marriage with women from matrilineal groups was forbidden unless these women were willing to accept the superordinate role of a husband who had control over both wife and children. "In *ba'al* marriage the offspring belonged to the husband" (Callaway 1987:74). Callaway (1987) illustrates that the insistence on patriliny in Islam liquidated earlier forms of matriliny in northern Nigeria.

Islam's theoretical predilection for patriliny and virilocal marriage, however, has not been adopted wholesale in Africa and is not consistent everywhere. Among the Mandinka of Senegal and the Yao of Malawi and Mozambique, for instance, matriliny and Islam are intertwined in the lives of many peasants. Spatial segregation of genders is muted among the Yao except in mosques. Muslim husbands and wives cultivate together in a field belonging to the wife's matrilineage, and Muslim women are as active as men in the local market trade. However, the Yao case is more the exception than the rule. Certainly Muslim groups in northern Nigeria and other parts of West Africa practice purdah and other forms of gender segregation (Schildkrout 1982; Callaway 1987; Joekes 1985). Mernissi's theory of sexual space, then, is applicable to some societies practicing Islam but not to others. More variation exists within and between societies than can be grasped by a single theory.

The Gendered Life Cycle

Having compared several African feminist theories regarding gender structuring, I want to approach gender through a different lens, one that looks at gender as a sociosexual phenomenon and as being socially structured over the course of a life span. Rituals that mark critical transitions along the trajectory of a life were, and still are in many cases, an integral part of the en-gendering process in an African community or group. As Amadiume (1987) points out, usually these rituals were/are planned and carried out by a prominant lineage or sublineage in a community or group. How do these rituals order the life cycle of females in contrast to males? Are there points in the life cycle where the genders converge?

My rendering of the gendered life cycle is drawn from my work and the work of others among rural peoples in southern and eastern Africa. Among urbanites, especially those with more than a primary school education, the scenario differs greatly. Also, in trying to capture normative patterns of behavior, past and present, I run the risk of masking differences among various groups. Great variation exists; we need to keep this in mind.

In particular, I want to capture the differences, where they exist, between matrilineal and patrilineal gender structuring. I use data on the Gikuyu and Bukusu of Kenya and the Shona and Ndebele of Zimbabwe as examples of patrilineal groups. The material on matrilineal groups comes from the Tonga of northern Zimbabwe and the Chewa, Mang'anja, and Yao of Malawi (also the Yao of Mozambique) with some historical reference to the Bemba elite and the Kaonde of Zambia.

Africans on both sides of the lineage divide have explained the gender-development cycle to me as one in which an individual is perceived as moving from a precarious state of infancy with little gender identity toward a period of maturity when gender becomes ritually and socially recognized toward a period of elderhood when gender distinctions gradually drop away. A description of this sequence follows.

The Ambiguous Child

A thin thread separates a newborn infant from the world of his or her ancestors. Historically, until an infant had lived long enough to indicate that it had a fair chance of survival, it was given either no name or a very temporary one depending on the religious orientation of the family into which it was born. The child's official naming ceremony came between six weeks and a year after birth. In some places this is still the case. Usually elder clan or lineage members organized the ceremony. Other lineage members and relatives were invited and a goat, chicken, or ram was slaughtered to honor the occasion. The child's place in his or her descent group was stressed in all aspects of the ritual.

Formerly, a postpartum period of sexual abstinence was observed by the mother after the birth. It lasted between two and four years or as long as the mother was breast-feeding her child. It was a way of ensuring child spacing. As a rural Kenyan woman in her early fifties related, "In our time one waited for four years before getting another child, giving time for the body to build up strength. . . . One can go to the river and fetch water, but can you fetch blood and energy from a river? We knew these things" (Davison 1989:125–126). Older Malawian women interviewed for a health survey in 1992 expressed the same view (Kaufulu and Davison 1992), and Weinrich (1982) and older Zimbabwean women narrators in Staunton's collection (1990) confirm a similar practice.

Currently postpartum abstinence is observed by some Malawian women and not by others. In a 1992 survey of seventy-five mothers ranging in age from seventeen to forty-seven, Kaufulu and Davison (1992:14) found that the average amount of time between children was eighteen months to two years for the majority of mothers and that most wanted five to six children. Women with some education (up to four years) were more apt to practice family planning than women with no education.

A child's birth is cherished because a new person has been added to the group in a cultural context that has historically measured wealth in people. The birth of a child, according to the Gikuyu and Shona, also ensures the continuation of an ancestral spirit reborn in the new person. In some groups a child was/is given the name of an ancestor whose identity she or he assumes.

Among patrilineal groups such as the Gikuyu and Shona a boy is highly valued as a link between past and present. Among matrilineal groups such as the Chewa and Yao, a girl is especially welcome; not only does she bring a new source of labor to female relatives but she will continue the fertility of her lineage through the birth of future children. A mother with several daughters is considered blessed. In matrilineal groups, most often a daughter is viewed as being responsible for looking after her parents in their old age, whereas in patrilineal groups this is the responsibility of sons. Of course, individual circumstances provide the exceptions. If a son in a patrilineal family has moved away, a daughter close at hand or one with financial resources may become her parents' support. Similarly, a son with available resources in a matrilineal context may assume responsibility for younger siblings and his aging parents if a daughter is unable to provide support.

As a toddler, a child assumes a nongendered identity. She or he is raised and nurtured by a circle of kin, including older siblings of both sexes, parents (when both are present), uncles, aunts, and grandparents. During this time, a child begins to learn the family's language or languages and kinship terms. Most Bantu languages do not make a distinction between the sexes in the use of subject or object pronouns such as he/she or her/him; the context provides the clue to a person's gender. Thus, in terms of communication—oral and written—language is less gendered than it is in Eurocentric societies (see also Amadiume 1987 on this point). In most cases only two or three of the classifying kinship terms are explicitly gendered in lineage groups—those referring to the mother (which includes all women in a child's lineage in the first ascending generation, that is, those in the child's mother's generation); those referring, in cases of patriliny, to the father (all men in the first ascending generation); and those referring, in cases of matriliny, to the maternal uncle. Other kinship status terms such as those for siblings designate whether the siblings are older or younger. The same is true of parallel matrilineal or patrilineal cousins. The term for grandparents of the second ascending generation of matrikin or patrikin is not gendered but may become gender specific in some cases.

Generally, boys growing up in rural areas have more time for exploratory play than girls do, but this depends greatly on the socioeconomic status of the family, whether the father is present in the household, and whether the children attend school.

Both girls and boys are expected to participate in caring for younger siblings and at times to help with the care of younger cousins in their lineage, who often live nearby. In reality, however, girls spend more time caring for infants and toddlers than do boys. For example, a modest time-allocation study of forty-two Malawian primary school pupils' participation in after-school labor activities found, using direct observation methods, that the girls spent 13 percent of a sixty-minute period in childcare compared to 8 percent for the boys (Davison and Kanyuka 1990:48). Combined with household tasks such as water hauling, food preparation, and firewood collection, girls spent 68 percent and boys 37.8 percent of a sixty-minute period on domestic tasks (1990:49). In a study of peasant children's labor in twelve Tonga families in northern Zimbabwe, Reynolds (1991) found that of the six children under ten who assisted their parents with childcare during peak planting periods, five were girls and only one was a boy. Moreover, the boy worked fewer days (only three) than the girls, who worked on average five days helping their mothers during these peak periods (Reynolds 1991:Table 2.4, 49). Reynolds also found that female children took over the burden of domestic labor for their mothers when peak agricultural periods demanded their mother's labor. In theory, then, both sexes are expected to help with young siblings and domestic chores; in reality, girls most often carry the burden and for longer periods of time.

Where children are not involved in schooling (the majority in Mozambique and Malawi, the minority in Zimbabwe), they participate significantly in agricultural tasks connected with maize, rice, or cassava production. In a labor-allocation study for tasks related to maize production in 120 rural households in Zomba, Malawi, I found that children in these households contributed 34 percent of the overall labor for production (Davison 1992:77). Tasks in which children most often participated were weeding, fertilizing, and harvesting. In Reynolds's study of labor allocation in twelve Tonga families in Omay, Zimbabwe, she found that during the peak agricultural period (November-January), twelve girls and twelve boys in these families spent an equal number of days (84) in tasks such as clearing, planting, replanting, and weeding, but that the girls together worked more hours (396) than the boys (372 hours) (Reynolds 1991:47). Further, the children's labor differed by gender: The girls spent 31 percent of their time on planting; the boys spent only 12 percent of their time on the same task. For replanting, however, the pattern was reversed. Boys spent nearly half their total time on replanting, and girls spent only 26 percent of their time replanting. For the other two tasks, clearing and weeding, the proportion of time spent was nearly the same for girls and boys, although girls spent a slightly higher proportion of their time than boys on clearing land. Similar to the findings in my Zomba study, Reynolds's study found that children's contribution to production was significant, accounting for over 33 percent of the labor hours worked during the peak season.

Where children attend primary school, household maintenance and agricultural tasks are limited to the afternoons and weekends, but boys are more apt to be in school than girls and have more time to study after school. They are also more likely to complete the final three years of primary school, a period when girls are beginning to feel the pressure to marry (in Malawi and Mozambique, girls are between twelve and fifteen years of age at this time). In Malawi such pressure is particularly intense if the girl has undergone Chinamwale, the initiation ceremony that occurs at puberty (Kapakasa 1990; Davison and Kanyuka 1990; Liwimbi 1992).

Initiation into Gendered Adulthood

Initiation historically was the single most important gender ritual during the life span. Victor Turner's study of Ndembu initiation illuminates the role that initiation played in making public reproductive roles that were otherwise considered private. He observed (1969:53) that "powerful drives and emotions associated with human physiology, especially the physiology of reproduction, are divested in the ritual process of their antisocial quality and attached to components of the moral order." Thus the ritual of initiation became a socially legitimate forum for amplifying the sexual reproductive roles of adult women and men and for teaching these explicit roles to adolescents in the process of transition from one life stage to another.

In some cases, boys and girls were initiated together (e.g., the Gikuyu), but in most cases they were initiated in gender-segregated rituals (Shona, Ndebele, Chewa, and Yao). Among the patrilineal Bukusu and Shona, rituals were held mainly for boys. Among the matrilineal Yao, Chewa, and Bemba they were held for girls, although in the case of the Chewa a counterpart ritual developed in the nineteenth century to complement Chinamwale, the girls' ceremony (Woods 1992).

The extent to which initiation ceremonies are still held varies by region and ethnicity. Writing in the preface to the second edition of *Chisungu: A Girl's Initiation Ceremony Among the Bemba of Zambia,* Audrey Richards (1982) wrote of the ceremony she had observed in 1931 that by 1956 "such ceremonies seemed to be dying out" (1982:xiii). Moore and Vaughan (1994) relate that the sixty women they interviewed in Northern Province, Zambia, in the latter part of the 1980s insisted that *chisungu* was rarely performed at that time. In contrast, initiation ceremonies for girls (and boys where they occur) remain a part of the annual "calendar" in rural areas in much of southern and central Malawi in the 1990s, even if in attenuated form. I observed two for girls during the three years I worked there (1989–1992).

Initiation for girls, where it occurs in rural areas in southern Africa, differs from initiation farther north in eastern and western Africa. Historically "female circumcision" (clitoridectomy or its more radical form, infibulation) was not a part of the ritual, nor is it currently.[1] This is in contrast to female initiation rites held in other parts of Africa (MacCormack 1977; Edemikpong 1988). Boys, especially among Muslims, are circumcised.

The initiation ritual marks the transition to an adult dual-gender system. When only one gender is being initiated, only members of that gender attend. Older, well-respected females of a matrilineage organize and implement these initiations and are paid for their roles as the girls' advisers. Whereas historically the ceremony may have taken several weeks, currently it is limited to between two and four days, at least in rural Malawi and Mozambique. With the uneven penetration of capitalism into the rural areas, among some groups the initiation ceremony has become commoditized. The capital outlay for initiation in one Yao community, including fees for sponsors, advisers, food, and new clothing, was equal to three years of school fees (MK25, or US$8) in 1990. In some cases this capital outlay competes with a family's need to pay school fees (Kapakasa 1990). When this happens, a girl may be forced to drop out of school.

Initiations characteristically are scheduled at the end of the harvest season in Malawi and Mozambique—prior to the beginning of the school year in either late August or early September. The specialized elders of the appropriate sex teach initiates what will be expected of them as adults in three areas: sexual behavior, responsibilities as gendered adults, and adherence to customs and the traditions of the lineage or clan. Recently initiated young women or men act as sponsors to support the initiates through their "ordeal." For those who attend the initiation, it is a celebration of the particular gender values and qualities that make them female or male, respectively. For those who officiate and act as advisers, it is a specialized job. In southern Malawi, *nankungwe,* the older trained female advisers for Chinamwale, earned a fee ranging from MK2 per initiate to MK6—US$0.75–$2.50 in 1992 dollars (Makambera 1992).

For rural girls participating in Chinamwale cha Chiputa, which occurs for girls between eight and eleven years of age, the ceremony initiates a sequential process leading to maturity. For those who have begun menstruating, Chinamwale cha Ndakula is a significant marker of their growing maturity and potential for marriage. Socially, for a girl these two ceremonies form a symbolic and ritual connection with her ethnic group and lineage. A university-educated girl whose Christian family prevented her from participating in Chinamwale because they had "left behind" such traditional ways expressed regret that she had not participated in the ceremony. "If I had gone for Chinamwale," she confided to me, "I would have learned more about my culture, about myself" (interview at Chancellor College, Zomba, 1990).

Marriage as a Sequential Process

Marriage prior to missionization and continuing into the colonial period was a process consisting of a number of sequential steps rather than a single event. Negotiations for marriage arrangements began even before a child was born among some groups (see Wilson [1951] for the Nyakyusa) or prior to a girl's initiation (see Richards [1950] for the Bemba and Bisa). More characteristically, however, they began once a young person had completed the initiation ritual. Families arranged marriages through specialized marriage negotiators in most of central southern Africa. Among the patrilineal Shona groups in Zimbabwe the negotiator was always a man, but among the Kalanga and Ndebele this role could be filled by either a man or a woman (Weinrich 1982:48). Among the matrilineal Tonga, the young man's mother's sister was the preferred negotiator, although a male relative could also fill the role (Weinrich 1982:50). Among other matrilineal groups the negotiator was/is usually a female relative (Ntara 1973; Makambera 1992).

Even though young people try to choose their own spouses, marriage is the concern of their two extended families, and usually their families must make the final decision. Currently marriage is viewed as "a voluntary relationship between a man and a woman or women, intended to last for their joint lives" (Armstrong et al. 1993:2). This definition covers monogamous and polygynous marriages but does not include other forms of marriage recognized by some African societies under customary laws.

Examples of customary marriages that may or may not be recognized by statutory law are leviarate and sororate marriages. In a leviarate marriage, a brother stands in for his deceased brother, marrying the widow and taking responsibility for his brother's family. Similarly, in sororate marriages, a widower may be offered his wife's sister to replace his deceased wife. Among some groups (e.g., the patrilineal Igbo of Nigeria and the Nandi of

Kenya), if a woman does not have a son to inherit her property, she may contribute bridewealth to secure a younger woman to bear children for her (Akpamgbo 1977; Amadiume 1987; Oboler 1985). Older Nandi women, like older Igbo women, assume male status, becoming *kagotogosta komostab murenik* ("she has gone up the side of the men"); they become female husbands (Oboler 1985:131). Similar cases of woman-to-woman marriage, although rare, have occurred in southern Africa.

The patrilineal Lovedu and Zulu of South Africa had a form of woman-woman marriage whereby a wealthy older woman might marry a young woman to take care of her and provide children in her old age (Krige 1974; Gluckman 1950). A related practice occurred, and still occurs, among some matrilineal groups in Malawi, such as the Yao and Mang'anja, whereby a childless woman may select another woman to produce children with her husband. The children, however, belong to the female husband, and the younger woman has no marital or family rights except through the older woman (Makambera, personal communication, 1992). These woman-woman marriages are customarily recognized but may not be recognized by statutory law.

Marriage and Residence

Marriage is still a sequential process in many African societies. Lineage representatives from both sides negotiate to ensure that the particular lineages or sublineages are allowed to intermarry and that the marriage is acceptable to all. These negotiations also include a determination of the bridewealth or brideservice demanded of the man, which is given or performed in installments. Co-residence may occur at any stage of the process.

The Role of Bridewealth. Bridewealth transfers from a man's family to a woman's were, and still are in many areas, the validating event in a marriage among patrilineal groups. It ensured control of a wife's reproductive and productive labor. It symbolized the man's right to take his wife to his or his father's home. Historically, a man's elder male relatives, assisted by his mother, made the first move toward negotiating with a potential bride's family. A token gift such as millet porridge, tobacco, or a chicken was sent to the girl's family to signal the man's interest. If the gesture was reciprocated, the two extended families, through senior males, began the negotiations for bridewealth, referred to as *lobola* in many southern African groups.

Associated with virilocality, *lobola* was a gift given to the bride's family (and distributed among descent-group members) of several cows, a bull or two, goats, or other valuable goods. In the late twentieth century in Zimbabwe and Mozambique, it more often takes the form of cash. *Lobola* signals the value of a bride in terms of her procreative abilities in sustaining the patrilineage and the labor she will provide to her new family. It also is a form of compensation for the labor her natal family loses. Symbolically, *lobola* binds the two families and two clans or descent groups involved in the marriage.

Lobola is transferred in installments, a few cows or a few Zimdollars at a time until the total amount agreed upon has been delivered. Until this time, the rights of paternity that go with being a father are not fully recognized; nor are the husband's rights to his wife. A woman for whom the *lobola* has not been fully transferred has an easier time of escaping her marriage than a woman for whom *lobola* has been completed.

Among the Shona groups of Zimbabwe, transferring *lobola* was and is a lineage matter; "ancestors are believed to be particularly concerned with lineage continuity, they are regarded as the guardians of the fertility of their descendants" (Weinrich 1982:39). Formerly, the prospective groom and his male relatives drove cattle for *lobola* into his future father-in-law's cattle corral, where the bride's father welcomed them and ritually called on his patrilineal ancestors, announcing that the cattle for his daughter had been delivered and that his daughter was thus freed to go to another village to bear children for the husband's lineage. The ancestors were asked to bless the man's daughter, making her fertile. Even where Zimdollars have replaced cattle, these are taken into the future father-in-law's cattle bier and the father shakes them and refers to them as "cattle to continue the patrilineage" (Weinrich 1982:39).

Lobola has become tied to capitalism and thus now is stigmatized among urban educated women who feel they, too, have become commoditized. Despite their feelings, the custom is almost universally practiced in Zimbabwe in the late twentieth century (Weinrich 1982; Msora 1992). It also continues to be practiced in southern Mozambique despite the Organization of Mozambican Women's campaign to eradicate it as demeaning to women (Guimaraes 1986; de Silva 1992). Patrilineal groups in northern Malawi also practice the *lobola* custom. The amount of *kwacha*, *metacais,* or Zimdollars transferred from the groom to the bride's father currently is evaluated in terms of a girl's education and earning power as well as her procreative and productive capabilities.

In Zimbabwe in 1980, *lobola* payments were not uniform by ethnic group. The lowest amount transferred in installments among the Shona, Ndebele, and matrilineal Tonga was between Z$5 and Z$95 (between US$2.50 and US$47.00). Only 28 percent of Shona paid amounts in this range; 55 percent of Ndebele paid in the same range (Weinrich 1982:41). The Tonga fell in between the other two groups. At the upper end of the scale (Z$185–$275), 24 percent of Shona, just under 1 percent of Ndebele, and 12 percent of Tonga paid in this range. None of the Ndebele paid amounts in the highest range (Z$275 and over), whereas 4.8 percent of

Tonga and 5.5 percent of Shona transferred bridewealth in this range (Weinrich 1982:41, Table 7).

Why are there differences among these three ethnic groups? Weinrich (1982), who carried out a close study of *lobola* practices among them in the late 1970s, argues that the Ndebele make less of an investment in *lobola* because patrilineal ideology has become less significant to them (the practice of bridewealth is directly related to the maintenance of the patrilineage in Zimbabwe) (1982:42–43). This minimal ideological investment in lineage goes back to the period when their military units, which were based on descent groups, were broken up by the British colonial administration. Once this happened, according to Weinrich, the Ndebele lost interest in sustaining their patrilineages and the descent group became less important and the family more significant (1982:43). Alternatively, economics may be a factor in their reduced commitment to patrilineages. The Ndebele suffered most under colonial capitalism in terms of land alienation in the nineteenth century and cattle alienation in the twentieth century. They inhabit the driest and least fertile land in southern Zimbabwe and, not insignificantly, suffered most under the new political alignment at independence (Ranger 1970, 1984; Werbner 1991). *Lobola* has retained its significance among the Shona and the Tonga; what has changed is the inflation of bridewealth transfers, which ran as high as Z$1,500 in 1992 (Msora 1992).

Once the entire amount of bridewealth has been transferred, a woman is virtually under the control of her husband, a form of patriarchal authority that predates colonial capitalism. Zimbabwean legal scholar Welshman Ncube (1986:117) maintains that among patrilineal groups this form of patriarchy can be traced back to three factors: a feudalistic system of production wherein certain clans and families dominated commoners, the customary control of land by men, and patrilineal gerontocracy. However, this preexisting patriarchy was reinforced by the colonial administration: "The colonial legislature and judiciary in their understanding of customary law held the view that according to customary law an African woman never attained full legal status" (Ncube 1986:120). Overcoming this legal constraint became one of Zimbabwean women's major goals with the achievement of independence in 1980.

Part of a woman's socioeconomic dependence was, and remains, the result of her being a "stranger" in her husband's village upon marriage. Through virilocal residence, she is totally dependent on him and his patrikin for a house and land to cultivate. If a man marries more than one wife, he gives each one a piece of land, a granary for storage, and a house to occupy with her children. Where land has become scarce in his paternal village due to consolidated holdings and increased population, a newly married man may decide to settle in another area where he can borrow or buy land. Or if he has marketable skills, he may decide to relocate to a town with his new family. Consequently, although in theory a woman moves to her husband's home upon marriage, the practice depends on whether land is available to cultivate and what employable skills the husband has. The children born of this marriage take the father's patriclan name and become part of his descent group.

The only form of property that belongs to women in Shona and Ndebele groups other than property acquired through their own labors (e.g., as potter, weaver, herbalist, midwife) is held by mothers of brides. Early in a marriage, after the wife has relocated to her husband's village, the husband goes to his mother-in-law with a cow, referred to as *mombe yohumai* (literally "mother of the cow") among Shona speakers and *inkomo yohlanga* in Ndebele (Ncube 1986). This gift is given to the mother for her female ancestors, who have the power to ensure that fertility will pass from mother to daughter (Weinrich 1982; Ncube 1986). The cow may not be used as part of a brother's bridewealth but is for the mother to keep. Ncube (1986:134) notes that although this custom was still practiced in both rural and urban areas in the 1980s, in urban areas cash was more often substituted for the cow.

Ncube (1986) argues that property relations within a given society and within a particular household determine the power relations within the household (1986:1). The spouse who "owns" and controls the land also controls the household insofar as control of its subsistence needs enables him or her to command obedience from other family members. In patrilineal households the oldest land-controlling male controls the recruitment and allocation of labor. In matrilineal households where uxorilocality persists, the oldest female or the avunculate (her oldest brother) has a similar position. The extent to which household heads in either category are able to recruit the labor of others outside the immediate family depends on the strength of interhousehold ties based on descent and financial resources.

In residential clusters or villages where men are linked through patrilineal ties, men may recruit the male labor of their patrikin, but their wives have less control over the recruitment of labor beyond their own children. Among some patrilineal groups where women have other links through initiation or through church or women's organizations, wives are more likely to have access to and control over labor beyond their immediate households. And as a woman progresses through the life cycle, her increased authority and experience enable her to more easily recruit and control the allocation of labor within her own household and to participate in collaborative labor outside the household.

In cases of divorce, a woman returns to her natal home. Sometimes she is forced to leave her children, except for nursing infants, in her husband's home to be raised by patrikin. However, in most cases women have custody of their children in Zimbabwe (Gwaunza and Zana 1990). In theory, any *lobola* transferred is supposed to be returned to the husband's patrikin. But in practice this may not be possible because the cattle may have been used for a brother's *lobola* or the money may have been spent. Whether it is repaid can influence whether a husband is willing to pay maintenance for his wife and children. In cases where a husband refuses to provide maintenance, a wife's only option is to seek redress through the maintenance court under statutory law. The process of bringing a case is not easy; it is expensive and time consuming (Gwaunza and Zana 1990), thus discouraging women from becoming involved in a court case.

The practice of giving *lobola* has made inroads in matrilineal groups that formerly may have practiced brideservice. Historically, bridewealth and virilocal residence have been identified with matrilineal groups such as the Lakeside Tonga in Malawi, the Plateau Tonga in Zambia, and the Gwembe Tonga in northern Zimbabwe (Colson 1951; Richards 1950; Roberts 1964). To illustrate the ambiguities in the relation between bridewealth and lineage ideology, Gouldsbury (1915–1916), a native commissioner for Northern Rhodesia in the early colonial period, observed that the matrilineal, matrilocal Bemba of that period practiced bridewealth. He also noted a change in bridewealth values. Whereas in the late nineteenth century the bride's father was given an ax, three hoes, six goats, and twenty arrows, by 1915 the commodities had changed to one cow and four dhotis; the commodities given to the bride's mother had shifted from three hoes, three goats, bracelets, and twenty arrows to one bull and three dhotis (167).

In Malawi, some matrilineal groups began in the eighteenth and nineteenth centuries to incorporate *lobola* into their marital arrangements as a result of intermixing with patrilineal groups that practiced bridewealth. In northern Malawi, the Tumbuka, formerly described as matrilineal, adopted *lobola* together with other patrilineal practices as a result of being conquered by the patrilineal Ngoni (Vail 1972). During the period of Ngoni domination, the Chewa, who continue to ascribe to matrilineal ideology, began to adopt an optional cultural practice referred to as *chitengwa*, through which "an ordinary male person may arrange to have control over his wife and children" with the payment of *lobola* (Phiri 1977:9). Virilocality was implied.

In some cases, *lobola* had only a minor influence on marital relations. Crehan (1994:10–14) notes that among the matrilineal Kaonde of northwestern Zambia, marriage did not historically include large payments of bridewealth that had to be repaid should the marriage end in divorce. The casualness with which bridewealth was (and is) treated may have had some bearing on the sequential nature of residence. The Kaonde tended to begin married life by residing in the wife's natal village with her parents, where the husband had an obligation to perform brideservice (a matrilocal pattern). Alternatively, the wife might remain with her parents and the husband would visit her regularly. The couple remained in the wife's village until the first few children were born. After some time, the husband would take his family to his natal village, a virilocal pattern. Thus the Kaonde included both matrilocal and virilocal patterns of marital residence.

To summarize, marriage often, though not always, includes both bridewealth paid in installments over time and virilocality. Nonetheless, how bridewealth is transferred, and in what amounts, varies by ethnic group. Bridewealth also varies for urban areas, where higher amounts of cash are demanded. Bridewealth may or may not be linked to lineage. In Zimbabwe it has symbolic significance for the continuation of a patrilineage. In Zambia among the Kaonde, it has little currency.

The Role of Brideservice.   Many groups defined as matrilineal north of the Zambezi historically practiced matrilocality or uxorilocality prior to European contact (Richards 1950; Mitchell 1956; Roberts 1964; Ntara 1973). No bridewealth was collected by the bride's kin. Instead the groom performed brideservice for his future in-laws in the form of agricultural labor, usually clearing land and hoeing over a period of time. Referred to in Malawi as *chikamwene*, this form of labor still exists in rural localities in the central and southern regions, Tete and Zambezia Provinces in Mozambique, and in some areas of Northern Province, Zambia (Welch et al. 1985; Stromgaard 1985; Konzakapanzi 1992).

In areas where brideservice is practiced, once a man has proven himself to be a competent worker, his future wife's parents, with the approval, often, of the mother's brother, invite him to stay in the village. The woman's matrikin help her husband to build a new house for the couple, and the principal uncle allots him a piece of land. However, should there be a dissolution of the marriage, the husband will leave the village and the land behind and return to his own natal village or hamlet.

Part of the problem of analyzing matrilocality and uxorilocality and their significance for women lies in the gender bias of Western observers, past and present. Women-centered residence patterns were and are viewed as an anomaly by Western observers coming from a Eurocentric gender system dominated by patriliny and virilocality. This bias is reflected in colonial ethnographies. For instance, a male missionary writing about brideservice in 1919 stated, "Many a young man becomes practically the slave of his avaricious mother-in-law, and spends years in her service, from which he receives no release until her death" (Anderson 1919:238, cited in Wright 1983:74–75). And thirty years later, anthropologist Audrey Richards, in referring to the "husband's precarious position" in Bemba society, observed, "He lives in a community based on kinship traced through women and he is economically dependent on his wife's people and working under their orders" (1982:41). That women in virilocal marriages also have had to work under in-laws' orders and are dependent on them seems to have been overlooked by colonial anthropologists—male and female. Our ability to analyze women's positions in societies ascribing to either patrilineal or matrilineal ideologies has been colored by androcentric concerns for the position of men in these societies. We do not have a comparable record for women.

Even in recent writings, there is a tendency to gloss virilocal residence for all lineage systems. For example, several scholars have argued that with increasing capitalist and Christian penetration, uxorilocality as a practice has given way to pressure for paternal authority and virilocal residence patterns (Phiri 1977; Poewe 1981; Marks and Rathbone 1983). In parts of Zambia and central Malawi, that is the case. Nonetheless, the transition to virilocality does not apply everywhere. Marks and Rathbone (1983:3) suggest that "the matrilineal system" has been overtaken by "the patrilineal/virilocal system," but this is not accurate if residence is used as the indicator.

Matrilineage and residence are not necessarily linked. Moreover, in some cases a man in a patrilineal group may elect to move to his wife's hamlet to escape paying bridewealth or because better land is available there (Duly 1946; Konzakapanzi 1993). Furthermore, in large parts of southern and central Malawi, northern Mozambique, and some parts of northern Zambia, uxorilocality has demonstrated a healthy persistence (Geisler, Keller, and Chuzu 1985; Stromgaard 1985; Welch, Dagnino, and Sachs 1985; Arnfred 1988; Mandala 1990; Davison 1993, 1995; Pitcher 1993; Peters 1994).

Ideology and practice do not always mesh in residence patterns. At times economic circumstances intervene to dictate where a couple resides. Currently in rural central and southern Malawi, even though in theory a husband is supposed to move to his wife's village when he marries, in practice residency may depend most on where land is available. If more land is available in the groom's matrilineal village than in the wife's village, the couple will live in the groom's village (Konzakapanzi 1992). If land is scarce in a girl's matrilineal village, her father or maternal uncle may go to a chief in a neighboring village to beg for an additional piece of land, as occurred in the case of one of the University of Malawi students whom I taught. If there is little or no land available, the couple may have to relocate to a periurban area to seek employment. Land scarcity has definitely altered marital residence patterns that in the 1960s were more firmly rooted.

Polygyny and the Production of Lineage.   The ability to support multiple wives is often linked to status or class. If a man has accumulated wealth in cattle or cash, it may be invested in bridewealth to increase his wealth in land and people (Meillassoux 1981). Historically, for men with a surplus in matrilineal societies, polygyny also was a possibility. On the whole, however, it is rare for a man in a matrilineal, uxorilocal group to take more than one wife because he must build each wife a house and provide labor to the in-laws in each wife's village—and this can become complicated. As a result, marriages, with the exception of chiefs and village heads, have tended to remain monogamous.

Newitt (1973), drawing on Mitchell (1956), suggests that the Yao of Mozambique may have practiced dual descent and virilocality. However, my reading of Mitchell indicates that the descendants of those who emigrated westward to Malawi were matrilineal (Mitchell 1956). It may be that through intermixing with the Mang'anja, Nyanja, and Chewa, the Yao peasants of Malawi became more firmly matrilineal and uxorilocal. Welch and others (1985) maintain that the Yao in Tete Province, Mozambique, are matrilineal with uxorilocality predominating. Among the Yao, status and position have a bearing on marital residence with chiefs and village heads often practicing virilocality. Yao men, who accumulated wealth through trading, often became chiefs over the Malawian villages they conquered (Mitchell 1956; Phiri, Vaughan, and Makuluni 1977). In such instances, they remained in their own matrilineal villages and their wives came from other villages to live with them, a pattern that persists. In such cases, some form of bridewealth was, and still is, transferred to the bride's family. Thus status can be an intervening variable that determines residence independent of lineage ideology.

The children of a marriage in which both parents come from matrilineal groups belong to the matrilineage of the mother; the father has limited control over his children, although he may contribute to their care within the household. Instead, he has authority and responsibilities over his sister's children. As with the Bemba (Richards 1982), the Yao (Mitchell 1956), and the Mang'anja (Mandala 1990), it is the mother's brother, what I refer to as the avunculate, who often provides for the children's well-being, including their schooling if financially possible (Davison and Kanyuka 1990). Strong matrilineal bonds link a woman and her brother. He takes a particular interest in the discipline of her children, has the responsibility to provide for their initiations, and is consulted about their marriages. Establishing paternity has historically not been an issue in matrilineal groups because the children belong to the mother's lineage. However, with educated, urbanized men in matrilineal groups, it does become an issue; they want control over their own offspring.

Like a woman in a virilocal marriage, a man living where uxorilocality is practiced has little security in land unless he marries someone from his own matrilineal village (cross-cousin marriage was the preferred arrangement until recently). He depends on his wife's family for land or he tills land jointly with his wife that she has inherited. For some men, conjugal

are men in matrilineal comm
more inclined to migrate for
wage labor (other things being equal)?

production is not a problem and a husband is satisfied with staying in his
wife's village. For others, especially those who have been influenced by
Western notions of male entitlement and capitalist production, uxorilocal
residence may provoke tension. Such men are more apt to be found in
towns during the week, earning money over which they have some control
rather than depending on income from land they acquired through a wife's
matrilineage. If they choose to work in a town, they return to their wives'
villages on weekends to help with cultivation. In some cases they rarely return, more or less abandoning their families (Skjønsberg 1989; Trivedy
1987).

Because a woman in a matrilineal, uxorilocal household controls land
and its resources, either she jointly controls the allocation of household
labor with her husband or she takes major responsibility for its allocation,
especially in households where the husband is absent much of the time. A
woman may recruit the labor of her matrikin, both male and female, to assist her during peak periods of the agricultural cycle. This ability to recruit
interhousehold labor is critical to women who head households where no
adult males reside.

In villages where matriliny is ascribed to in Zambia, where capitalism
has penetrated more deeply than it has in Malawi or northern
Mozambique, uxorilocal residence is less evident except in Northern
Province, and men are more apt to have authority over their children
(Poewe 1981; Milimo 1986). At the same time, Moore and Vaughan
(1994) point out that Bemba and Bisa peasants in Northern Province are
only partially tied to the market and that with the drop in the economic returns from mining, many men have returned to their wives' villages to take
up family farming. Men's access to wage labor has partially changed the
marriage and residence patterns in Zambia, as has increased urbanization.
Over 60 percent of the population worked and lived in urban areas by the
mid-1980s. In these urban centers, matrilineal ideology may have little
bearing on the way gender relations are ordered and marriage is practiced
(Milimo 1986).

Religion as a Factor in Marriage Practices

Religion, including Islam and various Christian sects, has contributed to
the modification of indigenous marriage practices. Islam, on the whole, has
had less of a disruptive influence on indigenous practices than has
Christianity. Muslims tolerated polygyny and other marital customs that
Christian missionaries tried to terminate. Islam has proved adaptable, integrating various cultural practices except for the notion that a woman may
head a family; the Muslim principle that the husband should head the family prevails. However, in matrilineal, uxorilocal Muslim families in Malawi,
this principle becomes subject to modification. There, the husband and

wife tend to negotiate family decisions, and the opinions of the wife's brother carry more weight than the husband's.

As a result of men's preeminence in Muslim societies and the sanctity of family in Islam, the Yao Muslim husband in Malawi is more apt to be a stable influence than is his Christian counterpart even though both are married uxorilocally. For example, in a sample of eighty students' households in rural communities in Zomba District, half of which were located in predominantly Muslim communities and half in largely Christian communities, the proportion of households where both father and mother were in residence was 68 percent for the Muslim communities and only 31 percent for the Christian communities (Davison and Kanyuka 1990:35–36). There was a significant percentage of women heading their own households (41 percent) among the Christians. Of this percentage, less than 11 percent were single or widowed. Among the Muslims there were almost no women heading their own households. Husbands in the Muslim communities tended to be subsistence farmers or petty traders; those in the Christian communities were farmers or wage earners with a slightly higher level of education than those in the Muslim communities. It appears, then, that religion and possibly educational status, in tandem, worked to keep more Muslim men at home. Although larger samples are needed to confirm the relationship between religion and marital stability among the Yao, the results for this sample are suggestive of ways that religion may shape marital status in matrilineal, uxorilocal households in Malawi.

A primary difference between Islam and Christianity that has significance for indigenous marriage practices is attitudes toward polygyny. In contrast to Islam, the tenets of Christianity have usually demanded that monogamous marriage sanctified by a church ceremony be the rule. Historically, Christian missionaries were not sympathetic to polygyny, though it has persisted in a minority of patrilineal and matrilineal groups (Ajayi 1965; Murphree 1969; Weinrich 1982). Those who want a church marriage are discouraged from taking more than one wife.

Additionally, Christian missionaries viewed some practices of matrilineal groups, especially the inheritance of land by women and uxorilocality, as in conflict with Christian patriarchal practices (White 1987; Mandala 1990). In contrast, Islam historically has allowed women to inherit land, though in smaller portions than men. Moreover, even though in theory Islamic tenets discourage uxorilocality, this appears not to have been an issue for Muslims in rural southern Malawi or in northern Mozambique, where uxorilocal residence continues to be the custom (Davison and Kanyuka 1990; Pitcher 1995).

Urbanization and Marriage

Among people in urban areas, Christian marriage is the accepted pattern, whereas in rural areas the Christian rites may or may not take place. An urban couple's financial situation has much to do with the decision as to when a couple will take the Christian vows. Sometimes a customary wedding may precede a Christian ceremony by many years because the latter demands a capital outlay. It may take a family, or couple, several years to save the necessary funds to have a Christian ceremony. The combination of religion and economics, then, impinges on decisions about marriage in urban settings.

Variations in Age at First Marriage

The social imperative to marry, for both sexes, is stepped up once a young person has been through an initiation ceremony. For males, accumulating a bridewealth contribution can take several years. Consequently, most tend to marry in their early to mid-twenties.

For girls in patrilineal and some matrilineal groups, the bridewealth accumulated as a result of their marrying will be used in the future by brothers. As a result, brothers, especially those less educated, tend to put pressure on sisters to marry young. Girls in urban Zimbabwe and Zambia are more likely to resist because they have more opportunities for advancing in their education than girls in Malawi and Mozambique. The average age at first marriage for girls in Malawi and Mozambique is roughly 17.7 years (Government of Malawi 1984; United Nations Development Programme [hereafter UNDP] 1993). In contrast, in Zambia it is 19.4 years and in Zimbabwe it is even higher, 20.4 years (UNDP 1993, Table 16).

Adulthood: Procreation and Production

To be a parent is to achieve full adult status. Even though a couple may be cohabiting in the wife's or husband's village or town, until they have a child, neither is recognized as being an adult even though they may have achieved the age of majority. The significance of this new status is recognized among many groups by the referential term Baba or Mai with the name of the first-born child attached—for example, Mai wa Chidzu (Mother of Chidzu) or Baba wa Chidzu.

For a woman in patrilineal groups, becoming a mother means legitimating her position in her husband's family by producing kin for the patrilineage. Once she has achieved motherhood, her position in her husband's family is more secure. She also is apt to be treated with greater respect by members of his family.

Among rural Ndebele and Shona in Zimbabwe, when a couple had their first child, the custom was to go to the homestead of the bride's mother and deliver two goats to her, a practice known as *masungiro*. One was for her female ancestors and one was for slaughter in celebration of the birth. The goat given to the mother's female ancestors was in gratitude for the fertility passed down from mother to daughter (Weinrich 1982). Twenty years ago, 81 percent of the informants in a study carried out by Esterhuysen (1974 [cited in Weinrich 1982]) were still practicing this custom in Zimbabwe. In 1995, the custom was waning.

The tenuous role that women in patrilineal groups experience prior to giving birth to a child is not as great in matrilineal groups, where women are among kin. However, with the birth of her first child, a mother is also given more respect and with time has a greater say in the affairs of the matrilineage. Among some matrilineal groups in Malawi, the pending birth of a first child is cause for a ritual event to mark the woman's transition to motherhood.

The ceremony is referred to as Chinamwali cha Litiwo in Chichewa. A newly pregnant woman is advised by elder women how to look after herself in terms of nutrition and behavior so that she will have a strong child. She is told to abstain from sexual intercourse with her husband at about the eighth month to avoid exerting pressure on the fetus and causing it harm. Her husband has been similarly advised. Most important, she is told what to expect through the process of childbirth and how to handle an infant. She is also advised to abstain from sexual relations for at least six to eight months after the child's birth in order to avoid causing the child's premature death.

As I witnessed when I participated in the ceremony marking pending childbirth and the future mother's entrance into adulthood, it is a joyous and rewarding event marking a woman's full acceptance as an adult in her lineage. At the same time, achieving adulthood means that in the early childbearing years a woman will spend many hours in productive and reproductive tasks that are interwoven into her daily life. She may get up before dawn to chop wood and light a fire for the early morning meal, feed the family, and then spend several hours, often with a child on her back, cultivating her crops. Afterward she prepares the family's midday meal. The only leisure time comes in the early afternoon, when she may mend the family's clothes or knit new garments. She returns to cultivation or to collect water for the family's evening meal in midafternoon. Her working day is not over until after 8:30 P.M.

Women in Malawi, whether they live in a rural, perirural, or urban area, worked on average a fifteen-hour day in 1991 (Kaufulu 1992). Kaufulu compared a sample of roughly eighty women in each type of area in Zomba District and found that although the labor activities they carried out differed somewhat, the number of hours worked per day ranged from fourteen to sixteen. What distinguished women's work from men's, she found, is that they often carry out multiple tasks, working concurrently on several. For instance, they might be breast-feeding a baby while cooking and at the same managing younger children's baths or processing grain.

Men in similar locations in Zomba tend to have more single-purpose tasks such as constructing a granary, making bricks, or cultivating. They do not have the multiple tasks associated with childcare and family maintenance that women have. Also, men are more apt to be involved in the formal employment sector, which takes them away from the home much of the time. When they are at home, men have more leisure time, and those who commute between urban jobs and their villages are caught between family demands on their time and their own desires for leisure, as Skjønsberg (1989) found in a Chewa village.

Finally, women's income generated from sales of grain, vegetables, and fruit or dried fish is less than what men generally earn from cash-value crops, fish and meat, or the sale of miscellaneous items. Women with little education earn supplementary income from raising poultry; keeping bees; and selling baked goods, crafted items, and home-brewed beer. Some also earn income from practicing midwifery. Men with comparable education have a broader range of income-creating activities to choose from, including processing fish; working as carpenters, masons, tailors, barbers, and herbalists; and repairing bicycles and radios. Consequently, even where education is held constant, rural women in central southern Africa have fewer options than men. They also spend their income in different ways.

Men are much more apt to spend money on a bicycle or radio, goods that connect them with the rest of the world. They buy beer to drink with friends and relatives (Geisler et al. 1985; Kariuki 1985; Pankhurst and Jacobs 1988). They also more often buy meat, clothes for themselves, and items connected with improving the house such as furniture or sheets of iron. Women are most concerned for their children and tend to spend their earnings on food items, clothing, and health care, which improve their children's lives and chances of survival. Both parents contribute to school fees, but fathers (or maternal uncles) contribute the most. In a household survey carried out by Peters in southern Malawi (1992), she found that two-thirds of the children's school fees were paid by men.

The years of early parenthood keep a couple extremely occupied, and it is only when there are older children to help out that parents begin to have a little more leisure time. They begin to look forward to the time when their first child will be initiated or married and they will begin the process toward becoming elders.

Becoming Elders

In some groups a special ceremony was held (and in some places is still held) when a woman and man's first child is initiated. For instance, among the Gikuyu of Kenya in the 1950s such a ritual was still being practiced. Referred to as *nyumithio*, it was conducted for both parents. Their heads were shaved and they were advised that they were now entering a new stage of life—becoming the elders of a grown child. Large ear plugs were put in their earlobes and they were told what was expected of them as elders (Davison 1989). In the late twentieth century this practice has largely been abandoned. Similar rituals have faded in rural Zambia (Richards 1982). However, among matrilineal groups in rural Malawi, a ritual to mark elder status at the time a first female child goes through initiation is still held in rural areas. The ritual is held during the girl's Chinamwale ceremony. She is brought together with her parents in a separate place. The parents are advised to respect the girl, in particular because she has become an adult. She, in turn, is advised not to go near her parents' bedroom and to respect them as elders.

Gender is not a significant factor in the transition to elderhood. Women gain credibility and stature as older women and are invited to advise younger women and men. A similar pattern applies to older men. Postmenopausal women are treated with deference and respect out of fear that they may curse one who angers them. Some elders, of either sex, are thought to have special powers to protect or cause harm; in particular, they can bless or curse a close relative. As a result, they are given total obedience.

Older people who have leadership skills, regardless of sex, are selected by senior clan members or their descent group to become clan or lineage leaders. Those who have demonstrated sound judgment and a generous outlook toward others may be promoted for chieftainship or become heads of villages. These elders have the potential for wielding considerable social and political power. They also are expected to share any wealth they accumulate with other members of their descent group. Elder status carries responsibilities and obligations as well as privilege.

In Malawi, a number of village heads and traditional authorities, or chiefs, are women in groups where matriliny predominates. They, like their male counterparts, exercise the right to allocate communal land parcels to lineage members, settle land disputes and inter- and intrafamily disputes, and function as ceremonial advisers and leaders for initiations, funerals, and other community events. Elders with customary positions such as traditional authorities (TAs) in Malawi and chiefs in Zimbabwe are in a position to accumulate both human and material wealth.

In Zimbabwe, customary leadership positions and political positions tend to be held by men, reflecting the patrilineal and patriarchal nature of that society. Because women until 1982 were considered legal minors, it is not surprising that they were not considered for political positions. With their elevation to full adult legal status, Zimbabwean women hoped they might assume more leadership roles. They have made very limited progress.

In summary, being an elder carries both prestige and responsibilities. Achieving elder status means that socially constructed gender differences begin to fade. Women have comparative authority with men in their lineages. Power and authority over younger kin have increased, compensating for the loss of physical strength. At the same time, middle and advanced age carries certain moral and financial responsibilities for those with special gifts and sufficient material resources. Elders are thought to be nearing ancestor status and the spiritual transition that comes with death.

The gendered life cycle is circular. Infants are born into the lineage with few gender differences. They move through an ambiguous period of childhood to puberty and initiation, when gender becomes sharply defined. Adult women and men assume roles in a dual gender system that works to structure much of their daily lives. But the gender divide can be negotiated. An older childless woman may take a wife, assuming the role of husband. Women with extraordinary talents on occasion rise to become chiefs or female headmen. Procreation and production are intertwined throughout adulthood, but males and females often remain spatially separated in many of their activities and rituals. As adults they progress toward the period of being elders, when gender structuring wanes, becoming muted again in old age.

Lineage ideology cuts across gender throughout the life span. It shapes gender relations in specific ways depending on whether a group subscribes to matriliny or patriliny. The direction of lineage affects whether a man intending to marry is required to contribute bridewealth or brideservice to his future in-laws. It may affect where a married couple resides. It determines to which descent group the children will belong and whether the father or the maternal uncle will have authority over them. Lineage ideology influences the productive resources that are available to each gender, how they use them, and who will inherit them. Finally, lineage elders play a significant role in funerals, reminding the living of their spiritual ties with ancestors, thus reinforcing the lineage's continuity.

Gender and Dimensions of Family Labor

Having discussed how individuals become gendered over the life cycle, I want to return to the household level to illustrate how labor becomes gendered at this level; this information is important to the chapters that follow. Three dimensions of labor are described here. The first is its relationship with land in the sense of producing food crops for use and cash-value crops for sale. The second is its relation to the family household, including herd animals and poultry owned by the family, the physical homestead and its maintenance, and the children the parents are responsible for until adulthood. The third dimension of labor involves sustaining ties of lineage, clan, and friendship within the community. These three dimensions of labor are in turn interrelated.

Labor on the Land

The primary purpose of labor related to land is to hunt and fish; reap the useful vegetation of the forest; and clear, cultivate, and plant agricultural areas. It is this last activity that dominates in central southern Africa. In the late twentieth century, the majority of women in the region earn their living from agricultural production. Further, the majority of children born into farming families become farmers. And evidence exists that in the 1980s and 1990s, some former rural dwellers who had taken up wage work in more economically prosperous times in urban areas, especially in Zambia, were leaving to relocate to their villages of origin to resume farming (Geisler et al. 1985).

Part of the ongoing debate over gender productive relations at the household level involves tensions in land and labor relations. These tensions concern three issues: (1) which fields and whose fields receive the most attention and cultivation, (2) which crops are attended to (food versus cash-value crops), and (3) who controls income generated from production—the value of the labor input. The way that labor is allocated with relation to whose fields or gardens get attention is taken up in Chapter 6. In the past, some fields and gardens were designated as "women's fields" and others as "men's fields." In some cases, the designation was related to the kind of crop grown on a particular field and in other cases it related to the spatial relationship of the land to household or settlement. If a man was a compound or village head, he might have fields that were cultivated communally and others that were cultivated by single producers, often wives and younger members of the household or village. The names given to these fields and which gender controlled them shifted over time and with circumstances. Rights to the use of certain fields at times became contested as their use and crops changed (see Carney 1988; Moore and Vaughan 1994).

Labor Connected to the Family Household

Much has been written about the labor that women provide in maintaining a household. We know that women are primarily responsible for wood and water provision, food preparation, laundry, and cleaning. But little is said about men's roles in the physical maintenance of a house—hauling timber for construction, chopping or sawing wood for the framework, and helping to plaster or make bricks for construction. Although women may haul grass for thatching in some places, men are primarily responsible for roofing a house—using either thatching or corrugated iron sheets. They must also repair houses and farm implements. Men also build cattle corrals, granaries, and pens for chickens and pigs. Men's work is more periodic and intensive, whereas women's work is never ending.

Men and women, with their children's assistance, tend their own cattle, goats or sheep, and fowl. Women are as likely as men to take care of cattle they own and keep close to the homestead. Women and children are largely responsible for fowl.

Finally, fathers as well as mothers spend time with small children when they are at home. Nonetheless, women and older siblings of both sexes are largely responsible for younger children. Older boys divide into peer groups; girls are more apt to stay close to their mothers. Older boys work for their fathers or maternal uncles as herdboys; thus male family members bear the responsibility for training and supervising them. Parenting is shared among several adult members; often the oldest adults are the ones most involved.

Community Labor

In rural areas, both women and men are community organizers. Often this role is an extension of roles women perform in the household. For ceremonial events, including namings, initiations, marriages, and funerals, women together with men are involved in "kinwork"—labor involved in sustaining and reinforcing matrilineal and patrilineal ties.[2] Women's labor takes the form of planning the arrangements, organizing the food and drink, and anticipating the needs of guests. Kinwork takes other forms as well. Negotiating marriages and transfers of bridewealth or brideservice is considered kinwork. Visiting sick relatives (mostly done by women) also is kinwork. Taking care of a sick mother's children and supplying her family with food and other necessities is included. Meeting to solve relatives' marital problems or problems over children is another form. And finally, community decisions regarding shared resources such as water, sanitation facilities, transportation, and a village market all take place within the context of kin networks. Together with labor on the land and labor in family households, community labor is a negotiated process by gender, age, and class. This, then, provides a snapshot of gender relations at the household level in the late twentieth century as a basis for looking at the ways they have changed over time in succeeding chapters.

Summary

In this chapter I have reviewed the issue of gender from various Afrocentric standpoints. It is apparent that gender assumes different guises depending on the needs and priorities of particular societies. Further, the constructions of gender in these societies respond to new exigencies. The significance of gender varies with each life stage, and gender bifurcation becomes most pronounced beginning with the transition to adulthood. This bifurcation is reflected in the dual gender system of many African societies. At the same time, it is not a rigid system but allows for exchanges across the gender divide. In the Zambezi region, people acknowledge and, to varying degrees, celebrate the changes occurring with each life stage. These celebrations take the form of communal rituals that emphasize solidarity and oneness—as an ethnic community, a clan, or a lineage. In this southern African context, then, one way that gender and lineage are linked is through social rituals that mark transitions within the life cycle. I also briefly looked at the way labor is currently gendered at the household level as a yardstick for tracing changes in gender relations over time in the region. In the next chapter I begin to examine some of the historical shifts that have resulted in changed gender relations.

Notes

1. There was an instance reported in Malawi's *Daily Times* (1991) of a girl "circumcised" in a Yao initiation that year; but this was highly unusual, and with the global campaign to end the practice, this incident and the practice were condemned.

2. I am indebted to Edith Gelles for the term "kinwork," which refers to work that mainly women do and that is connected with extended family rituals, ceremonies, visiting, and taking care of ill relatives and other social tasks related to reinforcing kin connections.

3

Excavating the Past

In this chapter and the next I concentrate on changing gender relations of power and production as they articulate through time. Excavating the past is always a difficult enterprise. Where few written records exist and material artifacts are scarce, the task becomes even more complex. Interpreting how gender productive relations were structured during a particular time in the remote past challenges the imagination. We can only speculate. Lack of verifiable written data, other than in Arabic, in southern Africa means that non-Arab-speaking scholars are forced to reconstruct the distant past largely from translated texts and archaeological evidence.

As we move forward in time, oral histories of southern African royal lineages and great clan leaders become benchmarks for calculating political change and significant events in the region. These oral accounts are corroborated by the early records of Portuguese explorers and traders such as de Barros (1552) and dos Santos (1609), who provided further evidence (Henriksen 1978; Lancaster 1981). However, Kayongo (1987:3) rightly points out that although the Portuguese accounts may offer broad outlines, the geographical details are sometimes faulty and descriptions of African social organization are almost nonexistent (also see Beach 1984:20). Likewise, the descriptions of Portuguese colonial officers such as Francisco Barreto (1667) offer clues to the way ruling clans lived but give little information about the lives of peasants and slaves.[1] Consequently, Portuguese documents provide a selective history, one focused on conquest, the politics of the Mwene Mutapa ruling elite, and the dynamics of trade in the region.

Another form of exegesis is the historical documents left primarily by British explorers, missionaries, and colonial administrators. Though these tend to be more inclusive in describing various aspects of social and political organization, they, too, have their limitations; the records tend to be most concerned with those aspects of African social life that are amenable to colonial intervention and control. Even the colonial anthropologists hired to document "tribal organization" often concentrated on political structure and male leadership based on interviews with male informants (e.g., Gluckman 1950, Mitchell 1956). With the exception of the work of Audrey Richards (1939, 1950) and, to a lesser degree, that of Elizabeth Colson (1950, 1951), women were largely ignored except as they figured in kinship accounts. Such an oversight means that to reconstruct gender relations as they might have been, we are forced to read between the lines and to rely on oral accounts of older female informants to flesh out gender relations as they existed in the colonial past.

I begin this chapter with a chronological overview of gender relations of production in the distant past, then move to the period of Karanga domination at the Great Zimbabwe (c. 900–1450), which was coincident with the ascendancy of Muslim trade along the East African coast. The subsequent rise of other feudal states (1400–1800) occurred during the period of the intrusion of the Portuguese (1500–1850), who were anxious to vanquish the infidel Muslims with their trading monopoly and gain control of gold and ivory supplies. In the latter part of the chapter I describe the role of Portuguese colonialism in restructuring gendered land and labor relations in Mozambique.

The Distant Past

Evidence from artifacts coupled with conjecture based on the behavior of the more recent Khoisan suggests that two groups of foragers and hunters occupied central southern Africa prior to the Bantu migrations—the early Khoisan and the Twa, the latter related to the so-called Pygmies. Little is known about their early relations of production; they left behind stone tools, and some inferences can be made based on mid-twentieth-century Khoisan and Twa social formations.

The hunting of large game appears to have been a communal enterprise; hunters used either spears or traps and nets in combination with group cunning to outwit the hunted. As for foraging, both sexes, either together or in gender-specific groups, probably gathered roots, fruits, and vegetable matter. It is equally likely that women, with their childbearing and -rearing tasks, more often prepared and cooked food while tending children. Men skinned the largest animals, and women assisted in staking out the skins and smoking them for use as containers, mats, and clothing. Based on more recent observations of the Khoisan, hunting and foraging decisions probably were made on a communal basis with a headman, possibly acting as facilitator. Whether women had a decisionmaking forum separate from men's is unknown. It is plausible that the smaller bands of Khoisan retreated westward with the arrival of the first wave of Bantu speakers from the north between circa 300 B.C. and A.D. 800 (Langworthy 1972).

A major change came to the region with the influx of the migrating Bantu, who were fleeing drought conditions and famine in the Sahelian region. They brought with them the knowledge of how to smelt iron and work it into implements such as axes and hoes and how to make pots. They also practiced rudimentary horticultural techniques. Evidence of early Tonga-style pottery and iron tools have been found in the Zambezi Valley (Langworthy 1972; Pachai 1972; Lancaster 1981). These early horticulturalists began to settle into hamlets and villages located close to rivers, lakes, and other ready sources of water in order to take advantage of irrigation. It is not known whether farming tasks were divided by gender, but men probably felled trees and cleared land for cultivation using iron tools crafted by male ironsmiths. Women undoubtedly processed cultivated grains and tubers and probably made the pots they used for cooking and storage. Beyond these gender-specific tasks, one can only speculate. For example, were women the sole haulers of wood and water or did men also participate in these tasks? Equally important, were tasks requiring special skills, such as distilling salt, processing cloth, and making pottery, gender-specific prior to the time for which written records indicate productive tasks by gender?

Garlake (1983) posits that the changes occurring in pottery between the early Iron Age, when Bantu migrants entered the region (c. 300 B.C.–A.D. 800), and the later Iron Age (c. 800–900), during which the early Zimbabwe kingdom-state developed, are attributable to a change in social organization from a matrilineal to patrilineal system (1983:13). As lineage ideologies are at issue, this thesis must be examined carefully.

Garlake suggests that the early Iron Age in Zimbabwe reflected an egalitarian, expanding society that depended on grain for its subsistence. "And if work in the fields was then, as now, primarily a woman's task," he argues, "it would have given women a dominant role in the economy. Matrilineality both expresses and is the most efficient form of society precisely because of these circumstances"(1983:13). Garlake appears to be confusing a matrifocal economy with matriliny. He goes on to suggest that because women were primarily responsible for agriculture, men had more time to devote to crafts such as pottery, which in his view accounts for some of the more elaborate pottery designs of the period. To suggest that men controlled pottery production in a region in which women, historically and currently, have been the major producers of pottery seems a leap of faith.

By the late Stone Age, Garlake contends, the society had become more differentiated, with men moving into new specializations such as cattle raising while women continued to cultivate. With the new specializations, suggests Garlake (1983:13), came "more responsibilities for men" and male dominance in the economy—hence the transition to a patrilineal system of descent and inheritance. The new gender division of labor, Garlake argues, explains why men gave up their earlier interest in pottery and why the craft reverted to women, who did not have time to make elaborate designs. That such a connection could be made among a horticultural mode of production, lineage ideology, and the development of pottery as a gender-specific task flies in the face of evidence.

Most matrilineal horticultural societies have depended equally on male and female labor until very recently (Rattray 1929; Richards 1939, 1950; Duly 1946; Kaberry 1952; Mitchell 1956; Basehart 1962; Berry 1975; Poewe 1981). It is true that matriliny is not found in great numbers among pastoralists, hunters, or societies requiring management of extensive irrigation systems, but there are exceptions (Aberle 1962:670). Among South American herding groups in the Andes mountains, for instance, descent has never been patrilineal. Equally important, matriliny is *not* a particular level of social organization; rather it is a type of membership criterion based on descent (Aberle 1962:658). Matrilineality has been found at all levels of political and social development and was predominant among the states that developed in central Africa. Finally, that a particular type of pottery crafted centuries ago can be explained on the basis of a gender division of labor for which there is no evidence smacks of ill-founded reductionism. Beach's contention (1984) that we do not know exactly how society was organized on the Zimbabwe plateau in 1400 because Arab documents contain little social data and the Portuguese did not refer to marital residence patterns or even say much about cattle (1984:20) puts such speculations into perspective.

Langworthy (1972) suggests that trade between the coast and inland groups was in progress in the seventh century based on glass beads, copper, and seashells found in archaeological sites at Dambwa and Kalomo (1972:10). Elkiss (1981:14), based on a review of Arab documents, places the Muslim trade as beginning in the ninth or tenth century. The Muslim traders were motivated by gold from the Zimbabwe Plateau and ivory, which they then traded for Indian glass beads and woven cotton cloth. Elkiss (1981:5) suggests that the Muslims also traded quality iron from the mines of southern Zambezia for Indian-made Damascus swords. Al-Idrisi, a Muslim geographer at the court of Sicily in the twelfth century, left a treatise describing the East African Coast in which he mentions gold and high-quality iron.

Unfortunately, those without knowledge of Arabic know little about the period of Muslim contact, as trading records in Arabic have not been translated into English at the same rate as Portuguese documents (Kayongo 1987). What is known from early Portuguese reports is that Muslim traders, who came from Arabia, Persia, and India, had inland markets, or "fairs," at Sena, Tete, Zumbo, and Zimbabwe (see Figure 1.2) for trading gold and ivory for Indian textiles and jewelry (Henriksen 1978; Elkiss 1981). These traders went as far as China to obtain objects such as porcelain bowls and brass gongs; these and the jewelry and beads from India found their way to the Karanga *dzimbabwe* (great center) kingdom (c. 1100-1450).

The Muslim traders set up a string of city-states along the Indian Ocean coast, which they referred to as the Zinj. From these city-states they exported ivory and precious metals for scarce items desired by Africa's early rulers. In Mozambique the most important coastal trading center by the thirteenth century was Kilwa Kisiwani, which also controlled the commerce of Sofala (Elkiss 1981). The trade between inland groups and the coast was strictly in the hands of men. Muslim traders did not bring women with them but rather married local women or had liaisons with them. The Muslims left a cultural legacy with the coastal peoples through the language they spoke, which when combined with Bantu words and structure became Kiswahili. They also left an impressive architectural heritage and their religion, Islam. They maintained their primacy as coastal traders into the beginning of the sixteenth century and were the primary rivals of the Portuguese for the Indian Ocean trade. As Henriksen observes (1978:25), "The extensiveness of the (Muslim) trade system and its profit can be verified by the avarice it excited in the Portuguese and by the tenacity and resilience with which the Muslims resisted European incursions."

The City-State at Great Zimbabwe

In the interval between the arrival of the Arabs (c. 900) and the arrival of the Portuguese (1500), an organized society arose. This society was founded by the descendants of an early iron-working group at Zimbabwe and was supported by a military wing (Chanaiwa 1973; Beach 1977, 1980, 1984, 1994; Palmer 1977b; Henriksen 1978; Peel and Ranger 1983). These patrilineal Shona speakers, who have been identified as Karanga (Henriksen 1978; Lancaster 1981), built what can best be described as a city-state on the Zimbabwean plateau south of the Zambezi and north of the Limpopo River (Figure 1.2). The architecture of this city-state demonstrates a sophisticated knowledge of stone masonry that enabled the people to build monumental stone structures without the use of mortar. How did the ruling elite conscript labor for such a project? Were the laborers peasant farmers or slaves? As there is no evidence of slavery (Beach 1984, 1994), Garlake (1983) theorizes that labor was tributary but that workers may have been compensated in cloth from India that had been exchanged for gold from the city-state's mines in the vicinity. The high price of gold between the tenth and twelfth centuries may have financed the building of the Great Zimbabwe, which was in place from A.D. 1250 (Garlake 1983:13). It is possible that both men and women participated in the construction (as both sexes participated in mining), primarily in the postharvest season when they were not fully occupied with cultivation (Beach 1984, 1994).

Within the monumental stone *dzimbabwe* was the semicircular Great Enclosure that housed the court and a religious center. In the latter, rainmaking priests presided over rites that connected the ancestors responsible for the health of the land with the ruling elite. By their spatial confinement to a great stone enclosure, the elite Rozwi were able to signal their exclusivity. Trade and mining of metals were part of the economy, but cattle were the primary measure of wealth, with agriculture being central to the survival of the Karanga kingdom and its people (Beach 1977, 1980; Henriksen 1978; Peel and Ranger 1983).

Outside the royal enclosure were peasants living in mud and wattle enclosures; they farmed and raised cattle, pigs, and goats (Henriksen 1978:5; Beach 1984). Beach (1984) speculates that the household, including a man, his wife or wives and children, and relatives from allied or different lineages, made up the basic subsistence unit. Several households or homesteads made up a *nyika*, or territory, under a hereditary chief who might have a tributary relationship with the ruler or might be independent (1984:20). Language, custom, and territorial linkages signaled their inclusion within the greater Shona-speaking Karanga state (Beach 1994:23).

Karanga's reigning lineage exercised leadership through a system of patrilineally related chiefs. Little is known about the gender relations of the ruling elite except that first wives of Rozwi elites had a privileged position and could command an army to protect their fiefdoms (Elkiss 1981). The literature concentrates on male-oriented military and trading exploits. Beach suggests that control and use of land, whether for surface resources—wild vegetables, game, vegetation suitable for grazing, land amenable to cultivation—or for underground mineral rights, was the basis for a ruler's relationship with his people (1984:21). It may be that peasants worked the land together regardless of gender. Women undoubtedly were responsible for household tasks and childcare, and men probably took major responsibility for herding and tending cattle, which were the wealth of their patrilineages. A class of bondsmen may have existed who had few or no cattle for bridewealth (Beach 1984). In such cases, these men may have indentured themselves to others, assisting in cultivating and herding and rendering services to the ruling elite in exchange for cattle or access to a marriageable daughter.

Zimbabwe's influence over the southern Zambezia region it controlled waned in the mid-1400s as resources necessary for its sustainability, including grazing land, arable soil, and timber, became depleted (Phimister 1976:4; Beach 1984), and other Shona leaders began to exercise military power in the region (Beach 1994).

There is lack of agreement as to which ruling clan or lineage assumed leadership of the Shona-speaking ruling elite after the death of the last *mambo,* or leader, in about 1450. It may be that competition for control of the minerally rich Zimbabwean plateau arose simultaneously from several points (see Beach 1994). Henriksen (1978) and Lancaster (1981) maintain that the later Karanga leaders, who in the first half of the fifteenth century initiated a new period of military expansion in southern Zambezia, were from the Mbire clan. However, a revisionist version coming out of Zimbabwe has argued that the Torwa clan at Khami, farther west, was the successor of the Rozwi dynasty (Beach 1977, 1980; Elkiss 1981; Peel and Ranger 1983). This version contends that the Mbire clan leaders were dissidents. In either case, the *mutapa,* or paramount ruler, was experiencing difficulty in maintaining discipline among those tributary chiefs who ruled over their own land in the beginning of the fifteenth century, when the Portuguese traveled up the coast of southeastern Africa.

A Portuguese flotilla under Vasco da Gama rounded the Cape of Good Hope in 1498, looking for new trading opportunities, especially in gold. From 1500 to 1750 the Portuguese were at war with the Muslim city-states in attempts to wrest from them control of the Indian Ocean trade routes (Hafkin 1973; Newitt 1973; Langworthy 1972; Elkiss 1981). From the perspective of peasants living inland, whether the traders at the coast were Arabs or Portuguese made little difference; in complexion they looked similar, they both spoke radically different languages from the Bantu derivatives spoken inland, and they worshiped different gods (see Ntara 1973). However, to members of the ruling clans, whose hegemony over other more dispersed, weaker clans enabled them to establish feudal states, the trade from the coast added a new dimension to their monopolization of local tributary economies. The history of these new states is shaped, in part, by their connection with regional trade, first initiated by the Muslims and later usurped by the Portuguese. However, trade was not the only factor in the development and disintegration of such states. Internal factors relating to succession and control over natural and spiritual resources as well as ecological constraints such as drought also contributed to a state's devolution.

The Rise of Feudal States: Clan Struggles

Before looking at the development of feudal states in the region, I must be clear about the choice of the term "state" to describe precolonial political entities that arose in the Zambezi heartland between A.D. 1250 and 1750. Beach (1994:70) has pointed out that there is no definitive way of deciding what constituted a state in the region during this period. Nonetheless, he goes on to suggest that the precolonial states had a set of characteristics that have been identified with feudal states elsewhere in the same period. These indicators include a highly stratified society with a powerful ruler who had the authority to exact tribute and who, through control of critical rituals and trade and through military might, had coercive power (1994:70–75). An understanding of state (in its feudal form) as including a ruling authority with tributary or taxing powers and the power to bring others under its control through military might has utility for describing the major political entities that arose in the Zambezi region in the period under discussion.

The period between 1450 and 1800 was characterized by the rise and fall of major feudal states in the region of Zambezia. Two interrelated factors contributed to their emergence, one ecological and the other sociopolitical. The ecological factor relates to changing environmental conditions farther north that prompted clan leaders and their followers to migrate south from the Kongo or outward from the Great Zimbabwe in search of safe havens, arable land, and water. It also prompted the ruling clan leaders in some states to expand their territorial base as the soil within their own localities became depleted and the population outgrew the land base. This was particularly true of states formed later, such as those in the Malawi (Maravi) confederacy.

The sociopolitical factor has two dimensions: One is related to succession disputes within reigning lineages or clans, and the other concerns the role of trade relations with the Portuguese. Disputes within dominant clans over claims to leadership between brothers in some cases, between brothers and sisters in others, and between matrilineally related men of different generations in still others caused some states to change course and others to wither and die. These disputes over clan leadership, which might be initiated by a clan leader's inability to secure food or water for his followers as much as succession squabbles, led to social fissioning as a potential leader broke off from the parent clan and with his or her followers established authority in a new area. Where preexisting groups were encountered, these were conquered and assimilated, often as slaves, contributing to the wealth of the conquering leader. In other cases a dispute, particularly after a strong ruler had died, might lead to fragmentation and demise of the state. In Zimbabwe and Malawi, not only succession disputes affected the history of a particular state; relationships with the Portuguese were also a factor, influencing a state's ability to maintain political domination over existing alliances, as the histories of the Mwene Mutapa and Malawi confederacies demonstrate.

A hierarchical, feudal class structure developed in the states that predominated during the period of Portuguese exploration and ascendancy. At the apex of this hierarchy was a supreme leader from the ruling clan who was capable of wielding both spiritual and military power; under this leader were the tributary rulers, chiefs, and headmen in descending order (Langworthy 1972:13). Not all rulers were male. In some cases, women with strong leadership capabilities or extraordinary spiritual powers as rainmakers, especially among matrilineal groups, emerged as "queens" or chiefs (see Ntara 1973; Sangambo 1979; Phiri, Vaughan, and Makuluni 1977; Lancaster 1981).

In *Kings and Clans,* David Newberry (1991:4) makes the point that clanship and kingship are complementary as well as opposed concepts, with each being defined historically by the presence of the other: "Current clan identities were consolidated within the context of kingship, but kingship in turn . . . has meaning only within the broader clan structure." Within the societies of central southern Africa between 1400 and 1800, a similar relationship existed among dominant clans, the coalescing royal states, and the broader clan structure. The ruling clan or lineage, led by its principal leader, conquered lesser clans and, in the process of setting up a hierarchical, feudal state, legitimated its own existence. However, that legitimacy was maintained only so long as the ruling clan was able to exercise authority within a broader social context. Should it falter in the provision of protective services or spiritual security, another clan might challenge its authority and assume leadership, particularly where succession was not a fait accompli.

Langworthy (1972:13) suggests that a "cycle of reciprocity" typified the feudal structure that emerged during the period of the feudal states. It was based on the centralized management and control of intra- and interstate trade by the ruler in power. The ruler received tribute from subordinate rulers and subjects not only in the form of labor but in the form of goods, which were then redistributed to regions where they were in short supply in exchange for their goods (1972:14).

The ruler's monopoly on trade enabled him or her to balance the flow of goods from areas of surplus to areas of scarcity in a cycle of reciprocity. A similar pattern arose in long-distance trade. Arab, Swahili, and, later, Portuguese trading agents acted as the conduits for such trade. As long as the ruler was able to maintain control over the flow of goods in and out of his kingdom, his monopoly was ensured. However, once the trade agents began to establish direct links with individual producers of scarce resources such as ivory and gold—a process to which I will return in a later section—the trade monopoly of the ruling elite was in jeopardy.

Three Feudal States in the Zambezi Region

Many states rose and fell coincidentally with Portuguese ascendancy in Zambezia. I limit my discussion to the Banamainga state in what is now northeastern Zimbabwe; the Malawi (or Maravi) confederacy, which encompassed eastern Zambia, Malawi, and Mozambique; and the Mwene Mutapa confederacy in Zimbabwe, which spread to southern Zambezia in Mozambique. In the analysis of these three, the relation of clan struggles to lineage ideology and gender is of primary concern.

The Banamainga Kingdom

In the mid-1400s, along the Zambezi River north of its confluence with the Kafue River, a prototype Tonga people, the matrilineal Banamainga, were beginning to consolidate their power under the leadership of Kasamba. Kasamba was a powerful female spirit medium who had been brought back from Soli Manyika, where she was a powerful tributary leader, to unite various factions that were threatening to fragment the Banamainga state in a period when it could ill afford to become weakened (Lancaster 1981:16).

Kasamba was an astute leader who through diplomacy brought peace to the region and established her authority as the spirit medium in residence at a prominent rain shrine on Njami Hill. She ruled jointly with her brother, Ntambo, an arrangement that proved fatal for Kasamba. Growing jealous of his "sister queen's" power, the male clan leader had her killed with fatal medicine and usurped her position, becoming not only the warrior leader but the shrine priest (Lancaster 1981:17). He and his warriors later turned to elephant hunting to meet the Portuguese traders' demand for ivory; the strategic position of the large Banamainga villages on the Zambezi River made them convenient way stations for these trade agents as well as for those transporting captured slaves.

During the Ntambo period, a south-bank leader, Nyamhunga, came to rule as the *mambo,* or supreme ruler. Within his territory lived the most powerful land spirit, thought to be the son of the original paramount leader of the Karanga (Lancaster 1981:18). It is to this land spirit that the Banamainga turned in periods of drought, calling on him to "make rain." Though the original Banamainga were Tonga rebels against the Karanga, later they became subjects in the Mwene Mutapa confederacy's Karanga-Mbire political hierarchy (Lancaster 1981:20).

What is significant about the Banamainga state is the gender tension between the leader and her brother. For the Banamainga and the matrilineally based Katanga and Lozi "kingdoms" farther north in Zambia, struggles between brothers and sisters at the top, and in some cases between women leaders and their maternal uncles or sons, seem to characterize the early histories of these states dominated by reigning matrilineages or clans. In each case a female leader of the original ruling matriclan is forced out by a jealous male relative. The accounts of how these female leaders lost their positions are filled with tales of deceit, treachery, and blackmail (see Langworthy 1972; Sangambo 1979; Mainga 1973). For men in patrilineal, patriarchal states, female leadership is not an issue—only males in the ruling clan are eligible to become rulers, as the emergence of the Mwene Mutapa in the next section illustrates.

The Mwene Mutapa Confederacy

About the same time that the Banamainga were consolidating their power on the Zambezi in the fifteenth century, a band of invaders known as Korekore, or "locusts," to the Banamainga for the way they devastated the countryside marched north to the middle of the Zambezi Valley—see Figure 3.1 (Henriksen 1978). It was possibly an advance guard of Nyatsimba Mutota, who had become the leader of the Mbire clan and who may have split with the Rozwi clan, that moved west from Great Zimbabwe to Torwa (Henriksen 1978). These Korekore migrated north to the middle of the Zambezi Valley, conquering those in their path and laying the groundwork for the Mwene Mutapa confederacy (Abraham 1962; Henriksen 1978). According to Lancaster (1981:15), the original Korekore were related to the Tonga and were rebels against the weakened Karanga rulers after the fall of the Great Zimbabwe kingdom circa 1450. However, Henriksen (1978) maintains that they were Karanga soldiers under the leadership of Mutota, aiming to extend Mbire clan hegemony north and eastward (1978:7).[2] In either case, they intermixed with the existing Tonga groups along the Zambezi River, who referred to Mutota as the Mwene Mutapa, or Great Pillager (Henriksen 1978).

The Mwene Mutapa confederacy was actually a string of Shona-speaking groups led by allied chiefs whose goal it was to control the inland trade routes in order to capitalize on the Arab-Swahili and later the Portuguese trade in southern Zambezia. Mutota's relations with the Muslim traders depended on their ability to provide him with cotton cloth from India—which he used to pay his soldiers—in exchange for precious metals mined from the royal quarries on the Zimbabwe Plateau (Beach 1984). Both he and his successor, Matope of the Mbire clan, were driven by ambition not only to subdue the peoples along the southern Zambezi Valley, in what is now Zimbabwe, but to expand their sphere of influence to include much of central Mozambique between the Zambezi and Limpopo Rivers, thus increasing their trading options (Alpers 1968).

The confederacy proved difficult to control because ambitious chiefs, ethnic divisions, and poor communication threatened fragmentation (Henriksen 1978). Coincidentally with the rise of the Mutapa state, a state

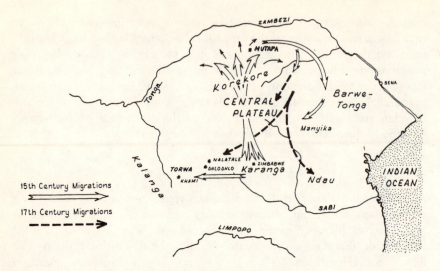

FIGURE 3.1   The early migrations of the Korekore, the Karanga, and the
Mutapa Confederacy. SOURCE: Langworthy 1972. Courtesy of Addison Wesley
Longman and Harry W. Langworthy.

under the leadership of the Rozwi clan's Torwa had been developing west
of Great Zimbabwe (Beach 1984). It was completely separate from the
Mutapa state and toward the end of the seventeenth century began challenging the Mutapa's hegemony in the region of the Zimbabwe Plateau.

There is some confusion about the Rozwi ruler Changa. Henriksen
(1978) and Elkiss (1981) relate that shortly before the death of Matope in
1480, one of the Rozwi provincial rulers, Changa, who commanded considerable mineral wealth, began to consolidate his power in a semiautonomous state. To emphasize his detachment from the Mutapa state and
honor his ties with Muslim traders from the coast, he assumed the Muslim
title "amir," becoming Changamire (Henriksen 1978:11). With the death
of Matope, Changamire began moving away from the Mutapa confederacy, according to Henriksen (and Elkiss), openly demonstrating his autonomy and rising to become a major ruler during the period of Portuguese
penetration. However, Beach (1984:39) contends that Changa, who had
begun as a cattle herder for the Rozwi Torwa and who rose to become a
warrior, broke off from the Torwa state at Khami to found his own state in
the seventeenth century. It is this state that challenged the hegemony of the
Mutapa confederacy in the waning years of its rule.

It is likely that by the sixteenth century other provincial rulers were similarly declaring their autonomy; thus the Mutapa rulers would have been
embroiled in regional battles. The Mutapa rulers' major ally from this period until the eighteenth century, when the last ruler of the royal lineage

died, seems to have been the Portuguese, who supplied the rulers with firearms in exchange for ivory—gold having proved to be an unreliable source by the beginning of the seventeenth century.

Class and gender were intertwined in the complex history of the Mwene Mutapa confederacy. For the ruling Mbire clan, according to Mudenge, wives were a status symbol of wealth and fertility; Mutapa rulers were expected to have many wives and might have between 300 and 3,000 (1988:104).[3] In the seventeenth century, wives were divided into nine major "houses" according to their seniority. Each of the nine had a name, with the first three wives having a special status (Mudenge 1988:104).

The first two wives were "ritual," or symbolic, wives; they were usually sisters or close female relatives of the Mutapa. Matope's ritual mate was chosen by his father, Mutota, who insisted that in order to keep the clan "strong," Matope must marry his half-sister Nyamhita, better known as Nehanda (or ruler of Handa), before he took the throne (Mudenge 1988:105).[4] This custom of brother-sister marriage was continued into the eighteenth century with the principal wife of the Mutapa always being a sister or close kinswoman who was referred to as Nehanda.

Nehanda had equal social, but not political, status with her brother-husband, and she treated her junior wives as subjects (Mudenge 1988:105). Although her position appeared strong to Portuguese observers in the 1500s and 1600s, it had limited utility, and her power began to wane in the latter part of the 1700s (108).

The second wife of the Mutopa was also a close female relative to ensure purity of clan and security. It was the third wife who was the choice of the ruler and fulfilled many conjugal duties. Regardless of their rank, however, all royal wives had their "own houses, land and vassals" (Bocarro 1964:358; Mudenge 1988:108). Among the Mutopa's many wives were the daughters of tributary chiefs; these alliances consolidated his power and prevented schisms.[5] As in European states of the same period, then, marriage became a means for the ruling clan to maintain its control over allied states.

As elite women, the wives of the Mutopa were not expected to do manual labor (Mudenge 1988:109). Tributary labor fulfilled the needs of the elite. Nevertheless, each of the Mutopa's wives was expected to manage a large retinue of female servants who carried out the domestic labor in her house. A similar pattern existed for wives of tributary chiefs, but subchiefs' wives were apt to be more involved in domestic and even agricultural labor (Mudenge 1988).

Specialized crafts were part of the Mutapa states' economies. Men smelted iron into ingots and in the dry season when they were not cultivating, worked it into implements (Beach 1977). Ironworking was the specialization of some ethnic groups. For example, the Njanja at Wedza were known for their ability to make sturdy hoes and fine axes, which they exchanged for cattle or even daughters (Beach 1977: 49). Men also accumulated and herded cattle, the latter being especially important for *lobola* (bridewealth).

Women helped their men cultivate finger and bullrush millets, the major staple crops. From the finger millet, women made a fermented drink that was used in rituals and ceremonies. As they were in control of distillation, women had a certain leverage with males, who controlled ritual events; they could always withhold production of the drink. Sorghum, being a supplementary (and drought-resistant) crop, was grown alongside vegetables in women's gardens (Gelfand 1971:40; Beach 1977:86). Female peasants also grew rice and, later, maize, groundnuts, and a variety of vegetables, all imported crops they learned to cultivate, process, and store. With the help of their children, they collected wild fruits, vegetables, and insects (Beach 1977). During periods of drought they also collected tubers, roots, and even edible bark. They distilled salt when the source of salt was nearby. Both sexes fished and made cloth; only women wove baskets and made pots (Beach 1977:86–87).

Both sexes and all ages participated in hunting, especially where grass burning to flush game was used as a method (Beach 1977:87). When pits and spears were used, men tended to predominate. Elephant hunting was carried out by men, who either hung from trees to spear the animal, prepared a pit to trap it, or distracted the animal while one man, in an individual show of bravery, ran up behind the animal's hindquarters with an ax and threw it to sever the hamstring (Young 1977; Beach 1977). When an elephant was killed, the ruler got one tusk and the other tusk went to the primary hunter (Beach 1977:53).

Most accounts telescope the history of the Mutapa confederacy by focusing on the paramount rulers, particularly Mutota and Matope, and their battles for political conquest. Women did not have key roles as founding ancestors, but female spirit mediums and rain-callers, or *chikara,* existed. Becoming a spirit medium was one way that a woman could achieve status. Female spirit mediums (*svikiro*) existed at the time of the Mwene Mutapa, but they tended to be possessed by *vadzimu* (lineage spirits) rather than *mhondoro,* spirits of royal ancestors—nearly always men (Schmidt 1992:24). In the late nineteenth century, a significant medium embodying the ancestor spirit of the former Mutopa's wife, Nehanda, became a leader in the rebellion of the Shona against the British South African Company.

At the other end of society from the ruling hierarchy and its support staff (including spiritual specialists, military professionals, and artisans) were four groups whose low position was linked to their lack of economic power and wealth: peasant women, children, bondsmen, and slaves (Beach 1977:55–56). Drawing on the work of Mtetwa (1974), Beach maintains that "both women and children played a considerable part in running the economy, yet they were legally classed as minors and received little more than the food for which they worked, their wealth being limited to a few belongings and, very rarely, a few beasts" (Beach 1977:55). He apparently is not referring to those women who acquired a cow (*mombe yohumai*) upon the marriage of each daughter or the goats they received with the birth of a daughter's first child (a custom referred to as *masungiro*). Women who had the resources accumulated cattle.

Bondsmen sold themselves to another man during periods of drought or because, as young men, they lacked the cattle to provide for *lobola* and so chose to become bonded to a future father-in-law to compensate for lack of bridewealth (Beach 1984:22). Beach fails to mention the role that females played as pawns. Females, particularly young ones from poorer families, were used to pay debts, as loan collateral to secure goods, or to secure food in times of drought (Schmidt 1992:30). Whereas bondsmen controlled their own personhood, female pawns were totally powerless.

Slaves, known as *akaporo*, were persons captured in war or sold by their communities in times of drought, although Beach suggests that slavery was not as widely practiced in the Shona-speaking states as it was in the states that arose north of the Zambezi (1977:56). Slaves had no rights, but the children of female slaves who were the wives of members of a royal lineage became members of that lineage, a pattern that prevailed for members of common patrilineages as well. The slave woman's lineage became "invisible." For men, such an arrangement simplified marriage because the woman was totally dependent on her husband and the "restraining influences and material demands" characteristic of a wife's patrilineal male relatives were overcome (Schmidt 1992:30). Women were also at risk of becoming pawns of war, cattle and women being the most prized objects of conquest.

By the eighteenth century, then, a patrilineal hierarchy was in place in which male and female members of the ruling clan were at the top and peasant women, bondsmen, female pawns, and slaves of both sexes were at the bottom. Whereas women in Shona-speaking societies generally had a politically peripheral role, the story is very different for women in the matrilineal Malawian states.

The Malawi Confederacy

The Malawi states began to form in the early 1500s and became most consolidated under Undi (c. 1750–1830), the best known of the ruling Phiri leaders. His ruling clan, the Phiri, owe their origins to the central role of a woman, Nyangu. As First Mother, she was responsible for producing an heir for Kalonga, first ruler of the Phiri clan. As Ntara relates, Nyangu provided Kalonga with "all the powers because she was a woman" (1973:11), a comment on the key role of women in this matrilineal clan. According to oral legend, when Kalonga could not produce an heir with Nyangu, Undi, who controlled the senior matrilineage, became her consort, providing the future Kalonga (rulers). All subsequent Chewa rulers came from the "house" (lineage) of Nyangu (Ntara 1973:12).

Nyangu's symbolic power was so great that even migrating Yao from Mozambique, who adopted Chewa and Nyanja clan names (Mitchell 1956), claim descent from Nyangu. In oral interviews carried out with Amachinga Yao elders in 1976–1977, K. Phiri and others (1977) found members of the Mbewe clan claiming descent from the "Great Headwoman Nyangu." Informants related that when the Yao came into the area, they found the matrilineal Nyanja; their chief, the woman Nyangu, granted them settlement rights (1977:34). Women continued to figure prominently in the history of the Chewa-Nyanja-Mang'anja ruling matrilineages. I referred earlier to Makawana, the spirit medium whose powers as a rain-caller won her acclaim and a large following, as reported by the early Portuguese observer A.C.P. Gamitto. Other women served as rain-callers attached to particular land shrines; some were clan leaders, for example, Chauva Banda, from whom all Banda claim descent. Some of the acknowledged female leaders had to raise armies to quell competing groups ambitious for power (see Ntara 1973).

As in the matrilineal kingdoms farther west, the greatest challenge to the Malawian women rulers' authority was their brothers, who out of jealousy challenged a sister's right to lead. When such a situation occurred, a female ruler had to depend on the loyalty of male military leaders in her matriclan to overcome the challenge. The sibling rivalry led to fissioning; usually the brother left to form his own lineage.

Women and girls, like their Shona counterparts, could become pawns who were used as tribute by chiefs or subchiefs to win favor or as collateral to gain access to scarce items such as cattle. By and large, however, females were more valued in the Chewa-speaking groups than among the Shona speakers. The birth of a girl was greeted with particular joy because it meant that the future fertility of the matriclan was ensured.

The Malawi confederacy of states included Chewa, Nyanja, and Mang'anja, as well as other groups brought into the confederacy such as the Chipeta, Zimba, Nwenga, and Nyassa. The later history of the confederacy traces its spread southward as two military clan leaders under Undi— Kaphwiti and Lundu—settled, respectively, in the upper and lower Shire Valley. Lundu founded the kingdom that had the greatest impact on the northern side of the Zambezi River and its territories. Lundu's armies spread eastward to control groups linked with the coastal trade, conquering the matrilineal Makua and Lomwe of Mozambique. By the mid-1700s, the Malawi confederacy controlled land and trade routes all the way to the Indian Ocean coast (Pachai 1972; Henriksen 1978; Elkiss 1981).

The rule of Undi and his successors was more indirect than that of the Mutapa rulers (Henriksen 1978). They relied heavily on subordinate chiefs who were granted land in exchange for tribute. These chiefs were not necessarily of the Phiri clan. They, in turn, relied on matrilineal village heads to provide tribute in the form of ivory and slaves, the two commodities of interest to Muslim and Portuguese traders by the mid-1700s. The regional chiefs had much more control over local trade arrangements than the provincial Mbire rulers under the Mutapa confederacy (Alpers 1968).

Of the states in the Zambezi region, the Malawi states were most vulnerable to Arab and Portuguese intrusion. Because of the machinations of the Muslim and Portuguese trading agents, who were most often Bisa or Yao, the Malawi confederacy's monopoly on trade north of the Zambezi deteriorated (Langworthy 1972:14). Ntara (1973) describes the Bisa traders, for instance, as playing off one Malawi clan chief against another. And he refers to the Yao as agents of the Muslims and Portuguese—agents who were feared not only because they had access to guns but because the Chewa, Nyanja, and Mang'anja lived in fear of being captured and sold into slavery by Yao trade agents. Yet the Yao and Chewa themselves were involved in an internal slave trade. Audrey Richards maintains that in the period prior to British colonization, a Chewa or Yao *asyene mbumba* (avuncular head of a matriclan) had the right to sell his sisters' children into slavery, a pattern she claims existed for other matrilineal groups in the region (1950:230). There were certainly linkages between the internal and external slave trade.

To further exacerbate the problems related to slavery, around 1750, Portuguese trading agents discovered gold mines in Undi's territory and made arrangements with the Chewa ruler to mine gold with slave labor in exchange for tribute (Henriksen 1978:77). Undi apparently attempted to control the Portuguese mining operations and the slave raids of the *sertanejos* (backwoodsmen) on local villages, but with little success.

Mandala (1990), in his historical study of labor relations in the lower Shire Valley, illustrates how slave raiding in the eighteenth and nineteenth centuries decimated Mang'anja villages. Not only were men in their prime productive years taken to work in the mines along with some women and children, but women as primary agricultural laborers were bought or captured by Yao and Portuguese traders to fulfill the labor needs of the *prazo* estates farther east along the Zambezi Valley.

Prazos were crown estates leased to Portuguese outlaws, to servants of the crown, and occasionally to the orphaned daughters of Portuguese officers for a period of three generations (Lobato 1957; Isaacman 1972; Newitt 1973). For the most part, the *prazo*-holders became robber barons who formed their own slave armies—referred to as *chikunda*—rather than going through Undi for the procurement of slaves. With these armies, they made war on local chiefs and village heads (Langworthy 1972:57). Illegal landholders also were involved in the slave trade, as Vail and White (1980) point out. The authors refer to a Portuguese woman, María Vas dos Anjos Varella, who had acquired farmland "illegally" at the confluence of the Zambezi and Shire Rivers; the farm served as a regular stopover for Portuguese traders to and from Sena and Tete because its "stockade offered protection for a large retinue of slaves" (8). Senhora María was a principal slave trader on the lower Zambezi River (7).

Villages on the lower Shire that did not cooperate in providing slaves were burned or pillaged. Mang'anja village leaders, who were just as likely to be women as men, found the relative stability they had earlier enjoyed eroded by slave raiding (Mandala 1990).

In sum, trading agents contributed to the destabilization of trade within and between existing states. By going directly to the producers of natural and human resources and buying from them directly in exchange for tribute goods from the coast, the traders undermined the authority of a ruler such as Undi to control trade and its redistribution. The cycle of reciprocity was broken, as was the ruler's power to control regional economics.

Gendered relations of production in the Malawian states were similar to those in the Shona-speaking states. The most basic unit of production was the hearthhold. Defined by matrilineal relations, it was referred to as the *banja* among Mang'anja, Nyanja, and Chewa. It was headed by a woman and included her husband and possibly her mother and younger, unmarried matrilineal kin (Mandala 1990). The woman's children belonged to her matrilineage. Should she produce no offspring, her husband would be asked to leave her household and another man, or in some cases a younger woman, would be solicited to assist in the production of children for the matrilineage. Children helped their mother and her husband with the cultivation of millets and, later, rice, maize, cassava, groundnuts, and sweet potatoes. Women were largely in control of the crops they raised, trading them for other crops scarce in their locality or for cotton cloth, pots, or other scarce goods. Men might control crops that they raised in gardens given to them by their matrilineal in-laws. Men cultivated indigenous tobacco for their own use and indigenous cotton was grown in small quantities by both sexes in the lower Shire Valley for weaving into cloth, a labor-intensive process (Mandala 1990).

Men had authority in avuncular roles once they had their own families; they could extend their authority to the protection of their sisters and their sisters' offspring. Occasionally these men rose to positions of power as village heads or regional chiefs. In some cases, mature, elder women also arose to such positions, negotiating the gender divide imposed by a dual-sex system. Only a few men from ruling lineages became paramount leaders.

There was a rich network of trade among groups in the Shire Valley, in the highlands, and farther north. Men who produced iron implements such as hoes and axes in the highlands of the Zomba Plateau traded them for cotton goods and leather goods from the lowlands. In the eighteenth and nineteenth centuries, salt was distilled by women and their families and traded for slaves and firearms with such groups as the Yao and, later, the Ngoni (Ntara 1973; Phiri et al. 1977). Basketry was the skill of men, pot making the skill of women, a gender division of labor that persists in the late twentieth century. Both items contributed to the array of goods traded internally among groups. Finally, fishing and hunting were male specializations, but once fish were caught, they were either sun-dried or smoked by women for sale in local markets. Women were the sole brewers of millet beer, which was used for rituals and ceremonial occasions. Hence, a rich economy existed within the Malawi states prior to European contact in which women were vital at all levels to the sustainability of the society.

With the introduction of firearms by the Portuguese, the balance of power between ruling clans in the region became even more destabilized as one group vied with another for control over resources and trade routes. The age of the clan-based kingdoms was coming to a close by the middle of the nineteenth century.

Gender and Class in the Feudal States

The feudal states that emerged between 1150 and 1800 were based on class relations that determined a person's position in society and that were a determining factor in intra- and intergender relations. A woman who traced her lineage to a founding ancestress or ancestor stood a much better chance of commanding services, labor, and goods than a woman belonging to a clan considered "commoners" or peasants. The same applied to a man. In cases of female slavery, a woman might have few rights, but her children, especially if they resulted from a liaison with a member of the ruling clan, might attain membership in that clan (Ntara 1973; Mandala 1990). Women captured as slaves were particularly desired because in becoming the "wives" or concubines of a member of a royal lineage, they further enhanced the authority and prestige of a ruler and his tributary chiefs (Ntara 1973; Mainga 1973; Sangambo 1979). Slavery had the effect of expanding the reigning clan's control over greater numbers of people. Female slaves given as tributary gifts to female members of a ruling clan enhanced the prestige of the latter.

The division of labor was influenced more by class than by gender. Within the ruling elite clan, regardless of sex, what can be described as administrative labor characterized this class. Males and females alike were expected to be responsible for and manage the labor of great numbers of people, usually of their same sex. In exchange for the obligatory services of their subjects, the ruling clan members provided protection and security from drought and disease through the powers of their spirit mediums and rain-callers. They also provided for their people's needs in time of scarcity. Village heads were respected and revered as long as they could intervene to heal the land by providing rain. When they could not provide rain, as occurred in the early 1860s during a severe drought, their authority was called into question. Female as well as male chiefs among the Malawians suffered humiliation in such cases and often lost their positions (Mandala 1990).

Even though women in the reigning clans were better off than their counterparts down the ladder, female leaders in matrilineal states were vulnerable to deception and even attack by male elites, often within their own families. Witness the case of Kasamba, ruler of the Banamainga. Even the rain-caller Makawana of the Chewa had problems balancing her leadership with that of Undi. Such a pattern suggests that women, who were central to the origins and leadership of these groups, provoked envy among their male counterparts. In struggles between women at the top and their male relatives, women most often were the losers.

In summary, the structure of society within the feudal states, whether the ruling clans were matrilineal or patrilineal, was asymmetrical and hierarchical, and the hierarchy affected gender relations. The dependency of this hierarchy on the control of spiritual and natural resources—including arable land and rain—made the ruling elite vulnerable to attack from within. The state's growing interaction with external trade agents made it vulnerable to external attack, a vulnerability that the Portuguese and their trading agents exploited.

The Portuguese in Zambezia

Motivating Portugal's quest for hegemonic power in eastern Africa were two forces: the Crusadic desire to vanquish Islam and its Muslim traders controlling the Indian Ocean trade, and a thirst for gold, the latter to be used as a scarce trade item for obtaining Indian spices for European markets (Henriksen 1978; Elkiss 1981). The gold sources dwindled in the late 1600s, whereupon the Portuguese turned to ivory and, to a lesser degree, the slave trade. With the opening of sugar markets in the Indian Ocean islands in the eighteenth century and in Brazil in the early nineteenth century, slaves became a primary preoccupation. In the meantime, the crown's twin interest in capturing scarce land and labor took the form of the *prazo* system, whose labor component later translated into *chibalo* (forced labor); the latter had far-reaching effects on Mozambique's social formation during the colonial period. I begin with Portugal's early quest for gold.

The Early Period: Visions of Gold

Sofala in 1500 promised more gold than could be produced. The Portuguese assaults on Muslim trading magnates on the coast proved unsuccessful, and the war against the infidels had to be carried inland. Part of the strategy was not only to replace strategic Muslim trading fairs with Portuguese fairs but to populate the fertile lands on either side of the Zambezi River and down the coast with settlers, giving credibility to Portuguese colonial conquest. Another goal was to gain control of the gold mines hidden within the Zimbabwe Plateau. Neither goal was fully realized.

By the time the Portuguese arrived, the hegemony of the Mwene Mutapa confederacy was beginning to disintegrate because of secessionist tendencies and regional wars. One of the early defectors was Inhamunda, "king" of Quiteve. The Portuguese were quick to woo him away from Muslim influence with tribute gifts and firearms (Elkiss 1981). The latter, firearms, were to have the greatest impact on internal trade between African states and the Portuguese in the following decades. At the time of his rule in 1519, Inhamunda used his considerable power to close the trade routes to and from Sofala port, effectively cutting off the states of the Mwene Mutapa and Manyika from trade with the Portuguese for six years (Henriksen 1978:31). The flow of gold from the inland states on the Zimbabwe Plateau slowed to a trickle. The gold trade with Portugal was also hampered by the Muslim traders' operations: In order to outdo the avaricious Portuguese, the Muslims exported gold from inland markets via a covert northern route that ended at Angoche (Hafkin 1973). How much the loss of trade harmed the economies of the inland states is debatable. Henriksen (1978) argues that they were hurt by the reduced trade, but Beach (1980) and Elkiss (1981) maintain that gold mining was an activity that supplemented other more significant economic activities such as cattle production and agriculture.

In a new tactic to seize control of the trans-Indianic trade routes, in 1600 the Portuguese tried—with little success—to force the Muslims to purchase trading licenses from Portuguese officials in Sofala and on Mozambique Island (Henriksen 1978:33). By that time, much of the trade in Mozambique had fallen off. The Portuguese and Muslim traders lived in uneasy truce until, in the second decade of the nineteenth century, the slave trade to Brazil and the growth of the Indian Ocean sugar trade rekindled Muslim traders' aspirations.

Southern Zambezia was the major arena contested by the two trading powers, as well as by major African leaders. There, a struggle for power lasted from about 1500 to 1800. In addition to the frustration the Portuguese crown endured over Muslim trade hegemony, Portugal's fear of Dutch, French, and British expropriation of the hidden gold wealth in the interior prompted its representatives in Sofala to seek an alliance with one of the last rulers of the fragmenting Mutapa confederacy. In return for military support against the enemies threatening the demise of his empire, the Mutapa Gatsi Rusere promised to transfer his rights in mineral wealth to the Portuguese (Elkiss 1981). Another major player in the region was Changamire, who was determined to extend his authority over southern Zambezia. During the 1500s, the states surrounding Sofala prevented either the Mutapa or the Portuguese from threatening their autonomy (Elkiss 1981:31). Among the principal groups involved were the patrilineal Chope (which included the Lenge, the Chopi, and the Gi-Tonga) and the Tsonga (which included the Ronga and the Tswa). Both consolidated groups were primarily horticulturalists, although early descriptions classify men as hunters and cattle herders and women as the cultivators (Fuller 1955; Young 1977).

According to the Swiss missionary H. A. Junod, who worked among the Tsonga in the early twentieth century, in Tsonga oral tradition, women's association with crops preceded men's with cattle (Junod 1962). Early Portuguese missionaries claimed that women provided all the food produced and that no man of any rank would turn a hoe (Fuller 1955:30). Men's interest was in cattle, which they accumulated for trade and bridewealth. Prior to 1800, women were the primary cultivators of staple crops such as finger and bullrush millet and sorghum (Young 1977:68). By the end of the eighteenth century, they had adopted new imported crops, including maize, cassava, and groundnuts, and were determining the best soil conditions and seasons for their growth (70). By the nineteenth century they had rendered cashew nuts edible and knew how to prepare beer from maize as well as millet (71).

Like other women in the region, women in southern Mozambique had a critical role as spirit mediums; their skills included rain-calling, on which their communities depended (Junod 1927; Young 1977). Equally significant, women with leadership skills were occasionally appointed as subchiefs in place of their brothers, suggesting that at one time the southern groups may have been matrilineal. There are accounts of a woman referred to as Zambi, who was purported to be the "Queen Mother" of Maputo (Young 1977:70). However, by the nineteenth century, reference to women chiefs or leaders in the records of Portuguese traders is nonexistent.

Stymied by the initial encounter with groups outside Sofala, the Portuguese consolidated their power at this coastal trading center. It was not until the first decade of the sixteenth century that a trader representing the Mutapa ruler Kakuyo Kumunyaka reached Sofala (Elkiss 1981). The meeting held out the promise of gold. It was followed in 1512 by a Portuguese trading mission inland to the Mutapa court (Henriksen 1978). What the Portuguese did not realize was that the Mutapa were in danger of extinction from warring factions on all sides. As a result, the Mutapa sought arms from the Portuguese. Other Portuguese traders followed. They began to participate in Muslim trade fairs. Some acquired land. The Portuguese set up their first trade fair at Sena in 1531 to compete with the Muslims. The *sertanejos* who followed were judged to be ruffians, and the Mutapa did his best to control them. But tension grew as their numbers increased and they were followed by Catholic priests eager for conversions (Henriksen 1978).

There were some conversions to Christianity, but as Henriksen (1978:37) points out, neither Christianity nor Islam had a major impact on the Shona speakers; the rain-calling and land-healing rites of Mwari fulfilled their spiritual and psychological needs. When the Catholic priests became too demanding, as did one Gonçalo da Silveira, they were apt to lose their lives (Henriksen 1978:38).

The retribution from the Portuguese was not immediate. Rather, they waited and plotted and then sent Francisco Barreto, a military leader of some stature, against Tonga villages along the middle Zambezi River because the Portuguese suspected the villages were Muslim. For three days in 1572 they fought; the Tonga, who were limited to spear warfare, lost. However, in a twist of fate, most of Barreto's army of 800 died during heavy rains and of subsequent illness the next year (Henriksen 1978). Nonetheless, the battle was seen as a victory for Christianity over Islam and set in motion a campaign of plunder and ethnic cleansing against Muslim villages all along the middle Zambezi River. Beach (1984) counts Barreto's campaign as one of two attempts made by the Portuguese to seize the Zimbabwe Plateau and gain access to the gold mines controlled by the Mutapa, Manyika, and Torwa states.

Three years later the Mutapa Nogomo, who had converted to Catholicism, gave Portugal the right to trade freely in the region and the right to mine gold, expel Muslims, and establish Catholic missions. By 1607, the succeeding Mutapa had signed a treaty to turn over to the Portuguese crown his gold, copper, and iron mines and had promised to educate his children in Catholic mission schools (Henriksen 1978). It was an uneasy alliance that brought retribution in 1631, when the Shona-speaking states and the Banamainga went on the rampage against the *degregados* (outlaws, disreputed) who had become *prazo*-holders, reducing the Portuguese population in the region from 300 to 40 (Henriksen 1978:41). Other rebellions took place under Mutapa Mukombwe (1663–1680). To the indigenes in southern Zambezia, the Portuguese were land robbers and tyrants. By the 1690s, most Portuguese had retreated to the coast, driven out by the campaigns of the Rozwi ruler Changamire.

Alienation of Land and Labor

A century after the Portuguese had ventured inland—and as they were reevaluating their quest for gold and their ambitions to connect Portuguese East Africa with Angola—a trader, Joao Pires, was slain in Teve territory. His death brought an unexpected response from his Portuguese widow. She raised a private army and marched into the interior, demanding land from the Teve ruler as compensation for her husband's death. Startled by her courage, he ceded her a large tract of land, which she later developed (Lobato 1957; Elkiss 1981). Women were among those who gained access to land in the fertile Zambezi Valley, whether they acquired it lawfully as widows or illegally expropriated it, as in the case of Senhora María referred to earlier.

Portuguese documents are largely silent on the subject of female land-holders. We know that Portuguese women gained access to *prazo*s as orphans or widows of Portuguese officers and for use as dowry with the expectation that they would marry Portuguese men—to whom the property titles would eventually revert (Newitt 1973). Contrary to expectations, these female *prazo*-holders did not always marry Portuguese men; sometimes they married Africanized Portuguese living in Mozambique. Newitt notes that a list of *prazo*-holders in 1763 showed that 43 out of the 105 listed were in female hands and that if church-held estates and those deserted by their holders were deducted from the 105, "it is clear that women were holding rather more than half the prazos" (1973:99). The *prazo* estates of these women were passed down through the female line from mother to daughter to granddaughter before reverting to the crown. If there were no female heirs, a woman's sons or husband was able to inherit the land (97).

The *prazo* system was especially repugnant to the Africans because it meant not only that their land would be taken away but that any Africans who happened to be living within the boundaries of a given *prazo* would be forced to work there (Mondlane 1983:25–26). I have already noted the enthusiasm with which *prazo*-holders commandeered the labor of slaves, forming them into armies that raided neighboring villages. The notion of conscripted labor set a precedent for later colonial policies.

Even though a liberal government in Portugal passed land-reform measures in 1832 that included the abolition of the *prazo* system and further grants of *prazo* land were, in theory, curtailed by edict five years later, the failure of the system to attract industrious Portuguese settlers had already been acknowledged. By 1859, according to Vail and White (1980:14), of the forty-seven *prazos* in the districts of Quelimane and Sena, only two small ones were occupied by the holders. The majority had been abandoned, others had been taken over by independent African rulers, and some were held by absentee landlords.

New laws were enacted to abolish the old *prazos* and curtail the size of new land grants; the law concerning land grants included a clause requiring the development of the land within a certain period. For the first time, free Africans within the colony were eligible for fifty-hectare allotments (Vail and White 1980:15). Attached to the new land deal was an annual "hut tax." Yet as Vail and White argue, the new reforms had little impact on the existing system in Mozambique.

The Perpetuation of the Slave Trade

Portugal's other area scheduled for reform by the early nineteenth century was the institution of slavery. Though some slaves had been exported for use in the Indian Ocean islands, the slave trade from Portuguese East Africa greatly increased in the early nineteenth century in response to Brazil's demand for slaves to work in the sugar plantations. Sugar, as a major export, had become a significant aspect of the Brazilian economy with the closing of other sugar markets in the Caribbean.

The traders in Mozambique responded to the demand for slaves with a will. From 1814 to 1819, 15,000 slaves were exported through Quelimane to Brazil, over 5,000 in the year 1819 alone, demonstrating the growing potential of the slave trade (Vail and White 1989:18). The slave trade had far-reaching effects on the villages up and down the Zambezi.

In the 1820s, however, Britain, which had curtailed its own slave trade, began agitating for its termination in other European colonies. In 1836 the British held their first negotiations with the Portuguese. By this time the Brazilian slave connection had become a lucrative business; thus Portugal dragged its heels in passing legislation that would terminate the trade. Finally in 1858, a law was passed outlawing slavery by 1878 (Vail and White 1980:19). However, the situation was such that in the Zambezi Valley the new law was virtually ignored; slave raiding and slave trading had become a business for *prazo*-holders and speculators throughout the Zambezi Valley.

Forced Labor and Migrant Labor: A Dual Burden

Though pressured into giving up the slave trade, the Portuguese sought other ways to institutionalize near slave labor in Mozambique. The result was gender specific, affecting mainly males. In 1899, a government commission was formed that drafted the labor legislation on which the colony's economic development would rest. The commission's report reflected the Portuguese attitude toward conscripting indigenous labor: "The state . . . should have no scruples in obliging and if necessary forcing these rude Negroes in Africa . . . to better themselves by work . . . to civilize themselves through work" (cited in Isaacman 1996:23). The labor code enacted that year required all African males to work for a minimum of six months a year (Isaacman and Isaacman 1983:34–45). Any adult male observed by African colonial police not working, or "idle," was apprehended and forced to work on European plantations, on public works projects such as road building, or in South Africa's mines. Known as *chibalo*, this insidious system of forced labor lasted in various forms until 1961 (Vail and White 1980; Isaacman and Isaacman 1983; Saul 1985; Harries 1994; Isaacman 1996). Even though the system was gender specific in targeting men, it affected peasant women who depended on male family members for labor in the central region, and it affected the wives of male peasant producers in the south by removing a husband's labor, often for long periods in the case of those whose husbands were conscripted to work in South Africa's mines. By 1904, these men numbered more than 50,000 (Isaacman 1996:24). Migrant laborers' contracts ran for renewable twelve-to-eighteen-month periods, so these adult male family members were also absent from home for a long time.

With male labor removed, women's responsibilities were extended and their labor time intensified. Women's primary role in agriculture in southern Mozambique became a rationale for justifying male labor emigration (Young 1977). Labor emigration and internal forced labor kept more than half the adult males away from their homes, and many did not return. Those who returned may have brought home cotton cloth, wool blankets, and cooking oil, but they also brought venereal disease and accusations of adultery against wives who remained at home (Young 1977:75).

The Portuguese colonial policy of leasing land with a promise of guaranteed labor was extended to concessionary companies in the late nineteenth and early twentieth centuries. Mondlane argues that the linkage between colonial land policies and forced labor was a primary cause of Mozambique's underdevelopment in the 1960s. He observed of the foreign concessionaires that they "not only acquired rights over natural resources, but they were also allowed to control directly the lives of all Africans living within these leased lands" (1983:29).

Concessionary companies were particularly interested in cotton and sugar. Portuguese demand for cotton doubled between 1915 and 1924 as a result of World War I. This increased demand led to an intensification of production in southern Mozambique, where 70 percent of the colony's cotton was produced by the mid-1920s (Pitcher 1993; Isaacman 1996). With most of their men involved in labor migration, the women of southern

Mozambique had the responsibility for cotton production in the area. In this region, women were required to work in the cotton fields four days a week under male supervisors; they cleared land, cultivated, destroyed insects, and harvested and marketed the cotton (Young 1977:77). A similar situation existed in the central region. In the matrilineal north, where peasants were much less affected by male labor emigration, a husband-wife team jointly produced cotton and other cash-value crops demanded by the state (Pitcher 1995).

During the period of the Salazar regime in Portugal (1929–1962), large tracts of land under Portuguese control were leased to British concessionary companies for plantation production of export crops such as sugar, copra, and cotton for European markets (Saul 1985). Isaacman's (1996) study of cotton production during this period documents the hardships that peasants of both sexes endured. Even though one of Isaacman's central premises is that peasants were able to "retain a degree of autonomy from the colonial state and from the cotton concessionary companies" (1996:8), he demonstrates that by and large they "were trapped within the cotton regime" (18). It was a regime driven by mandatory, forced production. With an intensification of concessionary company production, increasing numbers of Portuguese settlers also came to occupy land in the Limpopo and Zambezi Valleys. African peasants of both sexes found themselves forced into labor to meet the demands of European markets. As the demands of cash-crop production such as cotton increased, peasant women, in particular, were subject to coercion, sexual harassment, and abuse (see Isaacman 1996:53–57).

Women's Survival Strategies

Women managed their dual obligations of producing food and cash-value crops by extending their own labor day and week, particularly during periods of high labor demand (harvesting, clearing, planting). They also took on tasks normatively associated with men, such as chopping down trees, removing stumps to clear the land, and plowing (Isaacman 1996, 194–195). They depended more on their children for help. Not only were children involved in most tasks related to the family production of cotton, but girls were at times forced into production. "I was a young girl, perhaps twelve years old, when I was ordered to plant half a hectare of cotton. Many other girls my age had to grow cotton as well" (quoted in Isaacman 1996:194).

In addition to extending their labor hours, women in southern Mozambique faced ecological hardships in the first decade of the twentieth century that contributed to their economic burdens.[6] In 1908, the maize crop failed; it was only women's ability to collect edible roots and leaves that prevented their families from starving (Young 1977). In 1912, a severe drought hit; again, the women coped, this time by drawing on famine crops such as cassava. But in the following year, when the drought persisted, women visited Mwari shrines in order to learn how the land might be healed (Young 1977:76). According to the spirit mediums, the drought was linked to male labor emigration and men's corruption during their absence from their homes. The response was the *mourimi* rite, a spiritual cleansing; men who had been absent at the mines in the Transvaal were forbidden from entering their homes until they had undergone a cleansing period. Women believed that conformity to such rites was responsible for finally breaking the drought (Young 1977). The severe flooding that followed the drought was also attributed to Mwari—she was angry about the dry condition of the land.

Male labor emigration and increased demands for cash crops for export in the preindependence years (1928–1974) led to increased pressure on women farmers, who assumed sole responsibility for both contract-crop and food production. Women not only extended and intensified their labor but were forced to take a more active role in agricultural decisionmaking in the absence of male heads of households. In some areas the production of food crops suffered because women had to spend increased amounts of time producing cash-value crops for export (Kruks and Wisner 1981; Munslow 1983; Isaacman 1996).

In the 1950s, a reform was enacted that ignored women's central role in cotton production, especially in the north, where matrilineal patterns of landholding and uxorilocal residence historically had assured women of land and labor (Hafkin 1973; Arnfred 1988). The reform encouraged male *agricultores*, or progressive cotton producers, to increase production with larger plots of land and the use of state-distributed inputs. Women and older peasants were excluded from such measures (Pitcher 1995; Isaacman 1996).

Another incentive for increased production was the setting up of *concentraçoes*, settlement schemes whereby producers were concentrated in particular areas and provided with inputs and social services such as health and education. Pitcher (1995:6–7) points out that in Nampula Province, civil servants, chiefs, African police, and company agents—all males—were the beneficiaries of such schemes. These men tended to live at home, and their wives responded by concentrating their labor on their own family plots rather than cultivating their husbands' cotton. The *concentraçoes* were not successful in attracting progressive producers, and in some areas producers were coerced into joining (Isaacman 1996:138). In Nampula, only a small percentage of the cotton producers was involved in such schemes (Pitcher 1995:6). After 1961, when forced labor was abolished, larger peasant producers were allowed to gin and sell cotton themselves and thus were able to bypass the control of the concessionary companies.

They also began to switch to producing other cash crops, such as peanuts and cashews, that brought more favorable returns (Pitcher 1995). By 1970, the peasant sector was responsible for 12 percent of Nampula's total cotton production. Cotton production declined thereafter.[7] Without the cooperation and support of women (and, indirectly, their children), such colonial schemes were bound to fail.

The dual exploitation of peasant land and labor became a primary target for change in the liberation struggle led by FRELIMO, which resulted in Mozambique's independence in 1975. Primary among FRELIMO's goals was a socialist transformation that would, in theory, lead to restructuring gender relations as well as other productive relationships. How successful this agenda was will be taken up in Chapter 5.

Summary

In this chapter I have outlined major changes in gender productive relations from early settlement to the rise of major African states in southern Africa. I have illustrated that gender relations of power and authority in the states differed depending on whether matriliny or patriliny predominated. States' rise to power and the maintenance of that power were affected by external trading powers and their demands for natural resources that were previously considered supplemental to indigenous economies.

Major Portuguese colonial policies relating to land and labor adversely affected women and men in Mozambique. Primary among these policies were the *prazo* system, which guaranteed a labor force for the *prazo*s and for the mines of the Transvaal and Southern Rhodesia. Yet the impact of labor emigration was variable by region, and northern Mozambique was much less affected. At the same time, the intensified production of the colony's major cash crop, cotton, meant that both women's and men's labor was targeted for exploitation. *Chibalo* profoundly affected gender relations of production and reproduction in southern and central Mozambique; it also served to extend women's labor obligations and disrupted women's position in matrilineal, uxorilocal households in the north. In the next chapter I turn to British expansion in southern Africa and its effect on the areas that were to become Nyasaland and the Rhodesias.

Notes

1. There is a scarcity of reliable ethnographies for Mozambique in the colonial period. The only Portuguese ethnography is of the Makondes, *The Maçondes of Mozambique* by Jorge Dias (1948). In addition, the Swiss missionary H. A. Junod

carried out a study of the Thonga south of the Savo River, with specific reference to the Ronga of Rikathlha (1927).

2. Beach maintains that it is difficult to determine the lineages of the ruling clans because they are not clear from oral traditions. He supports the notion that the Rozwi moved west to Torwa in the sixteenth century and that one of their royal cattle herders, Changa, went on to establish the Changamire state that succeeded the Rozwi line (1984:38–40).

3. Mudenge (1988) bases the wealth in wives on his readings of Portuguese documents describing the Mutapa between 1500 and 1600. By the eighteenth century the court had been greatly reduced.

4. This is the same Nehanda from which the spirit medium and colonial rebel leader Nehanda Nyakasikana (referred to by Gaidzanwa [1992]) took her identity and inspiration in the late nineteenth century.

5. Similarly Elkiss (1981) refers to first wives among the ruling Rozwi of Torwa having the power to become tributary chiefs over particular areas in order to retain Rozwi territorial control.

6. Isaacman (1996:151) has rightly pointed out that the introduction of wage labor and cash-value crop production, along with colonial marketing policies, exacerbated constraints related to food security among peasants: When drought, pest infestations, and flooding occurred, women, who were largely responsible for food production, had an even greater burden.

7. Pitcher (1995) relates that in addition to diversifying production, the men in some peasant households also became urban workers or small-scale entrepreneurs while their wives continued to produce food and cash-value crops.

4

Changing Gender Relations of Production and Power: Nyasaland and the Rhodesias

The Portuguese thrust in southern Africa ran along an East-West axis; the Nyasaland border with Tanganyika bore much of the brunt of the atrocities committed in the slave trade (see Wright 1993). In contrast, the British thrust ran south to north. The two forces met in the upper Zambezi Valley, not without consequences. From the nineteenth century the British succeeded in becoming the dominant power inland, short-circuiting the Portuguese drive for westward expansion to Angola, which they already occupied. British expansion northward from South Africa into central southern Africa was spearheaded by David Livingstone and his early explorations of the Zambezi and Shire Rivers.

Even though the British occupation lasted scarcely a century, it significantly influenced gender relations in the region. Missionization presaged the occupation in Nyasaland, bringing new concepts of land tenancy and gender relationships, particularly in the area of marriage. In the Rhodesias missionization accompanied settler and mining development, not always happily. The settlers in Southern Rhodesia suspected the missions of coddling the indigenous population and of being too tolerant of its cultural mores. In some cases the Christian churches in the three colonies became the breeding ground for nascent nationalist movements in which both sexes were involved.

Colonial capitalism equally affected the native population. This process began with settler agriculture and commercial mining interests and spread unevenly through the three colonies. The fact that a commercial enterprise, the British South Africa Company, was given responsibility for administering the Rhodesias in the early years provides some indication of the crown's trust in capital and its mistrust of the rough-hewn settlers who formed the Pioneer Column, which advanced into Southern Rhodesia from South Africa. Interfacing with existing modes of production in various ways, capitalism became a formidable challenge to indigenous modes of production and land use.

Initially, settler demands for food grown locally stimulated peasant production outside urban centers. As a result, agriculture became commoditized and increasingly dependent on the settler and mining communities. At the same time, the best arable land was transferred into European hands at a rapid rate, decreasing the land base on which food could be grown for indigenous consumption. Cattle, too, became an issue. Indigenous herds were at the mercy of colonial administrators who were determined to control the spread of diseases such as rinderpest and bovine pleuropneumonia. Destroying a whole herd of cattle—all a man's wealth—was anathema to the peoples of southern Africa.

Spearheaded by missionaries and, later, by settler-planters in Nyasaland, the Pioneer Column in Southern Rhodesia, and commercial mining interests in Northern Rhodesia, capitalism with its attendant patriarchal ideology had a profound effect on gender productive relations even though its spread was uneven.

In this chapter I explain how colonial capitalism undermined women's economic roles differentially in matrilineal and patrilineal groups in all three colonies and argue that its adverse effects were felt most intensely by women in groups that practiced matrilineal descent and uxorilocal residence patterns. The chapter begins with a discussion of Nyasaland, where missionization had the greatest impact. Here, groups that largely ascribed to matrilineal ideology and uxorilocal residence patterns came into conflict with patriarchal Christian missionaries beginning in the 1880s. Further conflict centered on the colonial administration's hut tax, instituted as a means of financing services and, in theory, of capturing indigenous male labor to serve settlers and plantation owners. The hut tax was gender specific in that it was directed toward heads of households, who were presumed to be men in the Victorian received wisdom of the late nineteenth century. It was men who were expected to pay the tax, and it was men's property (the houses they had built) and their families who were at risk if the tax was not paid. The hut tax's effect on matrilineal households varied depending on where the men lived and the resources they had at their disposal.

The section on the Rhodesias begins with an analysis of the implementation of the hut tax by the British South Africa Company in 1894. Here I examine the effect of the hut tax on male labor recruitment. The intensification of agriculture and trade allowed Shona cultivators living outside towns such as Salisbury and Gwelo to raise the cash for tax payments; thus their households did not lose male labor contributions. However, marginal cultivators and those at some distance from urban areas were forced to emigrate. Among some groups in Northern Rhodesia, such as the Lozi, labor migration to pay hut taxes affected mainly peasants. The royal family and their *induna* (counselors) were able to pay their taxes through cattle sales through 1915. Thus the hut tax affected groups differently depending on class and gender.

My intent in this chapter is to paint a broad, composite picture of how British colonial occupation affected lineage and changed the gender landscape. In so doing, I draw on the work of historians who have specialized in exegeses of the colonial past rather than my own work, which is concerned with changes in gender relations in the recent past and is found in subsequent chapters.[1] I include the voices of the colonized wherever possible.

The Dawn of Nyasaland:
The Cross and the Torch

The mid-nineteenth century marks the beginning of the British intrusion into the territory they called Nyasaland. Inspired by Livingstone's promising accounts of his 1852 journey, the first missionaries to arrive in Malawi in 1860 were an ecumenical group—the Universities Mission to Central Africa (UMCA). They found a population in the lower Shire Valley decimated by war, slave raiding, and drought. Confronting a Yao slave-trading party, the missionaries forced the leader to free some of the Nyanja slaves (Linden 1974). This action set the tone for the work of the missionaries in the latter part of the nineteenth century, who had a captive audience, so to speak, in former slaves. The Nyanja and Mang'anja farther north had already been colonized by Mangochi and Machinga Yao. The Muslim Yao chiefs along the southern tip of Lake Malawi were less than enthusiastic about the UMCA's attempt to establish a foothold amongst them; the plan was defeated by malaria and Yao hostility.

By the time a Scottish missionary team led by Robert Laws arrived fifteen years later, in 1875, the last of the Malawi leaders of the Phiri clan had been killed by Mangochi Yao (Linden 1974:7). The matrilineal Mang'anja in the southern Shire (Tchiri) Valley had been partially colonized by patrilineal Kololo groups who had accompanied Livingstone as porters in his exploration of the lower Shire. The second attempt at missionization in Yao territory in 1875 resulted in the Free Church of Scotland's missionary presence at Cape McClear. The Livingstonia mission at the lower end of the lake was followed by other stations farther north. These mission activities became the rationale for Scottish commercial interests on the lake.

In 1879 the Scottish-owned African Lakes Company began supplying the missions along the Shire River and the lake with goods from the mother country or South Africa. The Livingstonia mission was followed by an attempt of the Catholics to found a mission at Mangochi in 1889—the same year that Nyasaland was declared a protectorate of the British crown. Catholic attempts to compete with the Church of Scotland for the support of the Yao chiefs came to naught, and the Catholics were forced to withdraw until 1901. Neither group of missionaries, however, made much headway among the Muslim Yao chiefs, who were cordial but wary of the Christians' motives.

In the central region the Chewa peoples had become subjects of militant, patrilineal Ngoni, a Nguni group that had escaped the worst of the militant campaigns of the Zulu which resulted in the *mfecane*. Marching north, the Ngoni conquered horticultural groups that came to be known as the Chewa, Nyanja, Lake Tonga, and Tumbuka, incorporating many of the young men into their military regiments. The Chewa-speaking groups survived Ngoni domination by raising food as tribute for their Ngoni overlords (Linden 1974). A similar relationship developed between the Chewa-speaking groups and the Yao chiefs in the south.

By the mid-nineteenth century, then, the two politically dominant groups in Malawi were the Yao and Ngoni. Neither was receptive to missionary activities. The Ngoni in the central and northern regions continued to raid the weakened Chewa, Tumbuka, and Lake Tonga even though the latter two groups had the support of the Livingstonia mission. In response to a call for help from the missionaries, the British established a military presence in the protectorate in the 1890s. The Ngoni twice attempted to challenge the new colonial power—once in 1896 and again in 1898—but they met with defeat. By the end of the century, Ngoni hegemony in central Malawi had been overturned by British imperialism.

In the south the Yao chiefs, who had benefited from the slave trade for two centuries, were deprived of this livelihood when the British colonial government, pressured by missionary groups, took measures to halt the slave trade once and for all. The Yao chiefs barely tolerated the Protestant and Catholic missionaries' work among the southern matrilineal groups, all of whom they had earlier subjugated. Ironically, after the unsuccessful revolt by the Christian convert John Chilembwe and his supporters in 1915, the Yao chiefs became the means through which the British colonial government exercised indirect rule in southern Nyasaland.

In 1900, just ten years after Nyasaland was declared a protectorate, there were only 314 Europeans in the colony, most of them missionaries—the largest missionary presence among the colonies (Linden 1974:119). A trickle of Boer and British settlers with visions of fertile land, export crops, and easy money began arriving in the 1890s. Once the settler foot had been planted, an administrative support system funded by local taxation was soon to follow. This pattern unfolded in most of the British colonies in eastern and southern Africa. Capitalism and Victorian notions of gender were an integral part of the colonial system that took root.

Prelude to Colonialism: Crises in Northern Zambezia

In his study of the lower Shire (Tchiri) Valley, Elias Mandala (1990) describes how the intersection of three historical developments—the East African slave trade, a drought that took place in 1862–1863, and the rise of Kololo power—began to undermine the economic stability of Mang'anja villages and the women who lived in them or headed them. I have already referred to the disrupting influence of slave raiding on Mang'anja villages during the waning years of the Malawi confederacy. Shadowing this was an environmental crisis—a two-year drought—that emptied women's storage granaries. Agricultural production in southern Malawi became negligible. Formerly, cultivators would have relied on a paramount leader such as Lundu to provide grain in periods of drought and to heal the land through his powerful rainmakers. The authority of the Malawian ruling class, however, had shrunk in the wake of Portuguese ascendancy and the powers of local rainmakers were sorely tested.

Women scoured the countryside for wild fruits, roots, and edible bark to feed their families. As mothers saw their children and old people weaken and die, they implored their local chiefs, who were also responsible for "calling down the rains," to intervene with age-old rituals that would appease the matrilineal ancestor spirits and bring moisture to the land. When the rains did not come the second year, the authority of local chiefs was weakened.

Drought in the region is cyclical, and several more droughts would appear during the colonial period, adding to the burdens of Africans in the midst of tightening economic conditions. One occurred in 1894 when the British had barely gained an administrative foothold in the region, and four more occurred in the first decades of the twentieth century—1903, 1909, 1912–1913, and 1917 (Linden 1974:56, 79). These droughts were regional, occurring in Southern Rhodesia and in Mozambique during the same periods, but their effect was uneven depending on the extent and depth of settler intrusion, the coincidence of locusts, and the policies of the colonial state (Iliffe 1990:10, for Southern Rhodesia). In the southern half of Mozambique between 1900 and 1902, drought and famine were accompanied by widespread disease, especially smallpox, making it the worst-case scenario in the region (Vail and White 1980:119–120). Other dry periods came in 1922, 1933, and 1942, but a major drought in Nyasaland (1948–1949) pointed out weaknesses in the agricultural policies of the expanding colonial state and the consequences for Malawians trying to survive the resulting famine (Vaughan 1987).[2] A similar scenario developed in Southern Rhodesia during the 1947 drought (Iliffe 1990). From the beginning of occupation, drought—the scourge of the land—came to be associated in the minds of rural Africans with colonial rule (Vambe 1972; Linden 1974; Vaughan 1987; Iliffe 1990). As the Africans interpreted the situation, matrilineal and patrilineal ancestor spirits were angry with the new invaders.

Traveling on the heels of the drought in 1862 was a political realignment in the villages along the lower Shire River due to colonization by the militant Kololo. The patrilineal Kololo were related to the Ndebele and had also migrated north to escape the disrupting wars resulting from the *mfecane*. The "mfecane," as it was known to its victims, referred to scorched-earth tactics used by the Zulu to conquer their neighbors. The Kololo had conquered many of the groups they came in contact with, including the Plateau Tonga (Colson 1951). Individual Kololo became porters for Livingstone's early exploration of the lower Shire River in the 1850s and later came back to conquer Mang'anja villages weakened from slave raiding and drought. When they found a village headed by a woman, she was dismissed and a sympathetic male head was found to take her place (Mandala 1990:83). A similar scenario occurred in Chewa villages conquered by the Ngoni in the central region. By the time British missionaries gained a hold in the 1880s, then, other forces within the wider southern African region were already affecting the erosion of Malawian women's authority and socioeconomic power.

The Impact of Early Missionization

"Missionization" in this book refers to the process whereby a particular Christian sect gains access to land for a mission station, the way that labor is recruited to develop the land and construct the mission buildings, and the means through which proselytization takes place, including outreach to indigenous communities through social services such as education and health. In the Shire highlands, missionization contributed to the erosion of Mang'anja women's power beginning in the 1870s. In Malawi the Christian sects of the British dominion—the Free Church of Scotland and the Church of England—got the lion's share of land, services, and funding during British occupation. Other sects such as the Catholic and Dutch Reformed Churches received less support from the colonial state.

Landeg White's (1987) case study of a UMCA mission at Magomero in the Shire highlands illustrates how the establishment of a mission could affect preexisting gender relations in the latter part of the nineteenth century. Noting that in "Mang'anja society, the custom was for a man to marry into his wife's home village," where they jointly cultivated land belonging to her lineage, White goes on to show that Church of England missionaries, in particular Bishop John McKenzie, directly undermined Mang'anja land tenure and marriage practices by allocating mission land to Mang'anja men and not to women when they adopted Christian marriage (33). "Despite all the Bishop's homilies about equality and fidelity in marriage," White comments, "what he had done in the eyes of the Mang'anja was to lend support to the pattern already evolving (at the mission) by which the most important rights and powers were vested in men, to whom women became subordinate" (37).

We do not learn what Mang'anja women's response was to this usurpation of their customary rights except that when deprived of their control over land, they began to steal peas from the gardens of local chiefs sympathetic to the missionaries (White 1987:39). However, it is notable that whereas Malawian men readily became Christian converts, Malawian women, who stood to lose much more, were less inclined to convert (Linden 1974).

To understand why Christianity was less appealing to women in matrilineal groups, we have to look at the differences between the gender ideology of patrilineal Christianity and that of matrilineality as it was practiced in Malawi. Christianity's mythic view of the origins of gender relations is very different from that of many matrilineal groups. For the Chewa and Mang'anja, the original human being was female; the blood line flowed from mother to daughter or son. In these matrilineal societies males were viewed as contributing to reproduction through their procreative ability connected with water (semen).

In Christianity, whose biblical origins arose from patrilineal herding societies, man was central and woman was an extension of that being—mythically created from man's rib. The centrality of females in one ideology and males in the other need not result in conflict unless the proponents of one mean to subordinate the other. In Malawi, the two ideologies were destined for collision because Christian missionaries were less eclectic than their Muslim counterparts and were determined, for the most part, to change the matrilineal beliefs and practices of the peoples whom they came to dominate. Christianity was associated with the presence of the colonial state in the minds of many Malawians, especially elders and women (Linden 1974). For others, especially younger men, Christianity became a means of getting out from under the yoke of matrilineal obligations and provided them with education and intellectual tools—in some cases, tools that enabled them to raise questions about the British occupation (Vail and White 1989; Chanock 1985).

The stories of two major Malawian dissidents in the first decade of the twentieth century illuminate that gender, lineage, and religion were interrelated factors in protest movements during the colonial period. One dissident was a woman and a non-Christian. The other was a male Christian convert. Both came from matrilineal groups.

The Chewa prophet Chanjiri did not belong to a Christian church and avoided mission contact. She depended on her spiritual ties with Mwari, the Chewa creator, and her ancestors for guidance and strength. In 1910, Chanjiri foretold the timely end of European rule in Nyasaland, especially the disappearance of Blantyre, the commercial center, if proper sacrifices were made to Mwari (Linden 1974:76). Her explanation to her Chewa followers was that Mwari had become angered with the way Europeans treated the land; to heal the land, tributary gifts should be made through Chanjiri, who by 1910 had escaped across the border to Mozambique to avoid capture by British colonials. Chanjiri had a large group of followers; they could be seen from one of the Catholic mission stations whenever they trekked across the border to visit her with tributary gifts (Linden 1974).

The other dissident was Eliot Kamwana, a Lake Tonga and a Christian convert who broke with the church to start his own sect. A member of the Watchtower Movement and a millenarian, Kamwana foresaw the end—on October 14, 1914—of the colonial state and its lackeys, especially the tax collectors. The latter were particularly odious; not only did they harass and beat those who were tardy in their payments but they burned down the houses of those who failed to pay (Linden 1974). Kamwana and his followers reasoned that since Western Christianity was not providing Africans with the wealth and power enjoyed by European Christians, there must be something wrong in the salvation that the European Christian church offered. Part of Christian salvation, in Kamwana's view, was to get free schooling for Africans so that they might achieve greater power (73–75). In 1909 Kamwana was deported for his millenarian views because they posed a threat to the colonial state.

That Chanjiri and Kamwana both came from matrilineal groups is significant. We have seen that among these groups, women had more economic security in land and labor. They also had a more secure place in their lineages. It is not surprising, therefore, that men in matrilineal groups were more attracted to Christianity with its patriarchal social values than were women (see also Poewe 1981; and Wright 1983 for Zambia). Even though the goals of these two prophets of colonial doom were similar, one chose a Christian solution, whereas the other employed a solution consonant with her indigenous religion.

Christians were not the only ones protesting the European occupation of Nyasaland in the early twentieth century. The multiple droughts in the first decade and the hardships associated with the hut tax led to a resurgence of Islam in 1912 with the spread of Muslim Brotherhoods (Linden 1974:94). Part of the problem was that land was rapidly being expropriated by Europeans.

Tensions over Land and Labor:
The Arrival of Cash Crops

By the 1890s in the Shire highlands not only were the missionaries challenging Mang'anja gender relations but British settlers and European companies had found a way to further destabilize these relations. With a recipe for land alienation wrought by Sir Harry Johnston, the British began gobbling up arable land belonging to the Yao chiefs who had earlier settled in Mulanje and the Shire highlands after migrating from Mozambique. The British excuse for territorial conquest was that ostensibly idle land would be put to productive use. By 1900, individual settlers, companies, and missions had been granted freehold title by the British crown to 15 percent of Nyasaland's land base of 26,000 square miles (Pachai 1972). The key crops were to be cotton and coffee. The linchpin for production, however, was labor, and labor was scarce.

The hut tax, tried successfully in Kenya, was proposed in 1894 as a solution to the labor shortage. Although this device forced the Malawians to pay the British in cash, it did not provide the "captured labor force" the planters had hoped for (White 1987). The alternative was hiring migrant labor from the central and northern regions, which provided only an illusory solution. Linden (1974:79) notes that half the male population of the villages surrounding the Catholic missions in the central region went off to Blantyre and Zomba, the provincial capital, to find work after the crops failed in the 1912 drought. A motivating factor was earning money to pay the hut tax. However, male labor from the north tended to be cyclical and sporadic. The Lake Tonga, the Tumbuka, and the Ngoni tended to migrate further south to Southern Rhodesia and South Africa, where salaries, especially in the mines, tended to be higher.[3]

A partial solution to the planters' labor shortage came when Anguru (Lomwe) immigrants escaping the punitive *chibalo* labor system in Mozambique crossed into Mulanje and began to "beg Yao chiefs for land." The Yao chiefs provided land in exchange for labor. Often Yao chiefs used the labor of Lomwe migrants to fulfill their labor obligations arising from the hut tax. Other Lomwe settled farther north near Chiradzulu, where they were allowed to settle on estate lands as tenants in exchange for *thangata* labor (Kandawire 1979). The precedent set by such a labor arrangement had far-reaching implications for gender relations of production in the Shire highlands.

In its original indigenous form, *thangata* amounted to collaborative labor provided to a village chief that was rewarded with large amounts of food and beer (Kandawire 1979; White 1987). However, under the estate system of production it was perverted into a dependency relationship; the dignity of male labor was compromised by an exchange system that left the *thangata* laborers on the estates with less land, less pay, and more work (Kandawire 1979). The women to whom they were married were differentially affected by the loss of male labor depending on residency and economy. Although in both matrilineal Yao and Mang'anja villages, uxorilocality was practiced, women in Mang'anja and Lomwe villages were more accustomed to relying on the labor of their husbands in agricultural production. In Yao villages, where there was a history of trading controlled by males, men were more often away for long periods on trading expeditions; thus women there counted less on their male relatives for agricultural labor (White 1987:49). Consequently, Mang'anja women in *banja* (matrilineal hearthholds, using Ekejiuba's (1995:51) term to designate a woman's hearth and those who eat food cooked there) felt more acutely the loss of male labor through the *thangata* system than did their Yao counterparts. In addition, elite Yao women, as the wives of former slave traders, were more apt to have slaves, captured in earlier raids, to assist them in production.

By the end of the nineteenth century, then, the incursion of missionaries with their attendant patriarchal ideas about women and property and the related capitalization of agriculture and labor through the advocacy of British settlers and planters (some of whom were descended from early missionary families) worked in tandem to significantly alter gender relations of production in the Shire highlands.

Gender Relations in the Lower Shire Valley

The situation in the lower Shire Valley was less disruptive of gender relations in agricultural production for two reasons. First, Mang'anja peasants intercropped cotton, the cash-value crop best suited to the region, with food crops such as millet and maize.

Second, from the income generated from cotton sales, they were able to raise cash to pay the insidious hut tax underwriting the Nyasaland colonial administration. *Thangata* as it was applied by British estate holders in the Shire highlands never succeeded in the lower Shire valley as a means of capturing indigenous labor because the peasant producers of cotton had other means of paying the tax than exchanging their labor. When labor raids did occur, potential workers hid in the villages or temporarily crossed the border into Mozambique (Mandala 1990). As Mandala (1990:130) points out, these largely smallholder peasant producers remained autonomous, and the failure of the colonial power to impress local labor for cotton estates meant, in part, that the settler estate sector in cotton was marked for failure by the 1930s.

A similar attempt by the colonial state to encourage smallholders in the central region to grow cotton as an export crop failed (Linden 1974:79). Chewa cultivators were more concerned with producing food, and tobacco was the cash crop that attracted European attention in the first part of the twentieth century.

Productive Relationships
in the Early Twentieth Century

The capitalization of labor was not uniform in the early twentieth century. Even though a few Sena growers in the lower Shire Valley became *zunde* owners of large cotton estates of 200 to 300 acres and employed wage labor, the bulk of the Mang'anja in the lower Shire Valley continued to produce as they always had, with women and men in matrilineal *banja* hearthholds cultivating cotton along with their grain crops (Mandala 1990:38). Other food crops and rice were grown in *dimba,* land adjacent to the river (Schoffeleers 1980). During the cotton era (1904–1936) women benefited equally with men as their role in production was ensured and they received a fair share of the proceeds, either in cash or in kind. Thus they experienced relative economic autonomy (Schoffeleers 1984).

Husband-wife teams met the new demands for cotton production by intensifying their control over their children's labor in three ways: first, through *chikamwene,* or brideservice, the uncompensated obligatory labor of betrothed male youths for their in-laws; second, through *chilere* (youth gardens), which they insisted be planted in cotton; and third, through the Sena-inspired *nomi,* or youth associations, whose members were required to help in the fields (Mandala 1990:130). This last form of labor included both girls and boys who, after fulfilling their obligations in their parents' gardens, offered their labor to smallholder peasants on a cash or kind basis. Women cultivators in particular tightened their control over the *chikamwene* labor of their daughters' husbands, which otherwise might have gone to the *ankhose,* the male elder responsible for the woman's *mbumba*—a group of related sisters who are of the same matrilineage (Schoffeleers 1968:52).[4] Even though gender productive relations in smallholder cotton production were similar to what had existed previously, what was intensified, then, was the use of youth labor.

In the larger households of Sena producers, where marriages were often polygynous, cotton was usually not intercropped but cultivated separately. It came under direct control of the husband, and wives continued to cultivate subsistence food crops (Mandala 1990:132). Consequently, in these patrilineal Sena households the association of cash crops with males and food crops with females, a phenomenon that led to the marginalization of women in the development process in much of Africa (Boserup 1970), was more prevalent than in the monogamous *banja* hearthholds of most Mang'anja.

Cotton production continued to grow in the lower Shire until the 1930s, when the world depression adversely affected local cotton prices. In 1933, 61.3 percent of the male *zunde* holders who had been growing cotton in 1932 stopped growing it, but production among smallholder Mang'anja peasants increased by 50 percent (Mandala 1990:163). When *zunde* holders dropped out of cotton, they divided the holdings among their co-wives and left to find wage labor farther south. The number of independent female cotton growers rose by 600 percent between 1932 and 1933, according to Mandala (1990:171).

In 1936 a large sand bar at the mouth of Lake Malawi broke up, causing a sharp rise in the level of the Shire River in the latter part of the 1930s. Prime cotton lands flooded, virtually ending the cotton boom (Schoffeleers 1984:191). The result was an outward labor migration of males—up to 53 percent in one chiefdom (Schoffeleers 1984:193). Some went north to Chikwawa District and others went farther south to the mines in Southern Rhodesia and South Africa. Some husbands among the migrants sent home remittances for their wives, but in other cases wives were abandoned and these women had to depend on other men—brothers or sons—for remittances. Moreover, their agricultural labor burdens were increased. Nevertheless, not all *banja* hearthholds were equally affected by the collapse of cotton. Many women continued to cultivate food crops on reduced plots, testifying to the flexibility of local farming systems.

An attempt in the 1940s by the colonial state to increase maize production through monocropping and soil conservation methods that included enforced ridging and contour cultivation met with stern resistance, especially on the part of women on whom "much of the burden fell" (Kettlewell 1965:239). Even though the enforcement policy was abandoned by the end of the decade, many had adopted the new methods despite initial resistance. Most hearthholds, however, continued to cultivate different plots of land using *banja* labor.

In the central region, European planters, through Crown Land Tobacco grants, began to grow tobacco, a crop that had long been grown by Malawians on an individual basis. Seeing the opportunity to make a profit, Malawian peasants also began to produce tobacco for sale. Through the Native Tobacco Board, a few Africans with large parcels of land were able to dominate production, pricing, and marketing policies for Africans and also dominated relationships with the colonial Crown Land Tobacco growers, who controlled the tobacco market in Nyasaland through the 1930s

(McCracken 1983). As the Malawian peasant growers proved to be successful growers of tobacco, they posed an economic threat to the European tobacco planters (Kachapila 1992). The latter worked as an interest group to promote state measures that would discourage peasant production of tobacco.

Not much is known about women's role in tobacco production during the colonial period. A 1948 report written by an acting director of agriculture mentioned that the strengthened demand and high prices for tobacco were leading to increased recruitment of labor, many of the newest recruits being women and children (cited in McCracken 1983:172). Hendrine Kachapila is undertaking a study that should fill the knowledge gap regarding the specific roles of women in tobacco production.

In the north, migratory labor was increasing, with consequences for Lakeside Tonga women. Older male village heads met their commitments to provide labor by recruiting younger men (van Velsen 1964). Younger men came to view labor emigration as a means of earning cash for their bridewealth commitments in this matrilineal society. In the 1930s, elders raised the price of bridewealth. As young men returned, they were not happy to settle down in their wives' villages, as Tonga men once had. Returnees preferred to settle on land they controlled, keeping their wives with them. Backed by their matrikin, these younger men attempted to usurp the authority that wives in Tonga society had by virtue of lineage. Tension between spouses led to increased cases of divorce in the 1950s as women sought autonomy by taking their children and returning to their natal villages (van Velsen 1964). Wives were also reluctant to remain in their husband's hamlet after he died, preferring to return to their own homes and the safety of kin. Thus, migrant males intensified ideological divisions over residence (uxorilocal versus virilocal) and lineage in Lake Tonga society when they returned and tried to enforce virilocality and take control of their children.

Interlineage Marriages, 1940s to 1950s

Increased mobility in the southern region by the mid-twentieth century led to an increase in intermarriage between different "ethnic" groups. If people came from groups that had the same matrilineal ideology and uxorilocal marriage patterns, such as the Mang'anja, Yao, and Lomwe, a pattern generally continued that stressed these features (Mitchell 1956; White 1987). In areas such as the lower Shire, where the patrilineal, virilocal Sena lived alongside the matrilineal Mang'anja, two patterns appear to have emerged. When Sena men married Mang'anja women, the marriage led to uxorilocality with no bridewealth being transferred. Sena men were appar-

[handwritten margin notes: — bridewealth paid goes along with virilocality — children belong to lineage of parent where they ...]

ently willing to relocate to a Mang'anja village at marriage, the compensation being that they did not have to pay bridewealth. The children of such a marriage belonged to the wife's *mbumba* (group of related sisters who share the same matrilineage). However, if a Mang'anja man married a Sena woman, her Sena patrikin required him to pay bridewealth, whereupon he was allowed to take his wife to his matrilineal home village (Duly 1946). In this case, the children belonged to his matrilineage. Thus although residence changed, the descent pattern remained matrilineal in both cases. What is notable is that lineage ideology involved proved flexible, adapting to the contingencies of the moment.

There were other cases where intermarriage involving contrasting lineage ideologies was less flexible; and there were still others where intermarriage between members of a matrilineal group and a patrilineal group was studiously avoided. Often the ethnic group and its economic viability determined the decision. In a comparison of matrilineal groups in Nyasaland and Northern Rhodesia in the mid-twentieth century, Richards (1950:235) observed that intermarriage between matrilineal Chewa and the patrilineal Ngoni, who had formerly conquered them, was becoming routine. Less frequent were intermarriages between the matrilineal Yao and patrilineal groups. In cases where a Chewa man married an Ngoni woman, the Chewa man transferred bridewealth and virilocality was observed. However, the children belonged to the husband's matrilineage. When a Ngoni man married a Chewa woman, he transferred bridewealth and took his wife to his village. The children, in this case, belonged to his patrilineage. In either case, the lineage of the father prevailed.

Yao men and women avoided marrying a member of any patrilineal group. Drawing on Mitchell's evidence (1956), Richards attributes the Yao reluctance to intermarry to three factors: (1) land shortage (women wanted to retain control of their existing land and the security that it represented rather than trade it for land elsewhere); (2) the greater permanence of Yao villages, including the preference for cross-cousin marriages within these villages; (3) the presence of heritable wealth obtained, often, through trade that the Yao preferred to keep within their own matrilineages (Richards 1950:236). Particularly women stood to lose should they marry a man from a patrilineal group. Intermarriage, then, was leading in some cases to flexible lineage and residence patterns, and in other cases it was avoided.

Banja *Family Hearthholds* *and the Impact of Migratory Labor*

Banja, a Chichewa term at times applied to family in a matrilineal homestead and at others to a woman's hearthholds in the mid-twentieth century

included few polygynous situations. A.W.R. Duly, a colonial customs officer who devoted much of his spare time to collecting information about agricultural production and social customs from Mang'anja informants, estimated that only 10 percent of the men surveyed were polygynous (1964:15). Roberts makes a similar observation for the Lomwe, noting that although polygyny was permitted, it was very rarely practiced (1964:25). Farther north in Machinga, a study of the matrilineal Yao (Mitchell 1952, 1956) between 1946 and 1949 revealed a similar pattern: Very few households, other than those of headmen, were polygynous, and "as a rule husband and wife cultivate[d] a garden together" (1952:23). That households were monogamous does not mean, however, that women and men limited themselves to a single partner over a lifetime. Separation, divorce, and remarriage were relatively easy. Male labor emigration meant that a husband could be absent for much of the time.

The mines in South Africa and Southern Rhodesia attracted Malawian males because the wages were higher than those they could earn locally.[5] Pressure from a liberal British government led to a law in 1907 forbidding recruitment of miners within Nyasaland; this law was changed later by the Native Labor Ordinance. Despite legislation to stop the flow of male labor from the villages to the mines, it was estimated that in 1910 there were 20,000 Malawian workers in Southern Rhodesia alone (Sanderson 1966:43). By 1913 emigration had risen to 25,000 by conservative estimates (Krishnamurty 1964, cited in Linden 1974:74). Evidence also exists of labor recruitment and extortion within Malawi.[6]

The need for labor on sugar plantations in Mozambique also encouraged emigration (Linden 1974:74). Catholic missionaries opposed emigration of men from the villages to the mines as disruptive of family life (172). However, the men emigrated, initially to meet the demands of the colonial state for tax payments and later as a means of raising cash to pay for commodities that formerly had been traded without benefit of cash. Another key factor was growing land scarcity in the southern region. Male labor emigration peaked in the 1950s and 1960s, but with the fatal crash of a plane carrying many Malawian males to South African mines in 1974, the tide was stemmed.

The rise in male emigration, whether internal or external, placed an increased burden on de facto female heads of households or *banja*, that is, those women whose husbands were absent for six or more months of the year and who, for all practical purposes, managed their *banja* without husbands.

With the growth of the estate sector in Malawi between 1966 and 1977, males in the southern region tended to shift away from smallholder production to take up wage jobs in the new national capital in Lilongwe or on tobacco estates in Kasungu. By 1977, 69.3 percent of those working on their own holdings in the southern region were women (Kydd and Christiansen 1982:358).

The consequence of male emigration for women in uxorilocal hearth-holds who are married has been the intensification of their own and their children's labor except in cases where remittance from an absent husband or grown son is sufficient to hire labor. An alternative is to induce male matrikin to assist them during peak seasons. The impact of migratory labor on married women's financial resources has varied depending on where the husband is employed (and the kind of work he does) and whether he sends remittances to his family. In cases where a woman's husband or son works in the mines of South Africa or Zimbabwe, where salaries are higher than they are in Malawi, families are likely to receive higher remittances than women whose men work closer to home (Peters 1994). Because these women have security in land, they gain independence from the decisions they alone must make in the management and distribution of production. In some cases, they may diversify their income-generating activities to include those that earn more income, such as brewing beer or raising poultry (on this point, see Moore and Vaughan 1994 for Zambia).

Women who are widowed, divorced, or single may or may not have to deal with a reduction in output because of male emigration; their situation depends on whether they have grown sons and brothers who participate in migratory labor. Generally women in de facto female-headed *banja* have fewer labor resources to begin with. Circumstances vary and much depends on whether a woman heading her household has depended in the past on male labor that may be withdrawn because of emigration. The degree of financial hardship also depends on the length of time a male family member is absent and whether a woman receives remittances. In short, when looking at the way migratory labor impacts Malawian women in uxorilocal *banja,* we must be careful not to assume that all women heading their own households fit into a single category and, therefore, are similarly affected. The strength of family ties, lineage ties, and existing social networks all contribute to a woman's ability to manage production in the absence of male labor.

The Rhodesias:
The Company, the Settlers, and the Mine

Three years after the death of Livingstone in 1873, a young British citizen with energy and ambition arrived in South Africa. He was destined to leave his imprint on the Zambezi Valley. By the age of thirty-five, Cecil Rhodes had amassed considerable wealth through activities in the Kimberley diamond mines, enough to found the British South Africa Company (BSAC). Eager to find new mineral wealth, he traveled north into Matabeleland in 1888. He found his match in the paramount chief of the Ndebele, Lobengula. The Ndebele had preceded Rhodes into Zimbabwe, escaping the dislocations of the Zulu wars. Arriving in the early nineteenth century, they conquered many of the Shona-speaking groups on the Zimbabwe Plateau.

When Rhodes met with the paramount chief, he was able to extract a concession from him that gave Rhodes's company rights to enter and explore mineral resources over a territory that included most of Zimbabwe and extended into southern Zambia (Ndlovu 1974). In the next two years he worked on a similar concession with Lobengula's principal rival farther north, Lewanika of the Lozi. The concession gave him the rights to what was then referred to as Northern Zambezia (Hall 1966). Through an additional concession negotiated by his agent, Lochner, Rhodes was ceded mineral rights within the entire Barotse territory, a concession that was extracted fraudulently—as were the mining concessions in much of Zambia. These agreements excluded the African producers and denied them trading privileges (Mutemba 1977; Van Horn 1977).

Rhodes was able to wrest a royal charter from the British crown that also gave the British South Africa Company (BSAC) rights to administer the territory of what was to become the Rhodesias. Among these rights—and responsibilities—was the promotion of trade, commerce (the development of mineral wealth), and "civilization and good government" with "materially improved conditions" for the "natives inhabiting the territories" (Mlambo 1972:1). The last objective was neglected; unlike the charter for Nyasaland, this one made no provision for a British administration to intervene on behalf of the crown or the "natives" should it be necessary—the BSAC had exclusive authority.

Particularly relevant to the preexisting groups in the Rhodesias were the clauses of the charter that empowered the BSAC to "develop, clear, plant and cultivate *any* (my emphasis) lands" (although as Palmer [1977b] points out, no provision had been made in the document for purchase or acquisition of land). Based on the charter, Rhodes put together a group of nearly 200 men from South Africa to trek to Zimbabwe, where they would be given land by the company to develop. Most men of the Pioneer Column, as it was referred to, were more interested in quick riches than in settling down to farm (Mutambirwa 1980:25; Schmidt 1992:36). As Schmidt observes, these men were "short on capital, education and skill" (1992:9). However, once these settlers gained a foothold in what was to become Southern Rhodesia, their numbers gave them the critical mass to demand an administrative voice in the operations of the BSAC, which administered the territory between 1890 and 1923.

The Jesuit missionaries who accompanied the Pioneer Column were more concerned with the BSAC charter's humanitarian aims. The men of the Pioneer Column and succeeding settlers clashed with the Jesuits over their "liberal" views toward the Africans and their efforts to extend education to them. The settlers feared African competition in all spheres—from education to agriculture (Schmidt 1991:9).

If the settlers were skeptical of the missionaries, so were the Africans. As one mission-educated Mashawasha (a Shona-speaking group) confided, "Now I know that the Church, both temporal and spiritual, helped the whiphand in all the tribal affairs of the VaShawasha people in the mission; it could, if it so wished, toss out of its lands any man, woman or family at any time and for any reason at all. . . . There was no right of appeal. . . . The Church owned the VaShawasha people" (Vambe 1972:14).

Whereas the missionaries in Nyasaland and in Northern Rhodesia often preceded the settlers and were a significant presence in Nyasaland, in Southern Rhodesia the settlers were a critical mass that countered the missionaries in the initial stages of occupation. This, then, is the backdrop for the development of the British presence in the twin colonies.

Implementation of the Hut Tax and the Africans' Response

Southern Rhodesia

The hut tax marked the first effort by the BSAC to secure funding for its administration in the Rhodesias. It was instituted in response to the settlers' need for protection after the 1893 Matabele War. Aimed at ousting the settlers, the revolt revealed that all was not well on the Zimbabwe Plateau.

Light rains in 1891 followed by locusts in 1892 had made for poor harvests, depleting the resources of the Ndebele, whose women had to forage for wild foods in the Hope Fountain area (Iliffe 1990:21). Having granted a concession to Rhodes, the Ndebele became nervous as more settlers arrived, accompanied by Jesuit and later Methodist missionaries committed to setting up mission stations. There was no attempt by the BSAC to negotiate between the Ndebele or Shona-speaking groups and the Europeans regarding land acquisition. Most land granted by the company was seized without attention to the "natives inhabiting the territories," who were given the option of remaining and paying rent or leaving. As one missionary with the BSAC observed, "We came and acted as sole proprietors. Often the Natives were simply driven away or told that they had to do certain services if they would like to continue to make gardens on their old place" (Richartz 1896, cited in Schmidt 1992:37).

The Ndebele rose up against the settlers and the company in 1893, the year rain returned. After the Ndebele lost the war, the BSAC annexed the remainder of Matabeleland and seized most of the Ndebele cattle. The first hut tax was instituted in 1894. Two remote, arid "native reserves" were set aside for the Ndebele. However, as much of the land demarcated for European settlement was not fully occupied, many Ndebele remained on their former land, supplying labor to the settlers on demand (Iliffe 1990:23). The only exception to this pattern was in the Melsetter area, where Afrikaner settlers brutally expropriated land and labor.

The Shona groups farther north were less affected by land expropriation than the Ndebele and were able to take advantage of European demands for food with increased production (Iliffe 1990:23). With increased production, Shona households, especially those situated close to administrative centers, did not have a problem in meeting the request for the ten-shilling hut tax in the first decade (Schmidt 1992). Increased agricultural production was largely accomplished by intensifying women's labor. Because the white settlers were not interested in producing food crops, the Africans had a virtual monopoly (57). As Schmidt's study of Shona women in Goromonzi illustrates, women sold green vegetables, potatoes, and groundnuts and made beer that they or their daughters sold in the mines and towns (58).[7] The intensified trading by women and girls led to higher incomes (56–57), not only enabling the Africans to pay the hut tax but alleviating the need for males to leave home in pursuit of wage labor. Concludes Schmidt (59), "The production of an agricultural surplus was the main bulwark against the breakdown of the social fabric through the out-migration of African men. The primary producers of this surplus were women."

In many rural areas of Mashonaland, however, 1895 brought both drought and an invasion of locusts, causing the first poor harvest since 1890 (Iliffe 1990). Although people clustered near towns were able to pay their hut taxes, Iliffe notes that by September 1895 "some villages were wholly dependent on wild produce and the collection of tax had to be suspended" (22). Adding to the burdens of Africans was an outbreak of rinderpest among Ndebele and Shona cattle in 1896. Thousands died and thousands more were destroyed—seemingly without reason to the Africans. Cattle represented a famine reserve that was traded for grain in times of need. They also figured prominently as a symbol of wealth and plenty. As Vambe (1972:2) has pointed out, "Cattle were as important to my people as the white man's bank account. . . . Cattle represented a man's or a woman's security, their livelihood." In another vein, Luponda, a Kalanga chief in southern Zimbabwe, told Werbner (1991:73) that cattle were so important that when he had to lend some to relatives, he preferred to use his principal wife's cattle rather than his own. Noting that the more cattle women accumulate, the more power they have as wives and mothers, he said that his principal wife had accumulated a lot of capital in cattle.

The cattle economies of Ndebele and Shona males were devastated by rinderpest disease in 1896–1897; those cattle that survived were destroyed by missions and the BSAC to prevent further spread of the disease (Schmidt 1992). The Ndebele and Shona revolted against the company between 1896 and 1897. Land alienation, cattle alienation, forced labor (*chibaro*), and the behavior of the "native police" hired by the BSAC to maintain order and collect taxes in the villages were among the root causes of the up-risings (Ranger 1967:105–113; Ndlovu 1974; Schmidt 1992:36–38). The BSAC had to call on troops from Britain, Cape Colony, and Bechuanaland to help contain the rebellions (Mlambo 1972). The violence in the coun-tryside led to famine; British troops destroyed crops and sought out Ndebele and Shona food stores in order to requisition maize (Iliffe 1990:24). By 1898, children—especially girls—were being traded in ex-change for food, and in Bulawayo "hundreds of girls sold themselves as prostitutes or concubines" in exchange for food, a behavior that the Europeans found scandalous (Iliffe 1990:27). The aftermath of the violence left both Africans and Europeans feeling weakened and fearful.

On the African side, Vambe (1972:17) explains, "this total, helpless fear did not exist in the Africans of my country before 1896. But after being ut-terly defeated on the field of battle and subjected to every form of control, subtle and violent, the entire African population lapsed into a state in which the passive instinct of self-preservation became predominant." After their crushing defeat, the Shona, in particular, acquiesced to the demands of a European settler economy that made competition from African pro-ducers impossible and contributed to the emigration of male labor to the mines of Southern Rhodesia and the Transvaal.

Gradually, however, the situation improved and African cultivators were able to meet increasing European demands for food and maize, the latter becoming the crop of choice for labor rations. People continued to meet their hut taxes, for the most part, without entering the labor market. In 1903, at the height of a new drought and famine, the BSAC opted to quadruple the hut tax to two pounds sterling per year (Iliffe 1990:33). The underlying motive was to push African males into wage labor.

Part of the BSAC's policy response to the 1903 famine was that "men should earn money to buy food by migrating to wage employment" (Iliffe 1990:39). Although the famine greatly increased the supply of mine labor in Belingwe District, Iliffe (93) perceives this to be a temporary response. Especially in the Mashona areas, there was no flight to towns for employ-ment. As Schmidt (1992) illustrates, in Shona households women intensi-fied their labor to offset the increased tax so that their men would not have to leave home. The situation was similar in the Kalanga areas—wives intensified their labor and diversified production to keep their men, husbands or sons, from having to migrate to towns and farms in search of employment (Werbner 1991).

In the Zambezi Valley, Gweru Tonga men hesitated to emigrate, fearing that their wives would reject them on their return; instead they remained at home digging roots, hunting, fishing, and gathering wild fruits with their families to tide them over the famine period of the early twentieth century (Iliffe 1990:40). Consequently, even where the hut tax was used to extract male labor, it met with limited success, a pattern that continued through the first two decades of the twentieth century.

The hut tax also was a liability for those assigned by the government to collect it. Werbner (1991:73–74) relates that during a later period, a tax headman who had several wives used or borrowed the resources of his more prosperous wives to meet shortfalls. When he sold the cow that he and his senior wife had jointly purchased in order to pay another wife's sons' taxes, he found himself in deep trouble and eventually had to resign his position. The incident illustrates that even within families, tax obligations were met in various ways depending on the resources of family members.

Northern Rhodesia

European settlement and the hut tax evolved differently in Northern Rhodesia. The BSAC was mainly interested in developing commercial mining in its northern territory, and it was not until after the South African War at the beginning of the twentieth century that white settlers from South Africa began drifting north. By 1904 there were only 850 Europeans in Northern Rhodesia, mainly administrators, missionaries, and mining prospectors (Mutemba 1977:350).

The hut tax was implemented for the first time in 1902 to support the BSAC's administration of Northern Rhodesia. Initially the tax was collected only in administrative centers, or *bomas*. It could be paid in kind, either in grain or cattle, or it could be paid through tributary labor (Mutemba 1977; Van Horn 1977). The hut tax affected people differently depending on their class and the strategies they designed to meet or avoid their tax obligations. For some groups such as the Lozi cattle-holding elite in Barotseland, the taxes were easily paid with cattle that had been accumulated through earlier raiding or with the tributary labor of their subjects (Van Horn 1977). But Lozi peasants had to pay the tax with agricultural produce or free labor.

As the need for additional administrative funding became apparent to the BSAC in 1906, it forced the Lozi ruler, Lewanika, to abolish slavery and extend the ten-shilling hut tax to include more areas, thus raising the revenue (Van Horn 1977:151). The Lozi responded by bringing more land under cultivation and by producing food that the white settlers, missionaries, and traders in the area wanted to purchase. Women producers, for instance, got imported seeds from Europeans and raised the vegetables, grains, and fruits that they knew the Europeans would purchase (Van Horn 1977:152). Nonetheless, wage employment became an alternative for some Lozi peasants who sold their labor in the mines of South Africa and Southern Rhodesia (Van Horn 1977:149).

The response to the hut tax varied by group. For example, Lenje peasants, like their Shona counterparts in Southern Rhodesia, responded to the hut tax by intensifying their food production and selling the surplus to raise cash so that their men would not be forced to emigrate. In Bulenje in 1915, only 61 people had left to work in South African mines; 210 were working in local mines and at the limeworks (Mutemba 1977:355).

Gender Relations of Production in the Early 1900s: Case Studies

The Patrilineal Shona-Speaking Groups

Few European missionaries, administrative officers, or traders thought to include the gender division of labor in their descriptions of indigenous peoples in the early colonial period (1890–1920). Relying on the observations of a German explorer, Karl Mauch, whose journals of his travels in the late nineteenth century were collected and edited by Burke (1969), and the Jesuit superior of Chishawasha Mission, Father Richartz (1905), Schmidt reconstructs gender relations of production in the Shona-speaking areas as being characterized by women and girls carrying out most of the more arduous tasks related to agriculture, including hoeing, planting, weeding, protecting crops from predators, harvesting, threshing, grinding, and storing the harvest (1992:45–50). Women and girls were also responsible, as they are in the late twentieth century, for hauling wood and water to the homestead.

The agricultural tasks of men and boys were more specific to particular slots of time in the agricultural cycle. Adult males usually cleared the fields, which included cutting down trees as necessary, clearing brush and rocks, and uprooting grass. With the help of their sons and other young male relatives, they piled the debris, woody matter, and brush onto a large mound and then when the brush and tree refuse had dried, burned it and mixed it with the soil. They dug furrows and then left the planting to the women and children. They would often return to the fields when the new grain seedlings had grown above the furrows. There they would build a temporary shelter on a slight rise in order to protect the growing crops from pests. The entire family was often engaged in crop protection, an activity that can be seen in rural areas in the late twentieth century not only in Zimbabwe but in Zambia and Malawi.

Men helped with harvesting and threshing grain crops (Schmidt 1992). They also were responsible for building the granaries. Some granaries were constructed of sticks, dried grass, mud, and wattle. The Shona built thatched granaries on solid rock or made pits in the rock; the Ndebele dug theirs under cattle kraals (Iliffe 1990:15). Among the Kalanga, women helped protect the granaries with a mud and dung mixture plastered to the walls inside and out (Werbner 1991).

The planning that went into crop storage was also reflected in the building of a cattle kraal, another primary task of men. Kraals were located close to the homestead and were constructed of interwoven thin branches; often branches with thorns were used for additional protection against predators. There was only one entrance, and the head of a family kept track of every animal that went in and out of the kraal. He knew which cattle were his, which belonged to his wife or wives, and which belonged to a brother or neighbor. Even though men raised, borrowed, traded, lent, and gave away as tribute or bridewealth the cattle they collected, they were not responsible for most of the direct care of the animals. The feeding, watering, and herding of cattle fell to their sons and other young patrikin. There were both gender and age divisions in labor. Older men and women assumed more of the management roles related to production, and younger adults and children did the more tedious, labor-intensive tasks.

Wives in these patrilineal groups were responsible for providing labor in their husbands' *zunde,* separate fields that were cultivated by the husband (Bullock 1913; Holleman 1951). Each wife also worked with her children on her own plot, or *tseu,* allocated to her by her husband. On this plot she raised grains and vegetables for her family. Any surplus was hers to sell.

Holleman (1951:366) maintained that there was no fixed gender division of labor in the 1940s. Holleman may have been referring to the labor connected with *zunde* production. How active men were in their wives' gardens beyond clearing and possibly harvesting is open to speculation.

Even though daily agricultural tasks were performed by members of the family, there were instances of collaborative labor of two varieties. One, referred to as *majangano* in Shona, involved members of different families belonging to the same locale working together in each other's fields for a given period on specific tasks for which they would be compensated in beer at the end of the day. The other form of collaborative labor was *nhimbe,* which referred to a group of villagers of both sexes working in rotation in a field (Holleman 1951). In neither case did the participants expect to share in the proceeds of their labor, as is implied in cooperative labor production.

The Matrilineal Bemba and Related Groups

Historically, women in matrilineal groups have had the advantage of gaining direct access to land through their grandmothers, mothers, and other

TABLE 4.1   Gender Division of Labor: Bemba Peasants, Circa 1910

Tasks of Wife or Wives	Tasks of Husband
Hoes	Cuts and burns brush
Harvests	Builds hut and granary
Stores grain	Makes bed or mat for sleeping
Winnows and grinds grain	Fences garden
Fetches or draws water	Makes baskets
Fetches firewood	Works for mother-in-law
Makes pots	Provides fish and salt
Plasters home, makes fireplace	Provides cloth for wife
Sweeps	
Cares for children	

SOURCE: Compiled from Gouldsbury 1915–1916:158.

matrilineal relatives rather than indirect access through husbands, as in patrilineal groups (Gouldsbury 1915–1916; Richards 1939, 1950; Colson
1951, 1970; Mutemba 1977; Poewe 1981).[8] In groups where uxorilocality
was the rule, women were "at home" among their fields because they remained in the matrilineal villages of their birth. In cases of virilocality,
women traveled to their fields to cultivate them. If they were elites in either
case, they drew on tribute labor or slaves to do the work for them. In both
cases, women maintained security of tenure regardless of their marital status. They also controlled the allocation of labor, especially in uxorilocal
households.

One of the earliest records of the gendered division of labor in a matri-
lineal group comes from the 1915 descriptions of the Bemba by
Gouldsbury, a native commissioner in Northern Rhodesia (1915–1916; see
Table 4.1). He recognized chiefly clans and commoners or peasants.

Gouldsbury's list leaves some gaps. For instance, who was responsible
for planting, weeding, and crop protection? My suspicion, based on
Richards's work in the 1930s, is that these tasks were undertaken by both
sexes in the early twentieth century. She makes the point that the division
of labor by gender was not rigid.

At the time of Gouldsbury's observations, Bemba peasants were using
the *citemene* system, shifting cultivation to a new location every few years.
It was a system, however, that as early as 1907 the BSAC authorities criticized as an inefficient use of land (Richards 1958; also Berry 1993). In the
1950s the colonial government initiated a scheme to settle the Bemba on
more permanent plots, but it proved to be a failure (Richards 1958:303).

In the *citemene* system of agriculture, which was still used in some areas
in the 1980s (see Stromgaard 1985; Moore and Vaughan 1994), refuse

heaps were covered with soil on which branches, cut down by men, and brush, collected by women, were piled by women and then burned by men. When the mounds were prepared, each household assembled its members and went to the field to watch its most experienced members, regardless of sex, broadcast the seed (Stromgaard 1985). In this way younger members learned from older ones. Weeding was done mainly by women and their children (Richards 1939, 1950; Stromgaard 1985). Threshing and winnowing were usually women's work, in contrast to the patrilineal Shona, who carried out their threshing, at least, with the participation of both sexes (Richards 1939; Schmidt 1992). Harvesting was done by both sexes and all ages. Tree cutting, hoe making, hunting, and fishing, identified by Richards as men's tasks (1939:383), were not mentioned by Gouldsbury (1915–1916). In the 1930s, Richards (1939:397) found that women spent over twice as much time as men on agricultural tasks.

The *citemene* system created a pattern of cultivation that was highly individualized by household, similar to *banja* production in southern Malawi. Richards observed in the 1930s that the unit of production was the household situated within a matrilineally related sororal hamlet or village. Women lived among supportive matrilineal kin and had a central role in resource allocation and decisionmaking. Although production was highly individualized by household, distribution and consumption processes involved social relationships that were communal (Richards 1939). The combination of individualized production and communal distribution, evident in many matrilineal groups, need not lead to a contradiction as Stromgaard has suggested (1985). That is a Western perception.[9]

Gouldsbury lists "working for the mother-in-law," brideservice, as one of men's tasks. *Chisanga* (brideservice) was still in place at the time Richards did her fieldwork in the late 1930s. However, whereas *chisanga* was performed for a mother or her brother in matrilineal groups in Nyasaland, among Bemba peasants it was performed for the bride's father. Richards (1950:235) contends that fathers had a more important role in matrilineal Bemba society than they did in Chewa, Yao, or Mang'anja society. Moore and Vaughan (1994:5) believe that the bilateral aspect of Bemba society was as strong as matrilineal ideology, which they theorize accounts for the greater authority of fathers.

Richards (1958) found that with the opening of the mines in the Copperbelt in the late 1920s and 1930s, many young men in the area began to emigrate. Because they were working in the mines, they were unable to perform the customary brideservice for their in-laws and sent cash so that their in-laws could hire labor in their place—a purpose for which the remittances were not always used (Chanock 1985). However, Moore and Vaughan (1994:161) contest this conclusion on the basis of interviews with thirty Bemba men, former migrants, who had returned to the Northern

Province; these men had married for the first time between 1925 and 1959. Twenty responded that they had performed brideservice; ten reported that they had not. Of the ten who had not performed brideservice, four had substituted cash payments. Two of these men were married in 1946, the other two later. How representative this small sample is of other former migrants is difficult to say, but it does indicate that the majority of men in this area continued to perform brideservice and that a small portion (13.3 percent in the sample) substituted cash for brideservice for the purported purpose of hiring labor. That older males tended to use cash remittances from their sons-in-law to purchase commodity items rather than to hire labor, as Chanock (1985) argues, and that this contributed to labor shortages and led to an intensification of daughters' labor in particular, is difficult to assess because time-allocation studies on women's labor figured little in colonial studies of rural farming systems from the 1920s onward.

A Comparison of Matrilineal and Patrilineal Productive Relations

Chanock has argued that observers during the early colonial period were confused about the distinction between matrilineal and patrilineal ideologies and their practices, a confusion to which he contributes by constantly switching back and forth between matrilineal and patrilineal groups in his descriptions of marriage practices (1985:150–180). At the same time, Chanock acknowledges that district officers (including those in predominantly matrilineal Nyasaland) in the early twentieth century did recognize differences in marital practices that they were hard pressed to explain. He cites the "*reluctant recognition* by some district officers that there was a valid kind of marriage in which a large bridewealth was not paid, and in which the *husband's control over the woman and children was not so great*" (emphasis in original) (175). These early colonial officers concluded that this form of marriage was a "lower and irregular form" and that its reemergence in some areas would be an "evolutionary step backwards" (175). This observation is critical because it reflects the inability of male colonials, whether missionaries or administrators, to perceive of marriage practices and lineage ideologies different from their own as anything other than an anachronism. In their view, matriliny and uxorilocality would be shed along the route of evolutionary social development from "primitive" to "civilized" and, later, from "traditional" to "modern." Given such an androcentric worldview, it becomes difficult to extract a truly gender-neutral description of matrilineal ideology and practices.[10]

Regardless, if we compare gender productive relations of the matrilineal, uxorilocal groups in Northern Rhodesia with the patrilineal Shona in

Southern Rhodesia in the first decades of the twentieth century, two major differences become clear. First, a woman in a matrilineal group gained direct access to land through close matrilineal kin. In contrast, a woman in patrilineal groups might or might not be granted a plot of land from her father prior to marriage. After she out-married, it was expected that she would gain access to land for family sustenance through her husband and that she would retain rights to this land only while she was married (Gaidzanwa 1988). If she and her husband separated, or even if she was widowed and married her husband's brother, she lost access to the land.

In matrilinies where virilocality was practiced, a woman might return to the land in her matrilineal village if she separated from her husband or became a widow. In patrilineal groups, a woman had no such safety net. Men in matrilineal societies, especially young men in uxorilocal societies, had less security of tenure than men in patrilineal societies. Nor could they pass their matrilineal land directly to a son or daughter, even in groups practicing virilocality, because land, in theory, was inherited by the matrilineage, usually by a sister's son. Similarly, women in patrilineal groups could not pass on to daughters land they cultivated because characteristically sons inherited their father's land. Ambiguities in lineage rules existed, however, and there were always exceptions to these rules within and among groups, as Amadiume (1987) illustrates for Igbo society. Overall, however, women in matrilineal groups had more security of tenure than women in patrilineal groups and men had more tenure security in patrilineal groups.

A woman in a matrilineal group also had more control over household labor than a woman in a patrilineal group. Whereas a wife in patrilineal Shona society was obligated to spend a certain amount of time on her husband's *zunde*, sometimes working with co-wives and their children, a woman in a matrilineal group rarely had such obligations except where virilocality had become the practice. In cases where uxorilocality prevailed, usually older women, as mothers-in-law, gained access to a young man's labor through brideservice. A younger married woman, often with children, had her husband's assistance and sometimes the assistance of younger brothers. In such cases, a woman, together with her older brother, controlled the labor of her children.[11]

In patrilineal groups the husband controlled the labor of both wives and children (Richartz 1905, cited in Schmidt 1992; Holleman 1951; Vambe 1972). Nonetheless, as Vambe points out, a woman's personality and age made a difference. In describing his Shawasha (Shona) paternal grandmother in the late 1930s, Vambe (1972:25) observed, "Grandmother Madzidza was impulsive, flighty, imaginative and as tough and outspoken as it is possible to image. . . . Thrusting, witty and reckless, Madzidza was more often than not the boss of our household, if not the whole neighborhood." Whereas his paternal grandfather was gentle and calm, his grandmother in her later years was domineering and even abrasive. Individual agency becomes a mitigating factor.

Finally, production in matrilineal groups tended to be more individualized by household, at least for peasants, who were the bulk of the population. Few peasants were in polygynous marriages, and the wife and husband—along with their children when they were younger and with the help of matrikin or grandchildren when they were older—formed the production and reproduction unit. But this production unit was porous, allowing for periodic interhousehold exchanges with related (and unrelated) matrilineal households within a hamlet or larger village. For example, in the collection of wild fruits, roots, and vegetables, as well as wood, women from several households might collaborate, a form of collaboration also found in patrilineal groups. Furthermore, women collaborated across households in the production of food and drink for ritual occasions such as marriages and funerals. But women in uxorilocal households did not collaborate, as a rule, with other women in agricultural production except during the harvest (Richards 1939; Duly 1946; Mitchell 1952; Schoffeleers 1968; Poewe 1981; Mandala 1990). Even specialized activities such as salt distillation involved the individual family, including children, rather than a group of women working together (Phiri 1984:15; Mandala 1990:44).

In contrast, wives in patrilineal peasant households were more likely to collaborate with wives from other patrilineal households, all of whom, like themselves, were strangers in their husbands' hamlets. These women often formed collaborative hoeing, planting, and weeding parties that rotated from one woman's fields to another's, giving women a sense of solidarity (Muchena 1979; Gaidzanwa 1988). However, even though the labor was collaborative, women did not share the proceeds of the harvest, as in cooperative production. Each woman controlled the products of her fields and gardens.[12] Pot making, basketry, and salt distillation might also be collaborative activities.

In addition to lineage, the socioeconomic status of a household influenced how labor was organized. The ruling elite's large households were maintained by several wives and their children, and household production was dispersed, involving the tribute labor of subject peoples. Households commanding greater resources in land, cattle, and people tended to specialize in their production activities. Social status had an impact on the gender organization of labor in both matrilineal and patrilineal groups, as discussed earlier in regard to the reigning Mutapa and Malawi elites. Amadiume (1987) also found differences that cut across gender (and lineage) in her discussion on status in Igbo society. In matrilineal groups such as those in Luapula in eastern Zambia, Poewe (1981) argues that women in peasant households had more authority in management decisions than women in elite households, who tended to be more subservient to their husbands.

Finally, age was a cross-cutting factor. Generally, older women and men within households and in the community were respected for their experience and wisdom. A young bride in a patrilineal household was not treated with the same deference as an older woman with grown children, who had greater authority in decisions about production and the allocation of labor. Nor was the young bride in a matrilineal hamlet treated with the same respect as her mother, who managed several parcels of land and had the authority to transfer portions of this land to daughters and to demand the *chikamwene* labor of her daughters' husbands. An older man in patrilineal groups gained status over the life cycle through his position as a father and then as head of a household; an older man in a matrilineal society gained status through his position as an avunculate rather than as a father. A household member's changing position in the life cycle, then, mediated his or her gender status with relation to other members of the household, lineage, and community. Together, lineage, socioeconomic status, age, and individual agency contributed in shaping the gendered productive and reproductive relations in a particular household or community during a specific period in the colonial Rhodesias.

Clinging to Self-Sufficiency
Against the Colonial Tide

Increased colonial domination in the Rhodesias in the 1920s and accompanying changes in the politics of land and labor crippled peasant households' ability to pay their hut taxes and buy commodities without being drawn into wage labor. By the 1920s, settlers (and agricultural concessionary companies) had become an increasingly strident interest group, convincing the Home Office to adopt measures in their favor. [13] Among the measures implemented were the Native Reserves Acts in the 1920s and the creation of maize-control boards in the 1930s in both the Rhodesias. In the process of taking increased control of factors of production and introducing measures designed to modernize indigenous farming systems, colonial authorities introduced a gender fault line that had far-reaching consequences for women farmers, as will become clear.

An order-in-council passed in the Rhodesias in 1920 legalized the expropriation of land from Africans and set up "native reserves" for their "benefit" (a phenomenon that was less evident in Nyasaland). As a result of the Native Reserves Acts, African peasants were relocated to agriculturally marginal land so that Europeans might have the most arable land. Few of the "native reserves" had accessible water or other services necessary for settlement (Kay 1965; Mutemba 1982). Relocation in Northern Rhodesia meant that women in matrilineal groups had to break their ties to ancestral land. Only in cases where government-appointed male leaders in these

groups respected women's hereditary rights and continued them in the reserves were women able to gain a sense of land security. Moreover, settlers
did not always use the "excess" land taken by the state when the reserves
were set up.

After peasants in the railway region of Northern Rhodesia were evicted
from their lands at the end of the 1920s, the territories they left behind became known as "silent lands" because they remained unoccupied; since
European settlers lacked the capital for development, these lands "attracted
only the tsetse fly" (Mutemba 1977:351). It was not until the tobacco
boom of the 1940s that the "silent lands" once more became productive.
Thus productive land remained unused while Africans were crowded onto
reserves where land was marginal at best.

That Africans during this period continued to use legally recognized
strategies to protest land and labor alienation is a measure of their pa-
tience. That these efforts were largely ignored points to the accelerating
rate of underdevelopment in southern Africa in the third decade of the
twentieth century (Ranger 1970; Arrighi 1973; Parsons and Palmer 1977;
Phimister 1988). This premeditated underdevelopment occurred despite the
fact that "it is now generally conceded that in unit terms [African] peasants
were more productive farmers than settlers" (Parsons and Palmer 1977:8).

In new African settlement areas set up in the late 1930s and 1940s to encourage "progressive farming," the state's agricultural programs ignored
women farmers in both matrilineal and patrilineal societies. Credit, improved seed, fertilizer, and, symbolically, the introduction of the plow had
the effect of increasing disparities between female and male peasants, resource-poor peasants and wealthier peasants. Key to obtaining improved
inputs was credit. Women farmers could not obtain credit except as wives.
This constraint especially affected women in matrilineal, uxorilocal groups,
who were accustomed to operating as producers independent from their
husbands. Lack of access to new inputs disadvantaged women producers in
general—single and widowed women as well as wives—and women with
few resources in particular.

The plow acted as a symbol separating wealthier from poorer peasants.
As men in wealthier peasant households purchased plows, often with
credit, they were able to expand cultivation. As women were central to the
cultivation process, men with resources (cattle) in patrilineal and matrilineal groups that practiced virilocality invested in additional wives (Wright
1983; Schmidt 1992).

Women rarely gained access to a plow—it was viewed as a "man's tool."
However, there were cases where women did plow, particularly when their
husbands or grown sons were absent. They also used the family's plow to
leverage other resources. For example, in some instances Shona wives used
access to a husband's plow to secure the labor of other men in the husband's absence (Schmidt 1992).

Whereas the plow reduced men's agricultural labor in clearing and preparing land, corresponding interventions to reduce women's labor were not forthcoming. In some instances women's labor burdens were increased with an innovation designed to increase production. For example, the use of steer manure to improve production in the "native reserves" meant collecting dung and hauling it to the fields, a backbreaking task that was expected of women and children in patrilineal households. Shona women in Goromonzi refused to manure their fields to increase maize production because to do so meant increased labor to transport it to the fields (Schmidt 1992:82). Just as important, these women reasoned that spreading manure would attract insect pests and increase weed growth, which women and children would then have to remove. The refusal of these Shona women to support an innovation because it would increase their labor (and because they would have no control over its benefits) is not unlike Malawian women refusing to use contour ridging as a soil-conservation method because it would increase their labor without providing commensurate compensation.

When men invested in new technologies, they became "progressive farmers." In some instances, their ability to bring more land under cultivation fueled a desire for security of tenure in matrilineal, uxorilocal groups. Bridewealth and virilocality began to make inroads in groups that had practiced uxorilocality with brideservice prior to the 1930s (Poewe 1981; Phiri 1984). The shift to virilocality weakened a woman's ties with her land and marginalized her authoritative role in production. Men also benefited from colonial land policies that favored male tenure in progressive schemes.

Male Emigration and Women's Labor

A rapid rise in the number of Africans entering the labor market in the 1920s acted as a potential catalyst for restructuring gender relations in rural households. In 1904 in Southern Rhodesia, only 7,154 Africans (roughly 4.6 percent of the African population) were working for Europeans, whereas by 1921, their numbers had grown to 140,304—16.3 percent of Africans (Rogers and Franz 1962:19). By 1923, 37,482 Africans—4.4 percent—were employed in the mines alone, many as *chibaro* labor under brutalizing conditions (see van Onselen 1976:114).[14]

Indicative of the degree to which capitalism had taken hold was the response of Tonga men to food shortages in the early 1920s. Prior to the 1920s, rural households had continued to meet food shortages during droughts through men's and women's foraging. With the 1922 drought, however, Tonga men, who had been willing to forage previously, shifted their survival strategies, emigrating to urban areas to seek employment (Iliffe 1990:71).

I have referred to the way that the *thangata* system in Nyasaland and the *chibalo* system in Mozambique led to increased male labor migration. The scenario was similar for the Rhodesias. As the hut tax increased and new taxes were added to control labor in urban areas, young men in particular were forced to sell their labor in administrative centers, mission stations, and the mines. By the 1920s, an increasing number were also employed on the plantations of European settlers for minimal wages (Weinrich 1982:18).

Scarcity of labor continued to be a problem for colonial capitalists throughout the 1920s and 1930s. To increase the labor supply, a gender- and age-specific strategy was used in Southern Rhodesia. Designed to capture young male labor, the Native Juvenile Employment Act was passed in 1926. It provided passes for boys over age fourteen to seek employment and, not incidentally, gave the state guardianship over "destitute" African boys under that age (Mlambo 1972). The latter provision meant that the police could put these "destitute" boys to work. When Africans protested the constitutionality of such a measure, the response was deceptive; the law was designed to protect African juveniles from "loafing, undesirable employers and undesirable companions" (Mlambo 1972:38). Girls who lost their brothers in this way had to take over more of the burdens previously carried out by males in the family. For example, in the 1930s girls under fifteen were seen plowing and herding cattle in addition to their other tasks (Schmidt 1992).

The colonial state did not encourage women to join their men in the migrant labor enterprise. In both Rhodesias it was believed that African women's major function in the colonial economy was to stay in the reserves and raise food for the workers. In this position they were joined by the chiefs who had been appointed by the state to maintain order in the rural areas, a duty that included controlling women whose husbands were absent (Chanock 1985; Parpart 1986; Phimister 1988). In particular, young, unmarried women were discouraged from migrating; in Northern Rhodesia prior to the 1950s only women who were legally married were permitted in the towns. The policy was changed in the 1950s to one of "balanced stabilization" (Epstein 1981; Heisler 1984). Increasing complaints, however, came to the state in the 1930s about young women who were "running away" to seek new economic opportunities or who were following their husbands or lovers to the mining centers in the Copperbelt. The state's solution was to return these "runaway women" to the jurisdiction of male chiefs and elders (Chanock 1985). As a result, the majority of women remained in the reserves and rural areas.

In Southern Rhodesia the state's attempt to control women's migration to urban centers was halfhearted and ambiguous (Barnes 1992; Jeater 1993). On the one hand, women were not required to carry identity passes, as were their male counterparts (until the late 1970s), but on the other, a number of measures were instituted by the state to exclude them from dwelling in urban centers (Barnes 1992). In practice, African women were able to slip through the boundaries erected to protect urban white enclaves in Southern Rhodesia (Barnes 1995:6). However, as in Northern Rhodesia, the vast majority of women remained in rural areas and reserves.

Three types of male migration labor that affected women in rural areas characterized the Rhodesias between the 1920s and 1940s: circular migration, terminal migration, and conjugal migration. The first relates to males who out-migrated periodically and returned to take up farming with their families during the peak seasons. The second refers to men who left their families and did not return; in some cases they sent remittances and in others they deserted their families, taking up informal "wives" in urban centers or in mining towns (Chauncey 1981; Chanock 1985). A third type of migrant labor existed mainly in Northern Rhodesia. I refer to it as conjugal labor migration because a man emigrated to a mining town and then sent for his wife or girlfriend to come and live with him. This conjugal form emerged only in cases where a mining company provided housing for married couples.[15] The difference between the two Rhodesias was that in Northern Rhodesia, married women were officially acknowledged as having a right to be in mining compounds, whereas in Southern Rhodesia their presence was discouraged. Each type of male migration labor affected household production, and especially women's production, in different ways.

Circular Migration and the Women at Home

Men employed in urban centers or working part time on estates were most apt to return periodically to their families—on a monthly or quarterly basis. In such cases, women carried out tasks in the absence of these men but welcomed them back for larger tasks connected with cultivation, especially when land had to be cleared or crops harvested. In patrilineal and virilocal matrilineal households, husbands or fathers tended to make critical decisions about the use of resources and labor, whereas wives and mothers made decisions about day-to-day tasks and children. When a husband returned home, he was expected to take care of major decisions regarding the household's resources, including labor. It was during these home visits that new granaries were built or a kraal repaired. If a husband was responsible, he paid the hut tax and other taxes, helped with school fees and clothing for children, and even provided a few items for the family. Younger, unmarried men who visited periodically were expected to help their mothers and sisters with specific tasks and might bring them a piece of cloth in exchange for looking after their cattle in their absence. Unmarried women with hopes of marriage looked to these younger men to save their earnings for *lobola,* which was necessary for marriage.

Food crops were raised, processed, and stored by women and their children in a man's absence. They also looked after the cattle and other domesticated animals. That they provided their labor free of charge and raised the food meant that they were subsidizing a man's maintenance as a laborer, making it possible for an employer to keep wages low (Chauncey 1981; Parpart 1986; Schmidt 1992). As a native commissioner in Umtali, Southern Rhodesia, observed in the early 1930s, "They [women] are required under the present [migrant labor] system to grow food for the greater part of the native population" (cited in Schmidt 1992:82). That women expanded their labor output to include the bulk of food crop production in the reserves cannot be ignored.

When a husband returned home only periodically, his wife was expected to treat him "like a visitor," cooking his favorite dish, being available sexually, and catering to his particular needs. Skjønsberg (1989) relates that a man who returned periodically to his Chewa village in eastern Zambia from his job in an urban center expected to be treated "like a king" by his wife and other villagers. His weekend activities consisted of sitting around telling stories and drinking soft drinks while the rest of his family cultivated the gardens. Hence conflicts could arise when a wife or wives had decisions that needed to be made or tasks that needed to be accomplished and the man was not receptive to the family's needs.

Even though a similar situation might occur in uxorilocal hearthholds that were dependent on a wage earner's income, women in these hearthholds were more likely to have more control over decisions related to the use of resources and labor than their counterparts in virilocal situations. The absence of a husband or son who periodically returned was taken in stride because a woman was accustomed to handling most of the household decisions related to production and reproduction (also on this point, see Moore and Vaughan 1994).

Young, unmarried women left at home had different needs. They hoped that unmarried male workers empowered by the independence of earning an income would not forget to return to their villages and fulfill their obligations to perform brideservice or provide bridewealth. The tension between a single male migrant laborer and a single woman left at home is captured in Tonga songs sung during the 1940s–1950s. Chipepo, a male laborer, sang:

> I love a woman called Mulongo
> and because I travel so much
> I never have time to see her
> (Tracy 1965:67)

Unmarried women from the same Tonga village sang tauntingly:

> You bachelors, how do you like sleeping alone?
> You go to the towns for work, but when you
> Return home you don't pay your brideprice.
> What queer fellows you are!
> I don't sleep alone, and I'm sorry for you,
> Oh let me go . . .
> I don't want to stay with you bachelors!
> You had better consult the diviners and ask them
> To tell you what your fate will be!
> (Tracy 1965:101).

The first song suggests that young men, despite Southern Rhodesia's pass laws, were peripatetic in their search for work.

The song of the young women criticizes their male counterparts for their inability to hang onto their wages, part of which would go toward bridewealth for marriage. Indirectly, they are complaining that these men are irresponsible in not coming back to the villages to marry. At the same time they are getting across to these men that their absence is not making the women lonely, that they have other sexual resources. The song is both a protest—a critique of male behavior—and a complaint that is couched in female pride.

Terminal Migration and Deserted Wives and Mothers

Stories abound of the husband, son, or lover who left for the mines or an urban center and never returned home. The conditions in the mines in South Africa and Southern Rhodesia were deplorable, as the multiple strikes of the 1920s and 1930s testify. In Southern Rhodesia male laborers were not allowed to bring their families to the mine; housing was provided only for men. Wives were expected to remain at home, raising food to sustain and reproduce more labor. Unmarried women were also expected to remain home, an expectation that was enforced by chiefs and African police. Some found their way to the mines and urban centers despite interventions of the state.

The unmarried male migrant might attach himself to a woman who provided for both his domestic and sexual needs outside the confines of the mine. Those who worked in an urban area found it easier to establish a liaison. In spite of the state's efforts in the 1940s and 1950s to encourage some of these men to return home, especially in Northern Rhodesia, most remained in the mines or in urban centers indefinitely (Moore and Vaughan 1994).

Most married migrants found a new life without their families and formed liaisons with local women. In some cases a married man sent home remittances to pay the hut tax and a little extra to buy clothing. In other cases he sent nothing. Most men expected to fulfill a labor contract for a specified number of years, returning home at the end of the contract to take up farming again. Some returned and others deserted their families.

In either case, women carried on as de facto heads of households, making all the decisions in the absence of their men. In order to accomplish tasks formerly handled by their husbands or sons, some women hired outside male labor or coaxed male relatives into performing these tasks in exchange for food or other favors. In some cases, brothers or brothers-in-law helped to support a family. Women who had no surplus resources had to depend on their own labor and that of their children.

In areas where uxorilocality and brideservice were practiced, married men who left to take up wage employment were likely to ignore their remaining brideservice obligations. Mothers-in-law, and in some cases fathers-in-law, lost the labor of these younger men. Richards (1958) found in northern Zambia that fewer millet gardens were sown, which she attributed to men being unavailable to perform the *citemene* labor necessary for the preparation of mounds for millet cultivation. She linked the decrease in millet production to increased malnutrition. However, Moore and Vaughan (1994:155) maintain that overall, agricultural production in the areas where Richards worked actually increased in the 1940s and 1950s even though in some areas 70–80 percent of adult males were away working. Large acreages were planted in cassava instead; it was easier for women to cultivate and less dependent on male labor. Although much less nutritious than millet, cassava produced surpluses that could be sold to local government *boma*s (administrative centers). Moreover, evidence exists that women were growing cassava along with other vegetables such as beans and pumpkins and were collecting a variety of edible foods that grew wild such as mushrooms, cucumbers, edible roots, and fruits (Moore and Vaughan 1994:n. 11, 239). In some cases women also diversified production, growing other crops from which they were able to realize a profit.

Women's social networks and special relationships with other women were crucial to their survival whether they were used for assistance in agricultural production or to provide other types of social or economic support. Richards observed that the custom of *ukupula*, whereby a destitute woman offered her labor to another woman (or man) in exchange for food, enabled some deserted Bemba women to sustain themselves and their families when their men began disappearing to the mines (1939:145). Moore and Vaughan (1994) criticize Richards's portrayal of Bemba women as victims, pointing out that women's circumstances differed and that some Bemba women were not adversely affected by male migration. Most women had their own land and gardens and were able to reallocate household resources and labor to compensate for the absence of male labor. There also were women who optimized and diversified their production to meet the new demands for food coming from the district administrative centers. Additionally, some took up or increased supplementary activities that earned income, such as beer brewing or baking.

Schmidt (1992) reports a similar situation for Shona women; by taking up supplementary activities such as poultry raising, beer brewing, or handcrafts, women were able to substitute income lost when a husband (or son in the case of a widow) disappeared. In all these activities they were assisted by their children. In sum, a woman's response to terminal male emigration depended on a range of factors, including her marital status, economic circumstances, available resources, and, not last, her own inclinations and ambitions. Human agency and social circumstances combined to shape women's responses to male migration.

Conjugal Migratory Labor

In Northern Rhodesia, some men took their wives with them when they left to work in a mining township. To prevent African men from migrating to Southern Rhodesia or the Katanga mines in the Congo, the Copperbelt mines offered men the choice of migrating with their families. Chauncey concludes that it was "in the context of this overriding concern about competition for labor that the copper mining companies initially decided to allow women and children into their compounds" (1981:137). Married men with wives in residence were more apt to produce a stable labor force than single men. Chauncey cites a government officer's view (1931) that the presence of women tended "to keep men more contented and prepared to remain for longer periods of work" (140). Social reproduction was part of the package—by maintaining the household and socializing miners' children to the "demands of industrial work," wives would contribute to the efficiency of mining production.

There is some disagreement about married women's migration to the Copperbelt. Chauncey argues that in the mines even though "the intention of management was that women remain dependent and subservient to their working husbands, women themselves were able to establish a different relationship to capital and greater autonomy in their relations with men" (1981:143). Parpart (1986) concludes, however, that women who followed their husbands to the mines became more economically dependent on these husbands. At the same time, she points out that the quality of their dependency was shaped by the class to which their husbands belonged—one class consisting of unskilled miners who worked underground and the other of the company's administrative staff. Women who were married to staff employees were more dependent on their husbands, who forbid them to work, whereas women married to unskilled workers were freer to earn income and had more options—both legal and illegal—for generating that income.

In summary, women left at home found they had to attract male labor to accomplish tasks previously carried out by a husband or son. Alternatively, their own labor increased. So did their resourcefulness. In some cases, they diversified production to crops that were not dependent on male labor and as a means of increasing income. They also took up new income-generating activities. Women who followed their husbands in conjugal labor migration had a different set of problems. They were dependent on their husbands for income—some more so than others. Any authority they previously might have had over the allocation of resources, particularly in uxorilocal hearthholds, was mitigated by the family's new dependency on capitalist production. Of the women who entered conjugal wage labor, some gave up the relative autonomy they had enjoyed in their rural villages for a steady income. Others gained a sense of economic autonomy through income earned from activities that remained separate from their husband's income.

In all three cases of male labor migration, women's concomitant labor was exploited by the state. As wives, mothers, and daughters, women were expected to subsidize the costs of household reproduction through household maintenance and childcare. At the same time, women's individual circumstances and proclivities shaped their responses to male emigration. Some women had to double their labor efforts to make ends meet, and their economic insecurity intensified. Others were little affected by male emigration. Still others profited in men's absence by taking advantage of opportunities to diversify production and find new ways of generating income. Women in matrilineal groups were more likely to control land and labor, which gave them an advantage. Nonetheless, individual women in patrilineal groups also found strategies that enabled them to sustain their families in the absence of male family members. For women who migrated themselves, the opportunities and constraints were indeterminate.

Women on the Move

Not all women remained at home, as was mentioned in the discussion on conjugal migrant labor. Women with dependent children and older women tended to remain at home more often than younger wives and single women, who found ways to join their men—whether husbands, lovers, or brothers—in the urban areas and mining centers. Female migration, even though it was discouraged by the state and state-appointed chiefs, was one response to terminal male labor migration. As early as 1913, unmarried girls in Southern Rhodesia were beginning to seek ways to improve their economic circumstances by migrating to urban areas such as Salisbury. A group of Manyika workers at the Argus Printing Company in Salisbury wrote a letter of complaint to the native commissioner in Umtali on

September 19, 1913: "There are three of Manica girls here and they have no thing to do. They are not working. Their work is to commit all sorts of evil, going from one man to another. We wish you could report it to Native Commissioner in Salisbury and have them sent back to Umtali" (quoted in Ranger 1989a:140).

That young girls who migrated to urban areas at this early date were identified with loose morals and prostitution was a precursor of more to come (see Schuster 1979 for Zambia). This was one reason the colonial state later sought, with varying degrees of success, to prohibit unmarried women from migrating to towns. By the late 1920s in both the Rhodesias, female rural-urban migration accelerated and continued to do so over the next decades (Schuster 1979; Parpart 1986; Barnes 1992; Schmidt 1992).

When single or divorced women migrated, they were encouraged to marry or return home. Urban courts and African police were used to control women's activities in the mining townships (Schuster 1979; Barnes 1992; Moore and Vaughan 1994). Even so, Barnes (1992:606) found that for Salisbury in 1936, of the total number of women living in the town, only 150 were married. Of the rest, 450 were in consensual relationships that provided male migrants with domestic and sexual services, and far fewer were unmarried or unattached. Thus the state's efforts to control the flow of unmarried women from the rural to the urban areas proved less than successful. Time and space limit further discussion of urban women's situations in the colonial period, but it is important to realize that although the vast majority of women remained in rural areas in the mid-twentieth century, the number of women in urban areas was increasing.[16]

Pulling the Threads Together

Colonial capitalism in central southern Africa was built on exploitative relationships between colonials and indigenous peoples and between males and females. Gender relations varied depending on lineage ideology and marital residence patterns prior to colonial penetration, with women having a higher status and more autonomy in matrilineal than in patrilineal groups. Where patrilineal, militant groups such as the Ngoni and the Kololo came in contact with matrilineal groups, the latter were subdued and often assimilated. Part of assimilation was the adoption of certain aspects of patrilineal ideology, for example, bridewealth and virilocality. Some groups escaped assimilation and retained their matrilineal, uxorilocal ways, including the Mang'anja, Bemba, and others.

The early Muslim traders left their mark not on lineage ideology but on religion; many of the coastal groups and indigenous trading partners took up Islam. In contrast, the Europeans, whether Portuguese or British, influenced both lineage ideologies and religion. Although the Portuguese were less concerned about lineage, when they married African women, those women took their surnames.

British colonial capitalism was marked by racism and ethnocentrism. The British, on the whole, did not intermarry with Africans, and where missionaries encouraged marriage between Africans, they made sure that a woman took not only her husband's surname but that he controlled productive resources such as land and labor. Missionization challenged social as well as spiritual norms among the matrilineal groups of Malawi.

Capitalist formations entered first through trading and later through agricultural development and industry. Driven by the interests of *prazo*-holders and traders in Mozambique and by settler and mining interests in Nyasaland and the Rhodesias, the colonials plundered land and exploited labor with equal impunity. Also patriarchal, they accelerated the erosion of women's authority, especially in matrilineal, uxorilocal groups.

In the colonies of southern Africa, the most exploited class was peasant women. The accumulation of surplus by Europeans—whether missionaries, settlers, or mining interests—depended, in theory, on the exploitation of African labor, particularly peasant labor. In turn, where exploitation was directed toward African male labor, it was further subsidized by exploiting the labor of African women—as wives, mothers, or daughters.

In the 1890s, militant uprisings in each colony against land alienation began the protest against colonial occupation. These were followed by the refusal of many groups in Nyasaland and the Rhodesias to be forced into wage labor. These groups used strategies that included increased production and trading—often supported by women's intensified labor. The hut tax, meant to provide revenue, did not become the mechanism for capturing indigenous labor that it was intended to be in the initial decades of colonial occupation. It was not until the third decade of the twentieth century that male labor emigration became a significant factor with variable consequences for household production.

Women in rural areas continued to till the soil, with or without husbands, depending increasingly on their children. Where agricultural development measures were instituted, they were directed toward men regardless of who controlled the land or managed family labor. Women in both patrilineal and matrilineal groups were disadvantaged by patriarchal colonialism, but women in uxorilocal situations stood to lose more because many lost their matrilineal land rights.

How women in matrilineal groups responded to male labor emigration depended on their circumstances. For those women who continued to retain rights in land, the withdrawal of male labor could result in either destitution or opportunity depending on available labor resources and a woman's industry. Some women, such as those in Nyasaland, had no choice but to remain on their land, intensifying their own labor and using various income-producing strategies to make ends meet. Others—those in Northern Rhodesia—had some choice depending on their circumstances and age. They could remain on their land, intensifying their labor, or they could follow their men to the mines or urban areas in hopes of improving their opportunities.

In Southern Rhodesia's patrilineal groups, male labor emigration prompted married women who had once depended on husbands for production decisions to take on more of these decisions. At the same time, it forced them to devise strategies for earning income that supplemented the sporadic income they received from absent male family members. There were fewer eligible men in the rural areas, so single, unmarried women began emigrating to the urban areas to seek income through domestic service and other forms of employment. In short, colonial capitalism was the catalyst for a dramatic restructuring of gender productive relations among all groups, a restructuring that was embraced by nationalist states.

Notes

1. I am particularly indebted to the work of Alpers (1968), Pachai (1972), Linden (1974), Phiri (1977, 1984), Schoffeleers (1968, 1980, 1984), White (1987), and Mandala (1990) on Malawi; to the work of Beach (1976, 1977, 1980, 1984), Chanaiwa (1973), Lancaster (1981), Ndlovu (1974), Palmer (1977a, 1977b), Phimister (1976, 1988), Ranger (1967, 1970, 1983, 1989a, 1989b), Mudenge (1988), Barnes (1992, 1995), Jeater (1993), and Schmidt (1992) on Zimbabwe; and to the work of Chanock (1977), Chauncey (1981), Epstein (1981), Cliffe (1978), Mvunga (1978), Parpart (1986), Richards (1939, 1950, 1958), Wright (1983, 1993), and Moore and Vaughan (1994) on Zambia.

2. By the mid-nineteenth century with an increased population in the southern region, Malawians who had formerly practiced a forest-fallow system (whereby forest refuse was burned and mixed with the soil in mounds prior to planting) were increasingly turning to bush fallowing because shifting village cultivation was rapidly becoming impractical (Vaughan 1987:51). Intensification of land use and labor under bush fallowing led to the rapid depletion of the top soil's thin layer, leading in many cases to erosion. Even though cultivators may have hedged against drought and insect destruction by planting staple crops in different ecological niches, during a widespread drought, few areas escaped the drying effects. This was the situation in 1862.

3. Van Velsen (1964) claimed that the Lakeside Tonga chiefs and elders controlled the flow of young male labor and that the absence of these young men had an adverse effect on women who had previously counted on them for brideservice. He attributes the trend toward virilocal residence as arising from returnees' greater independence and their desire to control the resources of their families, including income and children.

4. This is a different scenario than for the Lakeside Tonga, where brideservice was no longer practiced.

5. Men in Nyasaland were not faced, as their counterparts in Mozambique were, with the forced-labor contracts of a *chibalo* system (known as *chibaro* in Southern Rhodesia, where such contracts were in force) (see Schmidt 1992).

6. A legal case was brought by the protectorate in 1954 against Wilfred A. Foulds, a South African who was charged with three counts of recruiting labor without a permit. He was also charged with "inducing natives to leave the Protectorate without an identity certificate or travelling permit" (Rigby 1954:164). The case testifies to the tenacity of labor recruiters. It also indicates where the sympathies of the Nyasaland protectorate lay, as Foulds was acquitted on all counts.

7. Schmidt's (1992) study of Shona women in Goromonzi District is one of the more comprehensive studies in a growing literature on Zimbabwean women. Other recent studies include Pankhurst (1988); Barnes (1987); Moss (1990); Staunton (1990); Gaidzanwa (1988); Mashumba (1988); and Ncube (1986), to name just a few of the more recent works.

8. These include the Bisa and Lamba, as well as the Bemba. Moore and Vaughan (1994:167) refer to the Bemba as being "bilateral." Certainly bilaterality was one aspect of the way the Bemba interrelated on a daily basis, but it did not overshadow matriliny in its cultural significance for this group. Moreover, Moore and Vaughan's contention (5) that there was a "tension in Richards' account between matrilineality and bilaterality" does not seem justified. In my reading of Richards (1940:87–88), she seems to be pointing out that both matriliny and bilaterality are important, co-existing aspects of Bemba society and that neither one assumes an ideal form in practice. The bulk of the literature on the Bemba refers to this group as matrilineal (see, e.g., Richards 1939, 1950; Epstein 1975; Werbner 1967; Stromgaard 1985), a designation that I adopt in this volume.

9. Poewe (1981:10) has made a similar argument for the Luapula, where communal distribution follows individual hearthhold production. A similar situation exists for matrilineal groups in Malawi (Vaughan 1987), but where the crop has been food, it has not presented a contradiction for those involved.

10. Unfortunately, the tendency is still to write about "a man and his wife" rather "a woman and her husband" or the more equitable "wife and husband" when referring to the conjugal unit in matrilineal situations (see, e.g., Chanock 1985:7; White 1987:167). The problem is the assumption that husbands have legal marital authority over wives regardless of the situation.

11. Differences in women's authority and control did exist among matrilineal, uxorilocal groups, however, as Richards (1950) observed in her comparison of the Bemba and Bisa with the Chewa and Yao of Nyasaland for the same period. She attributed the higher status of the women in the latter groups to the central position of "the woman [as] head of family, and [to the fact] that women acted as heads of hamlets in both groups" (1950:234). Poewe (1981) notes that for the Lundu and Luapula, class made a difference with women in elite Lundu households having less authority than Luapula peasant women in uxorilocal households even though they were historically the subjects of the Lundu. As men achieved military and political power, they tended to demand virilocality, in which case a woman's authority and status tended to drop.

12. For a discussion of the distinction between communal, cooperative, and collaborative production in southern Africa, see Davison (1992:72–75). Collaborative production refers to tasks that are carried out by individuals who agree, either by invitation or by volunteering, to work together with or without remuneration for a specific time period (1992:73). The labor may carry a sense of obligation for those who participate depending on the proximity of relatedness to the person requesting it. Collaborative labor does not imply that the product of the specific labor will be shared or divided among workers though their labor may be compensated with beer, food, or both. Work parties typical of many African societies fall into this category.

13. In 1898 Europeans, mostly settlers, accounted for only 3 percent of the total estimated population of 463,236 in Southern Rhodesia. By 1920 this figure had risen to 5.5 percent of a total population of 793,098. Between 1920 and 1940, the rate of growth of the European population slackened; Europeans composed 4.5 percent of the population of 1,455,000 in 1940 (Mlambo 1972:14). In 1911, there were only 159 European farm holdings and in 1919 there were 250 European holdings in Northern Rhodesia, mainly along the railroad line linking the colony with South Africa (Mutemba 1977:350).

14. *Chibaro* was the pejorative term used by Africans to describe the system of labor recruitment used by the Rhodesian Native Labor Board to secure mineworkers in particular. It connoted not only a contract labor system but forced or slave labor (van Onselen 1976:99).

15. In Southern Rhodesia, a three-tier system of housing operated in mining compounds. The inner and center tier of housing was for temporary and longer-term single male laborers; the outer tier was limited to the fewer, and more stable, married men (van Onselen 1976:134). Officially, the Southern Rhodesian mines did not allow for women in the compounds; nonetheless, women (both married and single) did find their way into the compounds, earning meagre wages or shelter from housekeeping, cooking, selling beer, or prostitution (van Onselen 1976:175).

16. For studies of urban women in the Rhodesias, see Schuster (1979), Epstein (1981), Parpart (1986), and Barnes (1987).

5

Nation Building, Ethnicity, and the Gendered State: Men Build; Women Work

The independent states that emerged in the post–World War II period in central southern Africa adhered to the boundaries defined by the colonial states; Africans had little say in the boundary-making process. Continued colonial domination by the Portuguese in Mozambique and Angola until 1975 and the hardening of racist regimes in Southern Rhodesia and South Africa defined politics in the decades after the war. Borders in the latter part of the twentieth century came to symbolize differences between the freed and those still under the impress of colonialism. Gender, in particular, became submerged in the urgency of regional politics.

The degree to which gender has been recognized as a factor of state formation depends on the particular history of a nation's transition to independence within the context of an increasingly global community. In Malawi and Zambia in the 1960s and 1970s, state formation became "gendered male" (Lovett 1989). Women were relegated to auxiliary wings in the state party apparatus.

The gendered state that had been a feature of European colonialism continued into the postindependence period with African males replacing European males as the agents of change at all levels—from community development committees to national political party leaders and policy planners. Moreover, the gendered state was a model that fit comfortably within the global gender paradigm of the 1950s and 1960s. When male colonials left the ranks of the newly formed states, European and North American

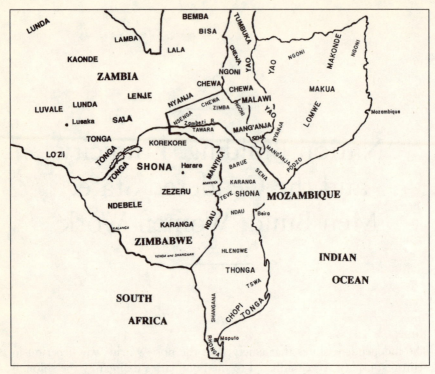

Figure 5.1   Ethnic groups identified at independence in the Zambezi region.
SOURCE: Compiled from various sources.

development "experts," largely male, joined hands with African elite males
to guide the new nations on the road to economic development. The
process was perceived to be gender neutral—what benefited males would
benefit females, class and ethnicity notwithstanding.

A ruling male elite became the dominant class regardless of the political
economy. In Malawi, Zambia, and Zimbabwe, educated male elites allied
with emergent capitalists formed the ruling class that shaped state formation. In Mozambique a male socialist cadre became the ruling group that
structured socialist transformation.

Even though on a regional level ethnicity was muted, on a national level,
ethnic identities began to coalesce and often became identified with political ones (see Figure 5.1). In Malawi, for instance, though theoretically the
Malawi Congress Party headed by Dr. H. Kamuzu Banda rose above ethnic differences, in practice the disparities between the more educated
Tumbuka and the less educated Chewa became a bone of contention in the
postindependence years. Dr. Banda, himself a Chewa, consolidated his

leadership, making sure that members of his ethnic group filled strategic positions in the state apparatus. With time, "regionalism" became a proxy for ethnicity and was closely identified with the politics of the 1994 election that ousted Banda.

In Zambia in the latter part of the colonial period, class and urban-rural differences began to have greater potency than ethnicity. But even so, the nationalist party that replaced the Zambia African National Party (ZANC), which had spearheaded the drive for independence, had its roots among the largely Bemba laborers of the Copperbelt and among the Bemba and Bisa of Northern Province. The coalition party that emerged, the United National Independence Party (UNIP), became the dominant power after independence and was accused in the early 1970s of becoming a "Bemba Party" (Smaldone 1979:38). An artifact of the colonial administration, ethnicity became identified with regionalism even though some groups spread across several provinces. Zambia's first leader, Kenneth Kaunda, attempted to overcome the politicization of ethnicity by calling for humanism based on unity and cooperative development.

Ethnicity was a critical factor of independent state formation in Zimbabwe. Growing ethnic awareness and its politicization on the part of Shona-speaking groups coalesced in the formation of ZANU-PF (the Zimbabwe African National Union–Patriotic Front). The major ethnic challenger for nationalist political power—the Ndebele—became linked with PF-ZAPU (Zimbabwe African Peoples Union) in the southern part of Zimbabwe. These two political groups and their armies vied for power during the war of liberation. (Not incidentally, women were as involved as men in this struggle; how they coped with and perceived this battle for dominance has only recently come to light and will be discussed farther on[see Staunton 1990; Kriger 1992].) The Shona majority took charge of the state apparatus and nationalist development at the expense of the Ndebele and their political allies (see Ranger 1984, 1989b). As Ranger points out, ethnicity became the terrain on which power and authority were contested in the early 1980s (1989b). ZANU-PF's struggle to consolidate its power base led to violence against the Ndebele minority and PF-ZAPU's supporters (Werbner 1991). It was a form of violence that came close to ethnic cleansing.

In Mozambique, although ethnicity officially was considered a negligible factor in independent state formation, differences remained between groups in the predominantly matrilineal north—where there were many similarities with Malawi's southern matrilineal groups—and those in south, which were patrilineal like their Zimbabwean neighbors. In the first decade of independence Mozambique had other problems besides ethnicity to contend with; primary among them was the destabilization campaign waged against the state by the Mozambican National Resistance (MNR) (also Renamo), which was militarily and financially backed by South Africa.

The foregoing provides the context for an examination of the juncture of gender and ethnicity in the newly emergent states. In this chapter I argue that the extent to which gender was addressed in state formation and national development, especially in Mozambique and Zimbabwe, was the result of a changing global climate and that issues of ethnicity were the product of changing regional and national forces. In examining state formation, I draw attention to the way that the state in the postcolonial era reframed and solidified trends begun under colonial occupation.[1]

I begin with an overview of the transition to independence in Malawi and Zambia and the continuation of the gendered state established under colonial capitalism. The overview is followed by an examination of ethnicity's role in nation building in Zambia, Malawi, and Zimbabwe.

Independence:
A Continuation of the Gendered State

Lovett (1989) has argued that state formation is a gendered process, one that is ordered and experienced differently by males and females in a particular society. She takes the position that the state in its ideal form is neutral but that through the historical specificity of certain processes, among them the penetration of colonial capitalism, the state and political economy of a specific country or region become gender structured.[2] The gender-structuring process is not without contradictions, tensions, and struggles, as we have seen for the colonial period in central southern Africa.

The post–World War II era left many of the European colonial powers in Africa in a weakened state. Spread thin by economic demands for reconstruction and development at home, Britain found it difficult to meet the competing needs of colonials for greater economic and political support and the demands of Africans for greater stake in the political process and ultimately an end to colonial occupation. Britain began to withdraw from its colonies in the late 1950s in western Africa and in the early 1960s in eastern and southern Africa. Malawi and Zambia were among the newly formed states in central southern Africa.

Malawi and Zambia broke from the short-lived Central African Federation, crafted and dominated by Southern Rhodesia, to become independent states in 1964. Armed with the security of British commonwealth status and new parliamentary systems modeled on Britain's own, the two countries moved quickly to formulate national development plans that were in harmony with the West's capitalist vision of economic growth.

National Plans for Development

The national development plans designed by Malawi and Zambia in the late 1960s and 1970s reflected differing resource bases and economic circumstances. As Malawi has few mineral resources, its development plans in the first two decades after independence aimed to build up an agricultural estate sector that was primarily responsible for producing export crops while at the same time encouraging nascent industry. Left behind was the smallholder sector, which included most of Malawi's population, including women.

Like other states in the region, Malawi was affected by South Africa's economic destabilization campaign beginning in the mid-1970s, particularly the closing of transportation routes through Mozambique to the Indian Ocean, which forced Malawi to depend on the much more expensive South African transportation routes. Equally, Malawi felt the impact of escalating oil prices and unfavorable prices on agricultural products such as coffee and tobacco in the late 1970s and early 1980s. As a result, Malawi began to reexamine the place of smallholder agriculture in the mid-1980s and to shift more of its development resources toward that sector in the late 1980s and early 1990s (Chisala and Mthindi 1989). In particular, the stranglehold of the agricultural, parastatal ADMARC on sales and pricing of agricultural products was addressed. Smallholder production of burley tobacco became a contested arena for allowing competition to enter the agricultural sector.

Until the 1990s, women figured little in Malawi's development plans. In the late 1970s, donor agencies such as the British Overseas Development Agency (ODA) and the U.S. Agency for International Development (USAID) began pushing for gender reforms in the agricultural sector to reflect the central role of women in production. The Malawian response was to set up the Women's Programme in Training and Extension Services Division of the Ministry of Agriculture, but this agency was given an advisory, gender-specific role rather than policy clout. It also was responsible for training female extension workers. The Ministry of Agriculture's agenda clearly reflected Western patriarchical attitudes: Training for female agricultural extension workers was directed toward "home economics" while their male counterparts learned innovations to improve agricultural production (Spring 1983). Not surprisingly, it was difficult to recruit Malawian women to become "home craft workers."

The national development agenda in Zambia was markedly different from Malawi's due to its rich reserve of mineral resources. The cornerstone of Kenneth Kaunda's first development plans was growth of the industrial mining sector, which in turn would underwrite the costs of humanitarian social welfare programs and technological advancement in the agricultural sector.

Two factors contributed to changes in Zambia's initial national development priorities by 1975—one connected with Zambia's strategic position as a frontline state and the other with its worsening economic position. Zambia's position in the regional politics of liberation struggles and South Africa's destabilization campaign made Zambia vulnerable: Kaunda made a commitment to majority rule in southern Africa and, as a result, was more than just a bystander in the liberation struggles developing in 1963–1964 in Mozambique and Namibia. Equally, the Unilateral Declaration of Independence by Ian Smith's party in Southern Rhodesia in the following year made it imperative that Zambia close its southern border. It was closed at considerable cost to Zambia's economic ties with its southern neighbors and at the risk of internal security because the underground liberation movements in Southern Rhodesia and South Africa used Zambia as one of their bases of operation (Dobert 1979:122). By 1975, the year that Mozambique and Angola gained independence, Zambia faced an economic and political crisis.

The second factor contributing to a shift in Zambia's development priorities was the worsening economic situation brought about by drastically reduced copper prices and escalating oil prices as well as the disruption of transportation routes to southern ports and the west coast of Angola. In response to the economic crisis, coupled with accusations of political corruption, President Kaunda outlined a series of changes. First, the country would shift from economic dependency on mining to greater reliance on agricultural production. Second, measures would be instituted to prevent capitalist accumulation of wealth, particularly among civil servants. Third, subsidies to parastatals would be reduced. A further reform involved converting freehold land titles to 100-year leases. And finally, the national newspaper, which had been owned by the British multinational Lonrho, was taken over by UNIP (Dobert 1979).

Even with such an array of reforms, Zambia's economic situation did not improve, and there was widespread inflation, adding to the state's financially precarious position. As a consequence, Zambia was forced to carry out further reforms in the next decade, largely orchestrated by the World Bank and International Monetary Fund (IMF) in keeping with structural adjustment. The austerity measures that were instituted as part of the economic reform package in part led to a further crisis and the demand for a multiparty system, a demand that brought the UNIP to its knees in 1991 and resulted in Kaunda being replaced by labor leader Frank Chiluba as head of state.

In both Malawi and Zambia the development plans crafted in the postindependence period bore the mark of major Western donor agency thinking and, as such, were geared to economic growth based on integration into a capitalist world market. The newly created state apparatus in each country was dominated by a small cadre of educated male elites. Initially, little attention was given in the development plans of either country to the neglected needs of smallholder peasants or women—often one and the same.

In the mid-1960s it was assumed in the West that economic development was "gender neutral" and that the benefits of economic growth would somehow "trickle down" to the most disadvantaged, including women. The trickle-down theory was one widely subscribed to by bilateral and multilateral agencies in the heady postindependence decade. Economic-growth goals with their presumed benefits were translated into national development policies with the cooperation of state elites for whom "development" spelled not only growth but upward mobility. In the first postindependence decades (1964–1984) in Malawi and Zambia, women, except for a fraction of the educated elite, made little headway either economically or politically. In Malawi they became co-opted politically under the Women's League of the Malawi Congress Party, and their opportunities for political participation at all levels were highly circumscribed (Hirschmann 1986). In Zambia, a similar situation existed (Schuster 1983), and Allen (1991) points out that women who showed an interest in pursuing politics that would advance women's interests were eased out of their positions in the UNIP Women's League. As Ferguson and Liatto-Katundu (1994:18) conclude, "The UNIP government generally channeled women's political participation in ways that supported party and state interests rather than women's own diverse concerns."

With the convening of the triple conferences of the U.N. Decade of Women (1975–1985), the governments of Malawi and Zambia were forced to recognize that giving women an auxiliary position in the sole political parties would not satisfy the global demand for the recognition of women as a significant group in national development. As a result, what the U.N. termed "national machineries" were created in both countries to implement the Forward Looking Strategies, created at the end of the Nairobi conference in 1985. In the two countries, national commissions for women were set up. In both cases they were charged with studying the obstacles to women's advancement and making recommendations to the state. However, small administrative staffs and limited authority for implementation hindered their effectiveness.

Moving Toward Political Empowerment

Zambia

By 1991 women in Zambia and Malawi had become more visible in politics. In 1991, prior to Zambia's national elections that year, a group of educated, middle-class women, many of them lawyers, organized a nonpartisan pressure group known as the National Women's Lobby Group. Their major objectives were to raise the awareness of UNIP's political leadership on gender issues and to address women's underrepresentation in political bodies at all levels (Liatto-Katundu 1993:80). The group received a negative response not only from UNIP and its women's section but from the newly formed opposition party, the Movement for Multiparty Democracy (MMD). The National Women's Lobby Group was accused of representing a small elite class of Zambian women. Nonetheless, it managed to gain a certain amount of public recognition, especially in mobilizing and training monitors for the national elections.

Only 7 women out of a total of 150 members were elected to the Zambian parliament in 1991 (4.3 percent), but they more than tripled their representation from 1985, when only 2 women were elected. In local government elections the following year, the National Women's Lobby's encouragement of women candidates contributed to a few women winning races for ward councillors and, subsequently, to 3 women being elected as deputy mayors, including 1 for Lusaka (Liatto-Katundu 1993). As of mid-1994, an additional woman had been appointed by President Chiluba to the parliament; there were 3 women cabinet ministers, 2 deputy ministers, and 8 permanent secretaries, of which 2 were acting permanent secretaries, for a total representation of 6.6 percent (Ferguson and Liatto-Katundu 1994:16). Also, one judge on the high court and three diplomats were women (Liatto-Katundu 1993; Ferguson et al. 1995).

In a study by Ferguson and Liatto-Katundu and their colleagues (1994, 1995) of Zambian women in government and politics since 1991, the researchers found that the transition to a multiparty democracy has provided a narrow range of professional women and well-financed businesswomen—often those with male relatives in political office—with an opportunity to participate. Often these women participated at a cost to their personal lives: Of the seventeen women in national government interviewed, eleven experienced financial problems and seven mentioned personal and family problems. Only eight out of the seventeen were married. The rest were divorced. Twelve of the seventeen agreed with the statement, "Most women who become active in politics experience marital problems" (Ferguson et al. 1995:13). Of those who were married, husbands' lack of support, often resulting in separation or divorce, and inadequate time for children and other family members were most often mentioned (14).

In addition to personal problems, the women identified social problems related to discrimination against women and sexual harassment. That discrimination is a continuing concern for female members of parliament is illustrated by a recent incident: Edith Nawakwi, the energy minister, was "chased out of Parliament" by the Speaker on November 23, 1995, because she was wearing "black sexy slacks which exposed her features." Speaker R. Nabulyato was quoted as saying, "I take strong exception to women who prefer to dress in men's clothes than their normal dress. May I ask the honourable member of the house to go and change" (Mukwita 1995).

Nawakwi was forced to leave, much to the embarrassment of other members of parliament. A similar incident with another female member who wore a sleeveless dress nearly resulted in her expulsion. These incidents amplify the social problems that women who choose politics must contend with once they are in office. Until Zambia's male politicians change their attitudes and make a concerted effort to accept women's participation in politics, the few women who are in office will continue to experience obstacles to their full participation and effectiveness.

Malawi

In Malawi, the National Commission on Women in Development (NCWID), housed in the Ministry of Community Services (changed to the Ministry of Women, Children's Affairs and Community Services in 1992), became the umbrella organization for tackling women's issues on a number of fronts, including legal issues, employment, and education, in the latter part of the 1980s and the early 1990s. It became the lead organization in lobbying for the inclusion of women's as well as men's civic rights in the new constitution under multipartyism in 1994. In its efforts it was supported by a number of other women's organizations that sprang up in the heady days of multipartyism. Together the NCWID and these groups were responsible for the inclusion of a section on women's rights in Malawi's new bill of rights.

In the multiparty elections of May 1994, out of a total of 177 members of parliament, only 10 women were elected (5.6 percent), a slightly better proportion than for Zambia but nonetheless way below parity, considering that in both countries women are slightly more than 50 percent of the population. Only 1 woman was named minister by the United Democratic Front (UDF), which won a majority of seats in parliament and also the presidency. Two women are deputy ministers and 1 woman is a high court judge. In addition, the NCWID has desk officers to cover women's issues in all ministries. The organization has rewritten its constitution so that it can move out of the Ministry of Women and Children's Affairs and Community Services (MOWCACS) as a parastatal organization with its own structure and employees and with control over its own funds (S. Funk, USAID/Malawi, personal communication, November 10, 1995). Moreover, NCWID, with support from a variety of women's NGOs, was responsible for the retention of the senate in a reformed national legislature outlined in Malawi's new constitution. This body is key to women's rights, because the constitution ensures that women will have 50 percent of the seats in the 1999 election (Funk 1995). Since the 1994 elections, Malawian women in the national government have concentrated their efforts on ensuring that women's legal rights in the home and the workplace are protected.

Mozambique

In 1975, ten years after Malawi and Zambia won independence, Mozambique finally broke the Portuguese stranglehold. The global development environment was now far different. Growing economic disparities—between rich and poor, men and women, urban and rural dwellers—amidst economic growth were becoming increasingly apparent in Africa and elsewhere. Tanzania, which had offered a safe haven for the development of Mozambique's liberation struggle, offered an alternative vision of nationalist development based on socialist transformation and economic self-reliance. It was a model that appealed to the FRELIMO leaders and led to Mozambique's guerrilla struggle for the hearts and minds of the Mozambican peasantry. Not incidentally, Mozambique's liberation struggle included women such as Josina Machel, who became part of the Women's Detachment, a defense force that was also highly effective in political mobilization. Having fought alongside men for liberation, women expected a return on their investment (Urdang 1984, 1989).

Significantly, Mozambique gained its independence in the same year (1975) that the U.N. Decade of Women was launched in Mexico City under the banner of "equality, development and peace." With FRELIMO leader Samora Machel's recognition that socialist transformation must include the liberation of women along with equitable development, Mozambique's new government wasted no time in enacting laws that made women equal citizens with men, in theory. However, the extent to which these laws have been implemented or even used by women has been uneven (Pinto and Chicalia 1990; Berg and Gunderson 1992). FRELIMO also launched an ambitious plan to convert former Portuguese plantations and estates into state farms based on collective production, a campaign that proved both financially and socially unviable (Arnfred 1988; Bowen 1993; Pitcher 1995).

Women were encouraged to apply for state farm jobs with a period of two weeks set aside when only women were eligible to apply (Urdang 1989:92). The few who were hired on these farms learned to do many of the jobs—including driving tractors—that men previously had controlled. They also earned the same wages as men for comparable work. At first men on the state farms resented women doing "their" jobs and earning equal wages. "The men kept telling us we wouldn't be able to do the same work as they did," related one woman (Urdang 1989:91). But with the women's persistence, men gradually came to accept women in new roles. Nevertheless, women were few in numbers on state farms, as they preferred to work on their own family farms (Davison 1988b; Pitcher 1995).

As part of the socialist restructuring, women were brought into the development process at all levels. It was assumed that with the withering away of capitalist relations of production, and even reproduction, there would be a greater share of power for women. To formalize their role in nationalist development, the Organizaçao du Mulheres Mozambican (OMM), the Organization of Mozambican Women, was initiated as the women's branch of FRELIMO. It was charged with formulating programs that met women's most critical needs. However, its authority was circumscribed to offering recommendations. OMM had a role in recommending action to address gender inequities, but it had limited power to implement such recommendations without the approval of FRELIMO. Even so, it contributed to women's advancement on a number of fronts, including increased literacy, cooperative production, and childcare. At the same time, both FRELIMO and OMM saw customary practices of land inheritance through women, associated with matriliny, and matrilocal or uxorilocal residence as being forms of "false consciousness," out of step with socialist transformation (Arnfred 1988; Pitcher 1995). Arnfred (1988:10) argues that FRELIMO and OMM explicitly promoted the virilocally based nuclear family and male land tenure, thus indirectly undermining the social authority of women in matrilineal groups that practiced matrilocality.

By the mid-1980s, Mozambique, racked by internal civil war and increasingly cut off from bilateral and multilateral development aid due to its Marxist stance, began to restructure its economy. First, as the smallholder sector was outproducing the state farms, the latter were broken up and turned into agricultural schemes for progressive—largely male—smallholder producers of cash-value crops. Not a few of these producers were elite males who held important local administrative or civil positions. Second, FRELIMO began moving away from socialism and more toward privatization. In some areas, joint ventures between the state and private companies or consortiums became the preferred model. In other areas private companies prevailed. Privatization affected not only the agricultural sector but the machinery set up for women's needs; OMM became a nongovernmental agency competing for scarce development funds along with other nongovernmental organizations in the latter part of the 1980s.

Women's representation in the national legislature has been better than any of the other SADC (Southern African Development Community) countries in the region (Davison 1996b). As of 1992, women represented 16 percent of the total membership of the national assembly, and one woman held a deputy cabinet minister position (UNDP 1993). As a result of the October 1994 elections, the percentage of women in the national assembly increased. Out of 250 total members, 26 percent are women (65 women). Most of them come from FRELIMO (51 women), with 13 from Renamo and one representing the Democratic Union, a coalition of three smaller political parties (European Parliamentarians for Southern Africa, *Mozambican Peace Process Bulletin*, April 1995). However, despite Chissano's campaign promises to promote more women in government, only one woman was appointed a cabinet minister—Alcinda Abreu, minister of social welfare (*Mozambiquefile* 1995:6–7). In addition, four women were appointed to positions as deputy ministers, up from one woman deputy minister in the previous Chissano administration.

Zimbabwe

By the time Zimbabwe won its independence in 1980—after twenty years of struggle in which women played a significant role—the global community's attitudes toward gender had shifted. Women had long been part of the struggle in Zimbabwe, as the case of Jane Ngwenya (1983) illustrates. A teacher with a small baby, Jane became involved in the political struggle as early as 1962 and was in detention from 1964 to 1972. She had a hard time, at first, convincing men in the movement that women should be taken seriously. "In politics," she relates, "I don't think anyone wanted women to be there. They just didn't think women would be interested" (Ngwenya 1983:79). But Jane was. And she was in and out of prison five times for her beliefs. Nyasha, a seventeen-year-old secondary school student, also became involved. She joined the struggle in 1975 when she crossed the border into Mozambique with other students to join the freedom fighters (Nyasha 1983). She relates that what pushed her to join the armed struggle was "the rule that said black girls were not allowed to be air hostesses, or bank accountants, or to be trained for public administration" (1983:99). In Form IV she had applied to be an airline hostess and was rejected on the basis of race. These are the voices of the educated and committed.

Other girls, often peasants with far less education, became part of a support wing in their home areas; they were purveyors of strategic information, bought food and cooked for the guerrillas, and provided clothing, cigarettes, and beer when requested. Referred to as *chimbwido*, these girls also were forced into sexual service by guerrillas representing both major opposition armies (ZANLA and ZIPRA), as two women who were *chimbwido* testify (Davies 1983; Staunton 1990).[3] They also lived in daily fear of being harassed, beaten, and raped by the Rhodesian Security Forces.

Similarly, mothers of all ages and economic circumstances were involved in the struggle. The narrative accounts of thirty Zimbabwean mothers collected by Staunton (1990) illustrate the crucial roles that these women played in feeding, clothing, and providing information to the freedom fighters. Their narratives also illuminate their vulnerability to exploitation and violence during the war years. At the same time, Kriger (1988:319) notes that Shona women in Mutoko were not above using their age status in relation to the young male guerrillas as a means of leveraging support for themselves against their husbands in marital battles, where women had little power. Yet for all their part in the liberation struggle, there was only one woman in the Patriotic Front delegation that met at Lancaster House to plan Zimbabwe's transition to independence (Ngwenya 1983:75).

The U.N. Decade of Women was half over by the time Zimbabwe achieved independence and it was widely recognized that African women had played a key role in the long liberation struggle. Development with equity had become the new paradigm of the multilateral and bilateral donor agencies. However, ethnic rivalries dominated the first four years of Zimbabwe's postindependence years, and women were faced with yet another war. Especially in rural areas, women found themselves embroiled on both sides of the ethnically politicized struggle for power as the civil war between Ndebele ZIPRA forces and the Shona-dominated ZANLA forces escalated. Women called to serve on either side found themselves again forced to provide domestic and sexual services, or they became pawns in the power struggle—a situation that not only was degrading but reinforced their status as minors with few rights.

In cases where a woman from one of the two major ethnic groups was married to a member of the other, she might be suspected of sorcery or treason—a case of guilt by association based on ethnicity. Werbner (1991:154), for example, describes the case of a Ndebele woman married to a Kalanga man who was suspected of practicing sorcery against Shona guerrillas. The woman was rounded up with other members of her Shona-speaking family and, in their presence, was kicked and beaten by ZANLA guerrillas until her teeth were knocked out and she lay in a heap, whereupon she was told, "Woman, today you will eat your own flesh." It is small wonder that Zimbabwean women began to question what they had fought for during the liberation struggle, and whether they would ever see the fruits of independence.

Under Robert Mugabe's leadership, Zimbabwe initially embraced a "socialist" model of development based on cooperative production that was similar to Mozambique's. There was talk of bringing women into the process. A critical mass of educated women existed in Zimbabwe at independence that, backed by the force of the Women's Decade, pushed for a national machinery capable of addressing the blatant gender inequities apparent in this patriarchal society. Paramount were legal inequities that cast women in the role of minors under the guardianship of fathers or husbands. The Legal Age of Majority Act was passed in 1982, giving both sexes majority status at the age of eighteen. Although a law was passed to give women full adult status, it took nearly a decade and constant pressure from women's organizations—both local and international—to force the gendered state to begin implementing changes based on the law. Nearly a decade later, in 1991, an amendment to the Deeds Registry Act was passed that gave married women the right to buy immovable property, including land, without their husbands' consent (United Nations Children's Fund [hereafter UNICEF] 1994b:55). Previously, they had to have a husband's consent.

Like the other states included in this study, Zimbabwe recently held national elections that allowed for multipartyism in principle, if not in practice; very few members of parties in opposition to ZANU-PF and very few women were elected members of parliament (MPs). In elections held in April 1995, out of a total of 120 elected seats (the president appoints an additional 30 MPs to make a total of 150 members), 18 women—all from ZANU-PF—were elected (Laasko 1995:13). The president appointed 2 additional women, bringing the total number up to 20 out of 150 members (13.3 percent), slightly better than their representation in 1992, which was 12 percent (United Nations Development Programme [hereafter UNDP] 1993). Out of 37 ministers and governors, 3 are women, and 4 of the 9 deputy ministers are women.

Of the four states, then, women have made the most progress in legislative representation in Mozambique, where they have nearly doubled the proportion of seats they hold, largely because of FRELIMO's commitment to put women forward as candidates (over 40 percent of FRELIMO's standing legislative candidates were women). In Zimbabwe, progress has been inch by inch; ZANU-PF shows little commitment to seeing that women are elected to parliament or hold ministerial positions. Mainly, it has displayed tokenism.

In Malawi, multiparty elections in 1994 made little difference in women's representation in the parliament, but with the constitutional reforms approved in 1995, women's prospects for enlarged representation through senate elections in 1999 are good. Only in Zambia have women seen negligible progress, despite the work of the Women's Lobby Group and Chiluba's campaign promises preceding the 1991 multiparty elections. Perhaps the 1996 elections in Zambia will tell a different story.

Ethnization in the Independent State

In this section I look at the politicization of ethnicity, or ethnization, first in Zambia and to a lesser degree in Malawi's independent state formation.

I then look at ethnization in Zimbabwe. In each case, my concern is with the way the politicization of ethnicity influenced state formation and in turn, economic and social development.

Zambia: Does Ethnic Identity Matter?

Zambia was attributed with having the largest number of recognized ethnic groups—seventy-three groups according to Hoover (1979) and seventy-two according to Burdette (1984)—in the postcolonial period. How did ethnicity come to be defined? To what extent did ethnic groups become identified with particular political parties or the state? With national development? Rather than discuss all groups, I take the case of the Bemba as illustrative of the ambiguities involved in perceptions of ethnicity in independent Zambia.

The Bemba, who alternately have been categorized as a caste of matrilineal elites (Richards 1940; Roberts 1973), a militarist order (Epstein 1975; Bratton 1980), and a horticultural group dependent on *citemene* cultivation (Richards 1939; Stromgaard 1985), began in the latter part of the colonial period to assume a new identity, this time related to nation building. Berry (1993:50) points out that the colonial state's campaign to abolish *citemene* and its accompanying strategy of constantly relocating the Bemba, Bisa, and other groups to discourage shifting cultivation and encourage permanent settlement in Northern Province made this region an easy target for organizing nationalist political party opposition in the 1940s and 1950s. Bemba peasants became linked to UNIP's disturbances against the colonial state in Chinsali District, Northern Province (Moore and Vaughan 1994:136). Bemba miners also were at the forefront of the political struggle for independence in the 1950s (Smaldone 1979). It is not surprising that the Bemba were highly visible in the coalition party that came to power after independence. In the ensuing years, the UNIP became increasingly linked with Bemba interests—both in urban mining centers and in rural northeastern provinces (Smaldone 1979:38).

The Bemba are statistically the most populous group in Zambia. Ethnic identity is based on cultural ties of language and custom rather than territory. They are spread across three postcolonial provinces—the Northern, Luapula, and Copperbelt. They do not adhere to any one recognized political-geographical unit even though others may identify them with Northern Province. They speak a common language and recognize matrilineal descent and inheritance rights. In marital residence patterns they are eclectic, some practicing virilocal residence with the transfer of bridewealth and others practicing uxorilocality. Because of their numbers and their early exposure to mission education, like the Lozi they have been prominent in the formation of political parties and have retained their high visibility. Other ethnic groups have accused the Bemba of "controlling national politics" as well as the copper mining industry after independence (Hoover 1979). As the copper-mining industry received the lion's share of development inputs in the postcolonial period, Bemba men often were the direct and indirect beneficiaries of these inputs.

Yet the Bemba are not a homogenous group. Significant economic differences exist among them (Hoover 1979; Moore and Vaughan 1994). Some Bemba form the backbone of the mining interests, as administrators. Others are laborers who became actively involved in labor organization. Still others are identified with the agricultural sector. Bemba rural dwellers are not a unitary group either; differences exist between commercial farmers and peasants. In the latter case, subsistence agriculture is the mainstay. The needs and development interests of commercial farmers and peasants differ. Consequently, although the Bemba may appear to others to be a single ethnic group, in reality they fill many niches across the social and economic spectrum. For the Bemba, then, ethnicity remains ambiguous.

My reading of Zambia's ethnic quilt is that ethnicity there has been overshadowed by other notable socioeconomic differences that grew in significance in the early years of independence and have continued to shape Zambian society. In particular, social class, based on educational status and income, has become a prominent factor of social differentiation. Often education is associated with the urban sector. The emergence of a class of independent petite bourgeoisie that cuts across ethnic identities has an impact on policy decisions related to development.

Another factor cutting across ethnicity is increased rural-urban migration between 1964 and 1984 (see Table 5.1). In particular, the migration rate for Lusaka more than doubled between 1963 and 1980, and there was a steady rise in migration to the Copperbelt. The Copperbelt, Central, Luapula, and Lusaka Provinces were most affected.

As unemployment grew in the urban areas in the 1980s, however, a countermovement began; many young people—in Northern Province, for instance—went back to their home villages (Geisler et al. 1985). This movement was encouraged by the state, which pumped development resources into Northern Province to encourage peasants in this area to grow hybrid maize (see Geisler et al. 1985; Evans and Young 1988; Moore and Vaughan 1994, ch. 8). Labor migration patterns, then, cut across ethnic groups and contributed to shaping Zambia's nationalist development agenda.

Hoover (1979:81) maintains that ethnic groups in Zambia represent broad coalitions of smaller groups competing for political power and scarce development resources. The Bemba (also the Bisa and Lala), for example, have been the major beneficiaries of Zambia's development of the copper industry. Together with the Lozi and Chewa, they also are identified with the administrative salariat (Hoover 1979). Tonga speakers in Southern Province, who are primarily commercial and subsistence farmers,

TABLE 5.1   Percentage Increase in Province Population Caused by Migration in Zambia: 1963, 1969, and 1980

Province	1963	1969	1980
Lusaka	5.6	8.7	12.2
Central	8.9	8.9	9.0
Copperbelt	15.6	20.1	22.0
Eastern	13.9	12.6	11.6
Luapula	10.7	8.3	7.3
Northern	16.2	13.4	11.9
Northwest	6.9	5.7	5.3
Southern	13.4	12.2	12.1
Western	10.4	10.1	8.6

SOURCE: Government of Zambia, Central Statistics Office 1981.

were among the first to benefit from government schemes designed to produce cash-value crops with improved technology (Wright 1983). More recently, agricultural development projects have been targeted for Northern Province to meet the needs of returning migrant workers after the collapse of the copper market (Geisler et al. 1985; Stromgaard 1985; Jiggins 1980; Jiggins et al. 1995; Sharpe 1990). In summary, although ethnic differences exist and are recognized by Zambians (e.g., Sangambo 1979; Mutemba 1982; Milimo 1986), other factors such as rural-urban migration patterns and socioeconomic differences cut across ethnicity and are equally important in determining the shape of Zambia's development and how its development resources are distributed.

Malawi: Ethnicity and Regional Balancing

In independent Malawi, the state legitimated a one-party system that was, in theory, to diffuse ethnization in the interests of nation building. At the time of independence, however, those favored with an early mission education were, as in the Lozi and Chewa communities in Zambia, in a more favorable position to assume posts within the new government bureaucracy. Because Tumbuka men had most often attended school and had learned English in the process, they were often the ones selected for low-wage civil service positions in the colonial state. They also were the first of those selected for government positions in independent Malawi. Consequently, the Tumbuka are perceived by other Malawians as having an educational advantage that translates into a potential administrative advantage within the context of the state bureaucracy.

In the Southern Region, the British had indirectly ruled through the Muslim Yao chiefs; once independence was won, a different ethnic power grouping emerged. Men (and sometimes women) who were members of Chewa-speaking groups (Mang'anja, Nyanja, Lomwe) were selected to act as local administrators in keeping with the Malawi Congress Party's intention to level the ethnic playing field in that region. In the process, priority was given to those who came from groups linguistically related to President Banda's group, the Chewa (see also Vail and White 1989). There is no question that much of the spoils of development went to the Chewa in the Central Region and to their linguistic relations in the Southern Region. Significantly, Chichewa (the language of Chewa speakers) was selected by the state to be the national language. As in Zambia, however, the official spoken and written language of government was English. Even though Chewa speakers lived throughout the Central and Southern Regions and crossed ethnic boundaries, in the minds of many Malawians those in the Central Region were the major beneficiaries of development. Ethnicity had become identified with regionalism.

Control of scarce development resources became an ongoing issue. One of the arenas where struggles over resources emerged was education, a key factor of individual advancement and national development. Primarily, the contest was one between men from different ethnic groups rather a question of education for females, which until 1990 was not a development priority (Ngwira 1989; Davison and Kanyuka 1990).

In 1988, it became evident in a national survey of education that the majority of trained teachers, overwhelmingly male in rural areas, came from the Northern Region, the home of the Tumbuka (Government of Malawi 1988). This was particularly true for science and mathematics teachers. In order to equalize teaching opportunities for other ethnic groups, all teachers were ordered to return to their region and district of origin to teach. There was a massive reshuffling as many teachers left the more populous Southern Region and returned to the much less populated Northern Region. The consequence was that schools in the Southern Region, in many cases, were left with a shortage of teachers and there was a surplus of teachers in the Northern Region.

Another critical aspect of Malawi's development—agriculture—also provides an example of the way development and ethnicity become intertwined. The case in point is agrarian reforms involving estate production of cash-value crops such as tobacco and hybrid maize, which were first introduced, not surprisingly, in the former president's Chewa-speaking Central Region. With the encouragement of the Ministry of Agriculture, the marketing parastatal ADMARC, and the Tobacco Growers' Association, an increasing number of elite male Chewa farmers obtained rights to large parcels of land through the state—land that enabled them to become estate growers of tobacco or hybrid maize in the 1970s and 1980s. Despite efforts in the 1980s to pursue a policy of "regional balancing" in national development, Malawi's state apparatus, backed by its sole political party, tended to favor some ethnic groups and regions over others. With the multiparty elections of May 1994 and the election of Baliki Muluzi, a Muslim from the populous Southern Region, it was hoped that the development playing field would be further leveled. Some preliminary reshuffling of development resources, particularly to the smallholder sector, has been noted, but it is still too early to tell whether this trend will continue and how it will affect the three regions.

Zimbabwe: Ethnicity and the Contest for Political Power

Zimbabwe became embroiled in a contest for political power between the two major ethnic groups—the Shona and the Ndebele—that emerged during the transitional and postindependence eras. As Ranger (1989a) has explained, through intraparty leadership contestations within ZANU, the Shona-speaking groups, including the Karanga, Zezuru, Manyika, and others, became consolidated as a broadly defined "ethnic group." Prior to 1971, a delicate tripartite leadership balance had existed within the party, but after the Zezuru leadership pulled out in 1971, the leadership of the Karanga and Manyika became polarized, with Muzorewa heading the Manyika Methodist entrepreneurs and Mugabe leading the Karanga (Ranger 1989a:118–120). On the eve of independence, Muzorewa left to form his own political party, leaving Mugabe in charge of a newly minted, ethnically identified ZANU-PF—a party that embraced all Shona. This broadly defined ethnic group accounted for nearly 80 percent of the population if the Manyika and other Shona speakers are included. Its major ethnic contender for postindependence national leadership was the Ndebele's Joshua Nkomo, who headed PF-ZAPU. The Ndebele accounted for about 15 percent of Zimbabwe's total population at independence.

With the first elections in 1980, ZANU-PF won the presidency and the majority of seats in parliament. However, the contest for power was not over and became increasingly polarized along ethnic lines. Led by the winning ZANU-PF, the state waged an often brutal campaign in the south to eradicate any vestiges of PF-ZAPU that might threaten ZANU-PF's military and political control. In the first four years of independence, thousands of Ndebele were hunted down as former loyalists of the Rhodesian Front (whether they were loyalists or not) and were harassed or tortured and killed (Werbner 1991). The bloodbath ended only when Nkomo agreed to join the ZANU-PF government, accepting the position of vice president under Mugabe.

The ethnic tension between the dominant Shona and the minority Ndebele was somewhat diffused by the latter part of the 1980s, but ethnicity continues to be an integral part of Zimbabwe's overall development in the late twentieth century in terms of who gets access to certain key positions in government and how development resources are distributed by the state. The Ndebele, in particular, have complained that more resources are not forthcoming for the development of water resources in the parched south. Even with an increase of development resources earmarked for Matabeleland, there is the perception among Zimbabweans—the Ndebele and others—that Matabeleland has been marginalized in the process of development.

Development, Gender, and Education

Before proceeding to a discussion of rural development and gender in the next chapter, a brief section is needed to explain the role of education as it impinges on women's chances for development. Education in the postindependence era became gendered male with the goal of training males for wage employment. This left most women with the bulk of agricultural responsibilities in the rural areas.

At independence the educational level of Africans in Malawi and Zambia was very low; less than 3 percent had completed primary school. The initial push in education was to provide schooling for those who, policy reformers reasoned, would be most likely to seek wage employment—males. It was assumed, as in the colonial state, that females would remain in the rural areas, attached to land and food production, even though increasing numbers of Zambia and Zimbabwe's younger rural women had been migrating in search of income opportunities since the 1950s.

Adopting the notion of *manpower* development, itself a gendered term, the new states of Zambia and Malawi began to build not only schools but vocational training programs. The latter were instituted to provide male school leavers with skills appropriate for capitalist development. Few programs other than in home economics or crafts were designed for women—a vocational gap that persists in the 1990s in Malawi (Liwimbi 1992). Even within the civil service, opportunities for advanced training and education were given to men.

The assumption that women would remain "at home"—on the homestead or in the urban house—as society became "modernized" was reflective of a patriarchal attitude that African males had adopted from European colonials. It was a perspective that especially appealed to educated, upwardly mobile elite males in the postcolonial era. Moreover, the belief that men should be the primary wage earners was reinforced, initially, by development agency consultants and personnel hired to assist newly emergent states in designing and implementing development plans. Especially for young men who were members of groups that ascribed to uxorilocal, brideservice marriages and matrilineality, the emphasis on male access to education and wage labor provided an escape from the insecure status that young men felt under matriliny until they reached elderhood.

As a result of the gender bias in education and training, national development became skewed toward male advancement to the near exclusion of females. The majority of women, especially in rural areas, lacked formal education at the time of independence, and thus they were barred from the political arenas where development decisions were being made. Equally, lack of education prevented women from qualifying for entry-level positions. And even where training was being provided, it was specifically limited to the "domestic arts." This combination of factors meant that most women were programmed to remain largely in the rural areas, fully engaged in agricultural production. The exception was the minority of women who had managed to secure education through the secondary level. These women most often lived in urban centers.

In Mozambique, where 93 percent of the population was illiterate at independence, although schools were opened to all children regardless of gender after independence, in reality more boys than girls attended school in the first decade (Urdang 1984; Marshall 1985). Initially, educational benefits and training went to men, although OMM spearheaded a major literacy campaign for women. Even in agricultural training courses men far outnumbered women.

Of the four countries, Zimbabwe had by far the greatest proportion of educated Africans at independence. Over 40 percent of the African population had achieved some literacy, although the numbers were skewed in favor of the urban population and males. Primary school education for both sexes was encouraged after independence, and literacy classes taught largely by female volunteers proliferated. Yet large numbers of women, especially in the communal areas, remained only semiliterate. For these women, agriculture continues to be the major arena of production.

Summary

In this chapter I have described the way the gendered state, as it took form through colonial rule, was extended to the independent state in central southern Africa. I have shown how ethnicity and gender became significant factors in postindependent state formation and how the confluence of these two shaped development policies and practices in the first decades after independence. Although political economies and state ideologies have varied by country in the region, efforts to structurally change gender relations at the national level have been characterized by ambivalence since independence. The problem lies partly in the gendered nature of postcolonial state bureaucracies and partly in these states' reluctance to take on ideas from the West that run contrary to African beliefs—especially about gender. Notwithstanding, some progress has been made in leveling the gender field of politics with the election of more women members of parliament in recent multiparty elections in three out of the four countries. Mozambican women have increased their numbers most significantly, but until more women are appointed to cabinet positions, where Mozambican women believe they have the greatest opportunities for affecting change, the gains they have made through the democratic process will be merely provisional. It is hoped that Chissano will appoint more women by the year 2000.

When we review the conjuncture of nation building and ethnicity in the four states, it is notable that ethnic identities in Zimbabwe became the most polarized with independence, plunging the new nation into uncertainty. Although ZANU-PF and PF-ZAPU were able to craft a truce in the mid-1980s, the weight of the Shona-speaking majority in nation building has been felt at many levels. Regional disparities in the allocation of development resources continue to be a source of contention. Matabeleland has gotten the short end of the stick. Some efforts have been made to address regional disparities through decentralization in the 1990s. However, the ethnization that occurred in the first decade of independence is not easily forgotten. Nor have ethnic identities easily been discarded in the other three countries even though their significance has been plaited into regional differences. Some regions have fared better than others in Malawi, Zambia, and Mozambique—development has become the measure. The way that development policies designed to increase production in various regions have affected those responsible for production in the rural areas—women and men—is the subject of the next chapter.

Notes

1. See Mohanty (1993a:16–17) for a discussion of the way post-colonial African states extended and reinforced the masculinist values and ideology inherited from their former European colonizers.

2. The notion of a "neutral" state negotiating competing interests does not withstand the test of history; states are not ideals; rather the state reflects the class and gender in power at a particular point in time, including values and priorities that are expressed in state action.

3. Even though the guerrillas had strict rules of conduct that included no drinking, drugs or sex (Kriger 1988:311), nonetheless from what the women's narratives report, it is pretty clear that these "rules" were routinely broken.

6

Rural Development and Shifting Gender Relations

The majority of the population in the Zambezi River region in the late twentieth century are rural dwellers, whether they live in Zimbabwe, Malawi, or Mozambique. Malawians and Mozambicans, overwhelmingly, remain in agricultural production. Even though the majority of Zambians now live in urban and peri-urban areas, this does not mean that they are equally involved in the wage sector. As of 1980, only seven percent of Zambian women were in wage employment (ZARD 1985, cited in Milimo 1986:102). The situation was roughly comparable in Zimbabwe with only 6.8 percent of women employed in non-agricultural employment (Made and Lagerstrom 1984:1). The vast majority of women in the region live and work in the rural areas. In the main, these women are agricultural producers.

Zambian scholar Miriam Milimo (1986) accurately describes the conditions that, beginning with colonialism, affected women's production. In referring to the feminization of rural households in Zambia (1986:101) she holds that "owing to the patriarchal nature of the colonial regime, the special role that women were *poised to play* [her emphasis] in agricultural production in the new situation, was not recognized and women's potential was never fully tapped—a legacy that was to be perpetuated by independent African governments." The gendered state ignored the potential for increased production that rural women held. In an effort to validate men's roles in controlling and managing production through agricultural development schemes, women's potential remained uptapped.

In this chapter I look at the gendered states and their quest to commercialize agriculture after independence. This process often served to continue women's economic marginalization initiated by the colonial regimes. In

161

Zambia and Malawi, the ethnic groups involved in the development schemes adhered to matrilineal descent, practicing either uxorilocal or virilocal residence. The trends initiated by the colonial agricultural agents that privileged individual control of land, preferably by men, and championed virilocal residence as the epitome of rationality were extended by agents of the newly independent states. As Ekejiuba (1995:56) has observed, regardless of lineage ideology, virilocality has become an issue whenever African women are concerned.

I begin the chapter by looking at groups practicing matriliny in Zambia and Malawi. Using agricultural development as the arena, I demonstrate that the confluence of ethnicity, class, and gender shaped particular groups' opportunities for advancing production once decolonization was achieved. In most cases, women were excluded as direct beneficiaries of agrarian reform. One way that the gendered state since independence has often precluded women from sharing in the benefits of development is by denying them access to land that the state controls—this includes agricultural schemes and resettlement land. The only exception, until very recently, was women who headed their own households. For women in matrilineal groups accustomed to having their own land, as in southern Malawi and parts of Zambia, being denied access to this vital resource except through a husband was tantamount to having their productive rights usurped. In Malawi, some matrilineal males refused to cooperate in such schemes.

Looking at changes in the allocation of labor in Malawi and Zimbabwe provides an opportunity to compare the way lineage ideology enters the arena. At the same time, case studies from Zimbabwe demonstrate that in making assumptions about labor and gender one must take into consideration other factors such as age and class to achieve a more balanced picture of women's and girls' opportunities in agricultural production. The chapter ends with a description and analysis of two agricultural cooperatives, one in Mozambique and one in Zimbabwe, to illustrate strategies used under socialism to increase production and juggle gender relations.

Agricultural Reforms in Zambia: Hybrid Maize Schemes and Women

The Gwembe Tonga, as noted in Chapter 1, are closely related to the Plateau Tonga, studied by Colson in the 1950s. However, some of the Gwembe, or Valley Tonga, had the misfortune to live in semipermanent villages within the area of the Zambezi River that was flooded after the Kariba Dam was constructed. The Gwembe Tonga of Mazulu village, for instance, were forced to relocate to high ground north of their former village, which was inundated by Lake Kariba (Scudder 1975). Thus they ended up in Zambia. Other Gwembe Tonga relocated south to Mola in Omay Communal Area, Zimbabwe (Reynolds 1991).

Prior to the building of the Kariba Dam, Thayer Scudder, following up on Colson's earlier work among the Tonga, in the late 1950s carried out an ecological study of the way Gwembe Tonga farmers of both sexes utilized their environmental resources in order to weigh the impact of their removal to another environment (Scudder 1975). The study is significant not only in the attention it gives to ecological conditions in the Tonga farming system but also because Scudder included in his survey both male and female farmers—a gender sensitivity that is remarkable in a period when most female farmers were subsumed within male-headed households and female-headed households were either ignored or barely acknowledged. The study is pertinent to this section because it acts as a baseline for tracing agricultural change in a matrilineal group.

Noting that the Gwembe Tonga are characterized by unranked matrilineages with specific kinship ties but shallow genealogies, Scudder found the Gwembe were held together by inheritance rights to land and property and the connection with ancestral shades, or spirits. In each *cisi*, or neighborhood, composed of between two and seven villages or hamlets, one matrilineage took precedence over others. Most Gwembe Tonga of both sexes remained in the neighborhood of their birth before and after marriage. Within each village the Gwembe lived with extended family members in homesteads consisting of one or more hearthholds structured around a married woman and her children. Virilocality was the norm, but there were cases of uxorilocality where a wife's matrilineal relatives had more land than the husband's matrikin. Nearly half the men in the two villages where Scudder carried out fieldwork were polygynous; each wife had her own house, granary, and gardens. Cultivators of both sexes most often obtained land for gardens from their matrikin (Scudder 1975:26–28).

The Gwembe Tonga farming system was highly flexible in the late 1950s, taking advantage of a variety of ecological conditions and climatic factors. Five different types of gardens, varying in their proximity to the river and in soil conditions, characterized the farming system. Bullrush millet, sorghum, and maize were the staple crops and were grown in the appropriate ecological niche for each crop's cultivation. Vegetables and tobacco were grown in the rich alluvial soil adjacent to the river. In four villages along the middle and upper parts of the river, Scudder found that women farmers tended to cultivate a greater variety of ecological niches than men in a farming system that differentiated men's and women's fields. There were also twice as many female as male farmers in these villages. Brideservice was still an aspect of Tonga social relations. Wright (1983:75) notes that the life histories of Tonga women in the 1940s indicate that women could command the labor of their sons and sons-in-law, thus increasing their productive output. This profile, then, provides a basis for assessing the impact of commercial agriculture on the Gwembe Tonga farming system and peasant households.

In the late colonial period, the Tonga were among the first in Zambia to embrace commercial farming, especially of hybrid maize (Colson and Scudder 1988; Wright 1983). Colson and Scudder (1988) found that state schemes to encourage production of hybrid maize privileged male farmers even though there were fewer of them in farming in the 1960s. As Tonga male farmers took to the commercial production of hybrid maize and, in some cases, increased the parcels of land they devoted to this cash-value crop, their demands on their wives to assist in maize production also intensified. Equally important, as sales of hybrid maize increased, tensions developed within male-headed households over who had the right to sell crops produced in fields that historically women had cultivated. Women had also cultivated a greater variety of crops in their fields before they were allocated to hybrid maize production. Thus not only was their labor expropriated for a cash crop over which they had little or no control but they lost their customary rights to central fields for food production. Women continued, however, to control millet cultivation, using this crop in the preparation of local beer. As beer is used on many ceremonial occasions and women also sell it to generate income (over which they have exclusive control), it is in men's interests to protect women's access to land for millet cultivation. Beer also provides a negotiating tool in wives' struggles with their husbands over the allocation of wives' labor; a husband's need for his wife's labor in hybrid maize production has to be balanced with his need for labor in beer production.

Wright's study of the Mazabuka Maize Scheme (1983) in Southern Province draws similar conclusions about the effect of growing hybrid maize on Tonga gender relations of production. Her study demonstrates that the practice of giving priority to male farmers in agricultural development schemes was initiated by the colonial state and continued with the postcolonial gendered state.

Joining the state-sponsored Mazabuka project in 1945, Tonga peasants found that the commercial maize scheme was far more rigid than what they historically were accustomed to in terms of land tenure arrangements and crop production. First, the scheme targeted male farmers and as such recognized only men's rights to land. Second, the separation between wives' and husbands' fields was ignored. Hybrid maize, according to the regulations of the scheme, had to be monocropped in a single field. However, women provided much of the labor. "By 1945," Wright observes, "there was a noticeable decline in married women's rights in land," with a wife's land being subsumed within a central field and her autonomy as a producer and trader eroded (Wright 1983:78).

The third outcome was that young men could become "progressive farmers" rather than working for their parents or in-laws. This had a generational effect on older adults' ability to command the labor of younger men. Finally, differences in access to resources—including land, technology (plows and mechanized cultivators), and cattle—led to increasing stratification among the male farmers (heads of households) in the scheme. Female farmers were not included as a separate category but were subsumed as "family labor" within male-headed households.

Three classes of male farmers emerged in the scheme. The poorest owned only an acre of land and little or no equipment; they accounted for 70 percent of the commercial maize sellers. A "middle class" that accounted for 26 percent of the farmers had more land, and half of these men had sufficient farm equipment, with a third owning a plow. The wealthiest maize farmers had the largest parcels of land, two to six plows each, and many farm implements. They also tended to belong to the local Seventh Day Adventist Church and, therefore, married monogamously according to its precepts. It was this resource-rich group of farmers that was behind a move in the 1950s to gain the right to bequeath property to their sons rather than leaving it to their matrikin (Wright 1983:78–82).[1]

Wives in the monogamous families of this wealthiest class found themselves with a greater workload because they could not draw on the labor of co-wives or grown sons. Additionally, the brideservice labor of sons-in-law proved unreliable. Only in cases where a husband had the financial resources to hire labor from outside was the family's labor burden eased. With the new wealth achieved from commercial production, women in these families tended to become more dependent on their husbands—and did not systematically challenge this dependency (Mbulo 1980; Wright 1983:83). It is interesting that by 1960—regardless of religion—this wealthiest class of male farmers and some of the middle-class farmers had begun to revert to polygyny as a sign of status and wealth. In terms of authority and control over decisionmaking, women in the resource-rich class lost more control over decisions related to the allocation of labor than women in the poorest households, whose roles remained relatively unchanged (Wright 1983:82).

Thus these hybrid maize schemes replaced a historically flexible farming system with a rigid one, changing gender relations of production and interhousehold relations based on matrilineal obligations. Moreover, social differentiation among male farmers became marked. It was a trend that continued with commercialization of agriculture in the postindependence period, as Poewe (1981) found in the Luapula Valley. Here men, who became involved in commercial fishing and small businesses, used certain aspects of their matrilineal ideology—especially as related to individualized production—as justification for the private ownership of land and re-

sources. Women, in contrast, emphasized the communal ownership of resources, which, it was argued, made communal distribution possible
(Poewe 1981:16). This gender scenario occurs in other matrilineal groups.

Poewe (1981:33) generalizes that women in matrilineal groups, whose
descent ideology reinforces the cultural and structural centrality of females,
fear a loss of control over their own reproductive resources (childbearing
and rights to children through the matriline), as well as the loss of critical
productive resources such as land and labor. In Luapula, women's concern
over control of reproductive resources and productive resources merged in
the 1970s in strategies to get around men's attempts to subvert their position, Poewe contends. In part, these strategies were related to women's insistence that the economic and social aspects of their lives remain separate
from men's. Poewe believes that by adhering to a dual gender system,
women were better able to maintain their autonomy. That gender separation is a viable solution in all cases is questioned by Amadiume (1987) in
her analysis of the state's impact on the Igbo gender system.

In postindependent Zambia, state-sponsored projects involving resettlement schemes—often promoted with funding and advice from foreign development agencies—have by and large resulted in women's loss of productive authority, including control over resources such as land and labor
in matrilineal groups.[2]

The Zambian state recognized through the Land Reform Act of 1975
that *in theory* all Zambian citizens, regardless of sex, should have equal access to unoccupied land. But how this policy was translated into practice
provides an example of the contradictions that may arise between government policies and their implementation.

The Land Convention Act 20 of the 1975 reform provided that all land
in the former reserves be "nationalized," with ultimate power to allocate
parcels being vested in the president (Milimo 1986:104). In reality this
power was delegated to district councils and the Ministry of Lands, administrative bodies controlled by men. Some district councils, as Milimo
points out, required the permission of a husband if a married woman applied for land. Often these husbands were reluctant to give that permission
because they preferred their wives to work on their cash-crop land
(1986:105). The irony was that women, who had formerly taken access to
land for granted, found that the state—and its male representatives at various levels—were thwarting women's rights to this basic agricultural resource. In state-sponsored hybrid maize schemes, male producers became
the designated landholders except where a woman headed her own household.

In a study of 400 women farmers in Mumbwa and Mazabuka in
Southern Province, Milimo found that women whose husbands were involved in a state-sponsored hybrid maize scheme funded by the Swedish

International Development Agency (SIDA) in the mid-1980s were more likely to be dependent on their husbands for access to land than women whose husbands were not involved in such a scheme. In Mumbwa, half of the women whose households were in the maize scheme obtained land for cultivating from their husbands, and 21 percent got land from their fathers. Women whose husbands were not in the scheme most frequently obtained land directly from a headman or chief or, secondarily, from their father or through inheritance. Only 10 percent obtained land from their husbands. Ninety percent obtained land through community leaders, their fathers, or matrikin. In Mazabuka, where the scheme had a longer history, the majority of women in the scheme gained access to land through their husbands. Of women in nonscheme households, although 37 percent received land from their husbands, 36.7 percent obtained land from a headman, chief, or father (Milimo 1986:127). Ten percent inherited land from matrikin. On the whole, women in nonscheme households had more options for gaining access to land and were less dependent on husbands for land than women whose husbands were involved in the hybrid maize scheme. Milimo (1986:104) found that nearly 70 percent of the women farmers earned income from production of staple crops and vegetables on land they controlled; they had no control over income earned from hybrid maize on their husbands' land even though they contributed their labor to production.[3]

A different scenario is painted for women farmers whose husbands are involved in hybrid maize production in Northern Province. In Moore and Vaughan's restudy of Bemba agriculture and nutrition, the authors observe (1994:11) that whereas women in Northern Province historically had rights to cultivate certain parcels of land, especially village gardens and *citemene* millet fields, in the late 1980s their rights to village gardens were being usurped by men involved in hybrid maize production. Moreover, the authors argue, women's chances for becoming landholders in their own right appear precarious because access to land and land registration are controlled by male stakeholders, including local headmen, chiefs, and members of village productivity committees (VPCs). Unfortunately, Moore and Vaughan do not present statistical data on how the thirty women farmers in their restudy, of whom seven headed their own households, gained access to land. We cannot assume, given changing circumstances, that they "effectively acquired land through marriage" (Moore and Vaughan 1994:214). The authors' interviews of thirty male farmers suggest that males obtained land through a diversity of means.

Of the thirty male farmers in Moore and Vaughan's study, 40 percent (twelve) had obtained land from the state through specific schemes designed to increase hybrid maize production; 43.3 percent (thirteen) obtained land through a village productivity committee. Two of the men got their land from brothers, one via a chief, and one from a father through the

VPC. Only five men acquired land directly from a chief, a headman, or a relative (Moore and Vaughan 1994:212, Table 8.4). Moore and Vaughan (251, n. 12) admit that the sample is atypical because of the research site's close proximity to a hybrid maize scheme. Perhaps if the survey site had been farther from a scheme, a different set of findings would have emerged, as it did in Milimo's (1986) comparative study of farmers in maize schemes and those not in schemes. Nonetheless, Moore and Vaughan's findings are suggestive of the extent to which commercial maize farmers in the late 1980s depended on the state and other male-controlled bodies, such as the VPCs, for rights in land. In such a situation, women farmers are doubly disadvantaged. Jiggins and others (1995:32) cite the observations of a male staff member of Zambia's Department of Agriculture: "Most women don't have the indicators necessary to be selected for inclusion in agricultural schemes." These "indicators" include rights to sufficient land, financial resources, and other inputs necessary for commercial production. Jiggins and her colleagues (1995:21–39) report on a program launched in Western Province to alter this situation in the 1990s (see Chapter 7, this volume).

The State and Land Reform in Malawi

The situation for women in Malawi is more promising. Land in most areas of Malawi is communally held—that is, it is under the jurisdiction of "traditional authorities" (TAs), or "chiefs," designated by the state. The state has ultimate jurisdiction over rural land, as in Zambia. For example, land cannot be sold without the state's permission except in urban areas. Equally important, legal statutes recognize a married woman's rights to own property independent of her husband and the right to dispose of that property, through bequests or other measures, in whatever way she sees fit (National Commission on WID [hereafter NCWID] 1993:10, 12). Where a woman has established her rights in one or more parcels of land in her natal village, her property rights include this land. How these rights are translated into practice depends on a woman's status in the community, her education, the attitudes of her male relatives, and her knowledge of the law. My impression from talking with both rural and urban women over a period of years (1989–1994) is that they are aware of their rights under matrilineal and uxorilocal circumstances but that sometimes they find them difficult to act on given women's disadvantaged educational and political position in postcolonial Malawian society.

Holding to the ideology of "communal land tenure" means that most rural Malawians tend to cultivate lands they have inherited through matrikin—including grandmothers, maternal uncles, and mothers—or they are allocated land by a chief or a village head. In the Southern Region, women retain more immediate control over the land they till than some women in the Central Region. In the latter region, it is the practice among some Chewa for a betrothed man to make a bridewealth contribution to the future bride's family that then allows him to take his wife to his matrilineal village rather than remaining in her village, as is customary according to Chewa matrilineal ideology. Unless husband and wife come from the same village, a wife must travel some distance to cultivate her own matrilineal land or gardens. By and large, until the mid-1980s state- and donor-sponsored agricultural development projects in Malawi ignored women's rights in land and their central role in production.

After independence, the state created seven major agricultural development divisions (ADDs) targeted for the commercial development of cash-value crops. Food crops, especially hybrid maize and rice, were grown for both profit and local consumption. To a lesser extent, tobacco and cotton were produced, mainly for export. Initially, in all state schemes, "progressive" male farmers were targeted for inputs. These were usually men with more land, access to family labor, and income.[4] Women were subsumed within the "male-headed" household farming unit. It was a model initiated by the colonial state under the senior agricultural officer, Richard Kettlewell, in the 1940s and 1950s to increase agricultural production that was subsequently extended by the independent gendered state in the 1960s and 1970s. Female heads of households were rarely considered until the sex of the household head was included in a 1981–1982 national survey of agriculture. It was then discovered that female-headed households, which constituted between 29 and 32 percent of the total farming households at the time, were a particularly disadvantaged category in terms of land and labor (Spring 1983).[5]

Land became a central issue in Malawi's rural development priorities. The state, which depended heavily on funding from the World Bank, was forced in 1972 to put into practice an agrarian reform that held sway with agricultural development theorists at the time; it was based on the assumption that to improve agricultural output, communal land tenure should be replaced with individual tenure as an incentive for increased productivity. In contradistinction to the state's policy of retaining "communal land" in rural areas, the Department of Land Acquisitions and Adjudication attempted to implement a land-reform measure based on individual registered ownership in the major project area in one of the ADDs—the Lilongwe Rural Development Project (LRDP) in the Central Region. The proposed system of individualized tenure in the LRDP was to become a model for land reform in other ADDs in Malawi.

The conversion of communal land to individual tenure in the LRDP proved to be a greater challenge than either development theorists or government agents imagined. The designated area was a patchwork of matrilineal holdings under the control of male elders and, in many cases, women. Working with the Ministry of Agriculture and the Department of Lands, World Bank consultants tried to "map" who the matrilineally related extended families were in the project area and then to identify the senior male in such families who would become the title holder on behalf of the family. The reform met with stiff resistance among Malawians, both female and male, concerned with "communally held" ties in land. As Nankumba (1989:4) observed,

> Some members of the Lilongwe Local Land Board acknowledge the fact that matrilineal succession rules continue to govern some aspects of rural land tenure in Lilongwe, and that a tenure system dominated by individual land titles was unlikely to emerge from applications for the partition of family land. The obvious reason for this is that the 1967 land-reform legislation . . . failed to break the strong [matrilineal] ties which exist between land and families.

Why did Malawians in the Lilongwe ADD balk? To many rural Malawians the network of *matrilineal social ties and obligations represented in landholding* makes sense, and they are not willing to compromise these ties in order to maximize production for the state. If land were to be individually held with only one person having ultimate control, these social ties would be rendered meaningless. Equally important, critical aspects of Chewa agrarian risk management based on taking advantage of parcels of land in different ecological niches would be lost by consolidating land into one holding. Finally, older women who controlled land were resistant to giving up their rights to this increasingly scarce resource. Not much headway was made with individual land registration in the 1970s or 1980s, and by the late 1980s the plan had basically been scrapped.

That individual land tenure will ensure improved production is debatable. As John Bruce (1993:38) has pointed out, individualized land tenure alone will not guarantee increased production. "If the freedom conferred by ownership is coupled with ignorance of proper land use practices and ecological stress, it provides only the opportunity to degrade the resource." He points to the American dust bowl as an example.

In Malawi women farmers depend on income earned from selling surplus from crops they cultivate on their own land, as do the women farmers in Milimo's (1986) study referred to earlier. Women with more resources cultivate and manage more food crops and are apt to include nonfood crops that have a market exchange value (Spring 1987, 1995; Hirshmann 1993b). As critical as land is, it cannot be utilized for production without labor. In the following sections I examine how labor recruitment and allocation of time at the household level have been affected by state-driven agricultural development since the countries in the region gained independence, using case studies from Zimbabwe and Malawi. I then move to the interstitial level between community and state in Mozambique and Zimbabwe to look at the way labor was recruited and allocated in two state cooperatives in the postindependence period.

The Allocation of Labor
During the Agricultural Cycle

It goes without saying that the recruitment and allocation of labor depends very much on the seasonal cycle. This cycle varies for different crops. Part of the ingenuity and adaptability of African farming systems is the repertoire of crops that are grown, either intercropped or monocropped, throughout the year. For instance, when the maize is ripening, another crop that requires more attention—say, millet, sorghum, or garden vegetables— may be planted. Peasants adjust the labor requirements for various crops according to their needs during the yearly cycle. I use maize, a staple crop, as an example for purposes of discussing labor allocation over a year's agricultural cycle.

For most of southern Africa the peak labor season occurs roughly between October and February, when fields must be cleared, brush burned and turned into the soil, and the land tilled and sowed with new seed. It is the most intensive labor period, yet the activities involved are mainly carried out by individual family units in uxorilocal households and by men and their wives with the possible assistance of younger male kin in virilocal households. This period usually coincides with the onset of the first rains in the region.

Once land has been cleared, prepared, and planted, weeding and hoeing become routine tasks that extend from January or February through April. In some places a second planting of maize is undertaken six weeks after the first (see Reynolds 1991). When the ears of maize have begun to form in May, members of a family often relocate to a temporary structure on a raised part of the land to keep rodents, monkeys, and birds away from the maturing crop until it has begun to harden and is ready for harvesting. Harvesting begins around the end of May or beginning of June and lasts into August. There is some overlap between maize and other crops; for example, maize is harvested before groundnuts or garden vegetables. Of course, seasonal fluctuations in rainfall, especially in drought years, influence this cyclical pattern. Maize is hauled back from the fields mainly by women and their children; if a cart is used, a man may also participate. The tedious task of storing and processing maize by removing the kernels from the cobs is undertaken almost exclusively by women. For other crops, such as beans, cow peas, and groundnuts, younger men may help in beating the dried plants to remove the pulses. Winnowing of crops such as sorghum, millet, and rice is carried out mainly by women.

Clearing the land, burning brush stubble, and turning it into the soil begin again in late August or early September on a leisurely basis and continue into October. This is the period when labor demand is at its lowest. This slack period allows household members time to repair houses and granaries or build new ones before the rains come in November. It also is a period when household members participate in kinwork such as initiations and weddings. Then tilling and mounding (or ridging) in preparation for sowing maize begins a new cycle. This cycle affects households in both uxorilocal and virilocal situations equally, but the way the labor demands for maize, or any other crop, are negotiated within these households often differs.

Labor Allocation in Uxorilocal Households in Southern Malawi

In this section I describe how women in one district in southern Malawi allocate family labor for the production of maize. State-driven agricultural projects that encourage women's collaborative production of cash-value crops are likely to be resisted among these women because they prefer individual production by household to collaborative production.

The majority of women in matrilineal, uxorilocal households in Zomba District, southern Malawi, are smallholder producers of local maize and, where they have adequate resources, hybrid maize. Zomba District is the fifth most densely populated district in the country with 171 persons per square kilometer (Government of Malawi 1987:1). On average, peasants have less than a hectare of land on which to grow maize as well as other crops such as groundnuts, beans, rice, and vegetables. Hybrid maize requires more inputs in terms of chemical fertilizers and pesticides than the local variety. The latter matures later in the growing season but has the advantage of being hard kerneled, drought resistant, and less perishable than hybrid maize. Peasant farmers in Zomba with a minimum of land (less than one-half hectare) grow primarily local maize for consumption and, when there is a surplus, may sell some. This was the case for 120 women farmers in Zomba District that I surveyed in 1992 (Davison 1993).[6]

Residing in their natal villages where they have married uxorilocally, Zomba women depend mainly on themselves, their husbands, and their children for labor. A secondary source is hired labor, particularly in jointly managed households (JMHs) where the husband was present. These women depend very little on collaborative labor and matrikin (see Table 6.1).

In my interviews of 120 female farmers, I found that 45 percent of the women headed their own households. This percentage is not unusual. A decade earlier, Hirschmann and Vaughan (1984) found that 45 percent of 70 female farmers in Zomba lived in FHHs, and a survey of 210 households in southern Zomba District carried out by Peters and Herrera (1989) revealed that 35 percent of the households were headed by women.[7] Of the 35 percent, 60 percent were de facto FHHs; the husband had either migrated to South Africa to take up wage work or was employed away from his village in Malawi and was absent over half the year. Those husbands who worked in South Africa sent higher remittances, and therefore these wives had the option of hiring labor to assist them (Peters and Herrera 1989). Wives whose husbands worked in Malawi had lower remittances with little to spare for hiring outside labor.[8]

Of the FHHs in my 1992 study, only 11 percent were de facto FHHs. Chipande (1987) argues that "fragile marriages," which Trivedy (1987) attributes to the "matrilineal system of land inheritance" and uxorilocality, contribute to male emigration in Malawi's Southern Region. Lack of security in land for out-marrying males, as well as increasing land scarcity, means that men are less willing to make a labor investment in *banja* (family hearthhold) production. They prefer wage labor as a more secure means of generating income and maintaining control over its distribution. However, this group was in the minority in the 1992 sample. In the majority of households (55 percent), husbands were present and the household was managed jointly by wife and husband.

In jointly managed households (JMHs), only 1.2 percent of total maize production was carried out by husbands alone; the figure for wives was nearly 30 percent. Wives and husbands working together accounted for 21 percent of the overall labor; children were responsible for nearly a quarter (23.9 percent) of the overall labor expended. Hired labor accounted for 13.2 percent of the total labor in maize production. Female relatives (sisters, 4.8 percent; mothers, 3.2 percent; and mothers-in-law, 1.9 percent) accounted for the majority of the remainder. Noteworthy here is that these matrilineal hearthholds depend little on recruiting matrilineal kin (sisters and mothers) for production even though they reside in the same village. By and large, *banja* hearthholds produce as a family unit. When they need to supplement household labor, hired labor is preferred.

In a time-allocation study of women in two Yao villages in Zomba District in 1991, Kaufulu (1992) found that only occasionally do sisters work together, usually during *kapale-pale*, the peak weeding season, and during harvesting. Most often women work alone with their children or

TABLE 6.1 Division of Labor in Maize Production in Zomba District, Malawi: 1992

| | | | | Percentage of Work Performed by: | | | | | |
Task	Woman	Husb.	WH	Childr.	Lab.	Sist.	Moth.	ML	Other
Land preparation	25.5	1.7	20.4	24.3	18.7	5.1	2.1	0.8	1.3
Planting	27.0	0.8	19.8	24.2	10.9	5.6	5.6	3.6	2.4
Weeding	27.1	0.9	22.5	25.2	18.5	3.7	0.9	0.9	0.4
Protecting crop	32.1	0.7	25.7	25.0	12.1	2.8	—	0.7	0.7
Harvesting	26.4	0.4	18.8	23.0	10.6	6.3	7.4	3.9	3.5
Storage	33.5	2.0	23.5	20.3	14.2	3.0	2.0	—	1.5
Seed selection	39.3	0.5	20.9	20.9	7.8	3.7	3.1	3.1	0.5
Fertilizing	25.1	2.1	20.2	27.2	11.9	7.4	0.8	0.8	2.5
Total percentage	29.0	1.2	21.1	23.9	13.2	4.8	3.2	1.9	1.8

Key: Woman = woman works alone; Husb. = husband alone; WH = woman and her husband together; Childr. = children help; Lab. = hired labor does work; Sist. = sister/s help; Moth. = mother helps; ML = mother-in-law helps; Other = others help.

Note: Based on interviews of 120 households in 14 rural villages in Zomba District, 1992.

they hire labor, usually young men, from outside their villages. A woman in her fifties said that women producers prefer to pay for labor rather than depending on matrilineal relatives because these same relatives might then make demands on their labor time. The female chief of one village remembered that families had at one time assisted one another during the harvest season in exchange for locally brewed beer. But this custom has since disappeared. Like the Bemba and Bisa in Geisler's study (Geisler, Keller, and Chuzu 1985), matrilineal women in Zomba prefer to avoid work parties that drain their resources and impose future obligations.

Another reason for preferring hired labor to matrikin was given by women in Kaufulu's study. She was told that a "competitive spirit" exists among women producers who now produce crops for cash as well as subsistence, and it is this competitive spirit that inhibits women from contributing to one another's profits in the form of a labor contribution. The women prefer to maximize their *own* profits by investing their labor on their own crops. The effect of crop commoditization and the need to produce cash income contribute to the preference for individual production among women who control the land they till and the income from its production.

Interviews with two women farmers in their seventies confirmed that women had rarely worked with female relatives in the past and that they depended most on the labor of their husbands and, more recently, their children. In informal observations of women working in their fields over a three-year period in Zomba and Machinga Districts, I rarely found instances of women working collaboratively with other women.

Tensions between sisters and other female relatives in a matrilineage may stem from competition over land. Pauline Peters, in a follow-up study to her 1987 survey, related that with increasing land scarcity in southern Zomba District, sisters who controlled adjacent plots of land in one village were experiencing conflicts over who would inherit which piece of land from the grandmother (Peters, personal communication, 1991). As land fertility dwindles due to soil depletion and overcultivation, control of the most fertile portions of a finite communal parcel becomes an issue. The daughter of a woman farmer in a Yao village related that her older married sisters had been given most of her mother's land. Her father had been forced to go to the chief of a neighboring village to ask for a parcel of land close to her mother's for the two younger, unmarried daughters. As less land is available, younger women may be forced to migrate elsewhere or seek employment in towns.

If we look more closely at Table 6.1, we find that women participate in all labor tasks related to maize production. Of the women who prepared land themselves without benefit of a husband's labor, however, nearly three-quarters were women who headed their own households.

Consequently, it is important to consider the added burdens in labor allocation that fall on the shoulders of FHHs without the financial resources to hire labor.

Even though husbands in JMHs were responsible for only 1.7 percent of the labor in land preparation, a greater proportion of their time was spent on fertilizing and storing maize. Children also spent the largest proportion of their labor time in fertilizing maize. In these smallholder hearthholds, fertilizing means hauling manure from a cattle corral to the plants, spreading it at the base, and working it into the soil. It is a labor-intensive task that family members share fairly equally, assisted to some extent by the wife's sisters.

Hired labor is used seasonally for the most physically taxing tasks—land preparation, weeding, crop protection, fertilizing, and storage—for several days at a time. In Malawi it is referred to as *ganyu,* denoting its temporary nature.

Seed selection is a task that involves decisionmaking at the household level. Notably, women farmers, usually on their own and in some cases with female matrikin, select the maize seed. In 20 percent of cases they select it with the assistance of husbands and children. Thus the labor involved in making judgments about the quality of seed and sorting it, as well as other labor allocation in Zomba's villages, depends on the task as well as the gender, age, and experience of the cultivator.

In a study of household decisionmaking in a matrilineal Chewa village in eastern Zambia, Skjønsberg found that husbands and wives in seven out of nine households—where both resided and were interviewed separately—responded differently when they were asked who makes agricultural decisions about when to clear new land, what crops to plant, how to cultivate, when to plant and harvest, and what to sell. In only two cases did the couple agree as to who made the decisions: the wife, the husband, or both (1989:216). Five of the wives thought they made most of the decisions, and two said that they and their husbands together made most of the decisions. Two of the husbands agreed with their wives that the wives made most of the decisions—these were husbands who were absent for much of the time. Two husbands thought they and their wives made decisions together (in one case the wife agreed and in the other she thought she made most of the decisions). Three husbands thought they made most of the decisions. One of the men's wives thought the couple made the decisions together and the other two wives thought *they* made the decisions. Even though the sample is small, it illustrates the liabilities of asking only one member of a household, male or female, about decisionmaking related to production.

What these case studies of labor allocation in uxorilocal situations illustrate is that in the late twentieth century, production is carried out by a wife and husband together in most cases, and when the husband is absent, the work falls on the shoulders of the wife. Children's role in production varies, with those not in school carrying a greater burden. Studies vary on the significance of matrikin in labor recruitment and allocation. Some, such as mine, Milimo's (1986), and Reynolds's (1991), reveal that matrikin are little used; others relate that matrikin continue to be an important factor for some households (Stromgaard 1985; Pitcher 1993; Moore and Vaughan 1994).

Southern Malawian female landholders' preference for working with their husbands as opposed to working with matrikin or other women has implications for development. In the 1980s, the state, prodded by bilateral and multilateral development agencies (the United Nations Children's Fund [UNICEF], ODA, the Food and Agriculture Organization [FAO]), attempted to cajole peasant women into joining agricultural cooperatives to increase production. It met with little success in central and southern Malawi because women preferred to allocate their own labor rather than working with other women. They also wanted to control the income generated from cash-crop production.

In 1990 the Ministry of Agriculture initiated a survey of 1,026 smallholder households in Malawi that included both jointly managed and female-headed households to find out their opinions about participation in income-generating activities, or IGAs (Culler, Patterson, and Matenje 1990). The study found that 59 percent had at some time been involved in an IGA project but only 25 percent were still involved in 1990. Of the projects mentioned, 62 percent were for crop production. When asked which type of IGA they most preferred—individual, family, or group—50 percent of women in the FHHs surveyed said they preferred individually operated IGAs, 44 percent of the JMHs preferred those that were family operated, and only a small minority in either category preferred group IGAs. These results indicated that smallholder producers (female and male in this survey) *least* preferred group production even when income was being generated. The findings confirmed that smallholders in Malawi have a preference for individual or family-based production over collaborative production, a point I will come back to in Chapter 7 in discussions on the role of donor agencies.

Allocating Labor in a Virilocal Context: Zimbabwe

One of the problems in analyzing data for labor allocation in households where residence is virilocal is that many studies carried out in the 1970s and even the 1980s did not disaggregate the division of labor in agricultural production by the gender of the *cultivator*. It was assumed that the head of household (male) was also responsible for production. Increasingly, data have been disaggregated by gender of the household head (MHH or FHH). What this leaves out, however, is the labor of a wife or wives, in the case of MHHs, and the labor of children. The tendency to leave out wives is particularly true for studies carried out in Zimbabwe, where it often is assumed that households are headed by males, whether these households are located in communal areas or in resettlement areas, and that the male head is the person responsible for production (see Pankhurst and Jacobs 1988 for a critique). Exceptions to this pattern are two studies. One was carried out in the early 1980s in a communal area, three resettlement areas, and two small-scale commercial farming areas where maize was the primary crop grown in all except one of the resettlement areas (Mazur 1985). The other was a village study carried out in one Tonga community in the late 1980s (Reynolds 1991). Mazur's study disaggregated data for labor allocation of those in residence in a household not only by gender but by age. The in-depth study of a Tonga community by Reynolds disaggregated not only adult cultivators in each household by gender but children who assisted their parents. I limit my discussion to Mazur's study.

In many areas of Zimbabwe, including the areas where Mazur worked, the household head is an absentee producer. The majority of agricultural laborers in communal and resettlement areas are women (wives, daughters, widows, single women), as men are absent much of the time working as wage laborers in mines, in urban areas, or on commercial farms (Mazur 1985; Pankhurst and Jacobs 1988; Truscott 1989). The Government of Zimbabwe (1991) estimates that male farmers in communal areas account for less than 39 percent of the total number of farmers, and of the 39 percent, most are men below the age of 25 and over 46 (Government of Zimbabwe 1991:Annex 3, 6). In Mazur's study, households with male emigrants constituted 63 percent of the total; the figure was as high as 82 percent for households with six acres of land or less (Mazur 1985:Table 8, n.p.). Differences exist among households in the communal areas. Households with fewer resources, including land, are forced to use strategies such as emigration for employment to ensure that their members survive.

One of the impacts of development has been the state's enthusiasm for resettlement schemes where the goal is to increase the production of cash-value crops while easing pressure on land in more densely populated areas. Studies by Mazur (1985) and Zwart (1990) illustrate the way Shona peasants in communal and resettlement areas allocated labor responsibilities in two different periods in the 1980s.

The Zimbabwean state at independence set aside land for resettlement schemes for the production of cash-value crops. The goal was to compensate Africans who had lost their land during the colonial period and to entice peasants from the increasingly crowded communal areas to resettle in areas where land was more available for development. Much of the land had come from the redistribution of commercial land formerly owned by white farmers. In contrast to the communal areas, land tenure in the resettlement areas is individualized, with each owner's parcel being registered. Parcels in the resettlement schemes were mainly awarded to MHHs except in cases where a woman was single or widowed and headed her own household. Male farmers, and many of their wives (Zwart 1990), in resettlement areas became members of farmers' groups.

In Mazur's household survey (1985) of the communal area of Madziwa, he found that labor allocation for some tasks challenged gender assumptions or stereotypes. For the youngest category of residents who participated in agricultural labor (those under nine years), 14 percent of boys and 16 percent of girls were involved in clearing land (see Table 6.2).

For youth in residence, he found a similar situation. Seventy-one percent of males aged ten to nineteen cleared land; 78 percent of females in the same age category cleared land. The same difference existed for males and females in their twenties: Eighty-three percent of males and 90 percent of females engaged in this activity. Only in the older age categories (ages thirty to forty-four and over forty-five) did the frequency of men's participation in clearing land exceed that of women. Thus the assumption that clearing land is more apt to be a "male task" is accurate in Madziwa only for producers thirty years old and above.

For the two resettlement areas, Nacala and Bemberi, the situation is somewhat similar in Nacala and different in Bemberi except for the youngest age group. In Nacala, girls and women are even more frequently involved in clearing land than their male counterparts in the same age groups until they reach the age of over forty-five, perhaps because, as in Madziwa, the major crop is maize. In Bemberi, male youth (ages ten to nineteen) are more frequently involved than female youth, and the pattern continues until the last two age groups, in which both sexes are equally involved (Table 6.2). In this resettlement area, half the land is planted in maize, roughly 40 percent is planted in cotton, and 8 percent is tobacco (Mazur 1985:Graph 1, n.p.). This may account for the greater frequency of male participation.

Next I look at another task identified as "male"—plowing. Again, in the communal area, females participate more often than men except for the two oldest age groups (thirty to forty-four and over forty-five). This is also true for the Nacala resettlement area, where over 60 percent of the land tilled is planted in maize (Mazur 1985:Graph 1, n.p.). The situation is similar in Bemberi, except that 92 percent of male youths and 84 percent of female youths handle the plowing. It appears, then, that where maize is the major crop grown, females under thirty more frequently handle tasks re-

TABLE 6.2 Participation Rates in Agricultural Tasks by Gender and Age: Comparison of Communal and Resettlement Areas in Zimbabwe

	Madziwa (Communal)										Nacala (Resettlement)										Bemberi (Resettlement)									
	0–9		10–19		20–29		30–44		45+		0–9		10–19		20–29		30–44		45+		0–9		10–19		20–29		30–44		45+	
	M	F	M	F	M	F	M	F	M	F	M	F	M	F	M	F	M	F	M	F	M	F	M	F	M	F	M	F	M	F
Agricultural task																														
Clearing land	14	16	71	78	83	90	94	88	94	60	3	14	76	92	67	95	90	92	100	81	12	16	96	84	86	92	100	100	100	100
Plowing	14	16	71	73	89	93	100	88	97	60	3	14	71	89	67	95	90	92	100	81	12	16	92	84	86	96	100	100	100	100
Planting	13	16	80	85	89	93	100	88	97	65	3	14	76	86	67	95	90	92	100	81	12	16	96	84	86	96	100	100	100	100
Weeding	12	15	82	85	89	90	100	86	97	65	3	14	76	86	67	95	90	92	100	81	12	16	96	84	86	96	100	100	100	100
Harvesting	12	13	80	81	89	87	100	88	97	60	3	14	76	86	67	84	90	85	100	81	12	16	96	84	86	96	100	100	100	100
Marketing	5	3	16	15	17	30	94	30	97	35	0	6	14	11	33	11	70	15	94	25	5	4	4	3	29	16	100	45	70	22
Tending cattle	25	25	48	45	17	30	67	35	59	30	30	19	10	25	0	21	30	8	11	6	37	30	28	29	14	24	47	40	50	22
Number of individuals in age group	84	88	79	80	18	30	18	43	32	20	40	36	21	36	3	19	10	13	18	16	59	50	25	31	7	25	17	20	10	9

SOURCE: Compiled from Mazur 1985, Tables 5 and 6.

lated to preparing the land for planting than do males under thirty. Thus age is a factor in determining gender allocation of tasks.

Weeding is often identified with women, and to a lesser degree, children. In Madziwa, girls and female youth are slightly more involved in weeding than boys and male youth, a gender allocation that continues through the twenties. However, in the group spanning thirty to forty-four years of age, the figures are 100 percent for men and only 86 percent for women. In the Nacala resettlement area, girls and female youth through their twenties are more apt to weed than their male counterparts. However, between the ages of thirty and forty-four, men and women are about equally involved. In the oldest group, as in Madziwa, men are more involved than women. The differences are roughly the same for Bemberi, with the exception of the two oldest age groups. In these two groups, all are involved in weeding regardless of gender. As with the tasks of clearing land and plowing, we cannot assume gender differences in the allocation of labor for weeding. Mazur's study reminds us that the age of household members is as important as the crop being produced in determining labor allocation by gender.

In Zwart's study (1990) carried out in a resettlement area in Mashonaland, he found that most of the men, in whose name the land was registered, were, in fact, absentee farmers. Their wives managed many of the farm operations and attended the farmers' group meetings.[9] As a result, Zwart interviewed mostly wives whose husbands were absent and a few women heading their own households. These women were equally involved in subsistence crop and cash-value crop production. Table 6.3 demonstrates how labor for cash-value crops (hybrid maize, cotton, and sunflower seeds) was allocated in MHHs in comparison to subsistence crops including sorghum, groundnuts, and vegetable.

Unfortunately, the study does not give the percentage of time spent on each task, nor does it disaggregate the data by age; but it does demonstrate that in this resettlement area a husband spends little time in labor related to cash-value crop production other than tasks that have to do with technological inputs (plowing and pest control). The labor he provides in subsistence crop production is carried out with his wife and includes specific tasks at the beginning of the cycle and threshing when the crops have been harvested. Thus his labor is limited to very specific points in the agricultural cycle and to very specific tasks. The wife, working on her own, provides most of the labor for cash-value crop production. And she is responsible with her children for producing subsistence crops. *Nhimbe* (work party) labor, which is historically connected to subsistence production, is used only for the most labor-intensive tasks and is not provided for cash-crop production. Compensation for *nhimbe* takes the form of food and beer. Commoditized production does not have a cultural history in the area. Labor contributed toward cash-crop production assists only the

TABLE 6.3   Division of Labor for Cash-Value and Subsistence Crops in
                 One Resettlement Area in Zimbabwe

	Cash-Value Crops		Subsistence Crops			
Task	Husband Only	Wife Only	H/W	H/W/Ch.	W/Ch.	Nhimbe
Land cleaning	x	—	x	—	—	—
Plowing	x	—	—	—	—	—
Hoeing	—	x	x	x	x	—
Planting and first fertilizer application	—	x	—	—	x	—
Weeding	—	—	—	x	x	x
Fertilizer application	—	x	—	—	—	—
Pest control (spray)	x	—	—	—	—	—
Harvesting	—	x	—	x	—	x
Threshing and shelling	—	x	x	—	—	x
Winnowing	—	x	—	—	—	—
Transport to market	x (oxcart)	x (headload)	—	—	—	—

Note: H/W = husband and wife; H/W/Ch. = husband, wife, and children;
W/Ch. = wife and children; Nhimbe = collaborative with neighbors, relatives
SOURCE: Adapted from Zwart 1990:6.

MHH, as the ultimate producer of the crop, rather than a wider circle including family and patrikin. An absentee producer depends mainly on the labor of his wife or wives for the production of crops from which he earns income.

Overall, Zwart (1990:7) found that women and children contributed 80 percent of the labor required for all farm-related tasks, including household maintenance. He did not indicate whether hired labor was used. It may be that MHHs with more resources were able to hire labor seasonally and that those with few resources, wives and their children when they were not in school, provided the bulk of the labor for both types of production.

That labor for agricultural production in Zimbabwe's patrilineal, virilocal households is carried out largely by wives and their children of both sexes, with some seasonal assistance from work parties, has been recognized by the state (Government of Zimbabwe 1991:20). The introduction of labor-saving technologies for women in rural areas has been suggested, but implementation has been slow. Two other issues equally plague women farmers and preclude their advancement. One relates to lineage ideology. Women in communal areas are especially disadvantaged because, as the state acknowledges, "traditional communal property rights and inheritance systems based on patrilineal kinship ties severely restrict women's abilities to capture productive resources" (Government of Zimbabwe 1991:Annex 3, 7). In other words, lack of direct access to land and the patrilineal practice of bequeathing property to patrikin rather than to a widow act as tangible obstacles to these rural women's economic development. The situation is little better for women in resettlement areas, as in most cases husbands hold title to land. In its Framework for Economic Reform, the Government of Zimbabwe indicated that ways to improve women's access to land needed to be included in the next development planning phase (1991:20).

The other issue that concerns women farmers is control over income. When a male producer is married and the head of a household, he controls income from sales of cash-value crops in which a wife or wives invested their labor. He is likely to invest the income from production without his wife's consultation (Pankhurst and Jacobs 1988). Only when a surplus is realized from subsistence crops may a wife sell the surplus and keep the income. Of course, for female-headed households the script is different; women have less access to improved seeds, fertilizer, and a plow but more control over the proceeds. It is clear that the gendered state of Zimbabwe has not adequately addressed the needs of women as wives in MHHs. Nor has it addressed the needs of youth and children. Patriarchy goes back to precolonial times in Zimbabwe (May 1983; Pankhurst 1988; Gaidzanwa 1992; Kriger 1992) and was reinforced in the colonial period; thus it cannot be reversed in a single decade. It persists in the postcolonial period and is reflected in the state's attitude toward agrarian reform and development, as these case studies have demonstrated.

Access to Labor-Saving Equipment

Women throughout the region have been neglected in development schemes in which technological inputs were directed at male farmers. In the 1960s and 1970s very few female farmers were targeted as beneficiaries, as the case studies from Zambia demonstrated. Often these state schemes included access to labor-saving equipment that benefited Zambian men's production and reduced their labor. Included were plows, pesticide sprayers, harrows, and other equipment. Although some Zambian women did use plows, they usually did so with the permission of a husband or in the husband's absence. Very few female-headed households had access to plows or other labor-saving equipment. Access to plows is still a problem for Zambian women.

The situation may be the reverse in Zimbabwe, if Mazur's survey (1985) is any indication. By the first part of the 1980s, girls and women were using plows as much as if not more frequently than boys and men in at least one communal area and two resettlement areas. What these cases point out is that it is necessary to take into account the country and location in making conclusions about gendered use of certain equipment and technologies.

In Zambia and Malawi, reforms of the postcolonial state were based on goals of privatizing land and maximizing production through progressive-farmer schemes. In Zimbabwe and Mozambique, improved production was sought through cooperative schemes based on a theoretical socialist model.

Cooperative Production and Gender in Mozambique and Zimbabwe

At the beginning of this chapter I referred to socialist transformation in Mozambique as a way of restructuring gender relations among employees on state farms. Women were brought into the wage sector as equals for the first time and received training in what were formerly considered to be male occupations, including the operation of mechanized equipment such as tractors. In so doing, some women made headway in meeting their strategic gender needs, that is, those needs that relate directly to overcoming gender inequities that act as constraints to women's (or men's) social and economic advancement in a particular society (see Moser 1989). Collective production was one strategy used by the FRELIMO government in Mozambique to transform gender productive relations. Another strategy was participation in producer cooperatives that targeted both sexes as beneficiaries. Zimbabwe, partially influenced by Mozambique's socialist experiment, also encouraged cooperatives in the 1980s. In this section I compare two agricultural cooperatives, one in Mozambique and the other in Zimbabwe, launched in the 1980s. The intent is to analyze the extent to which gender inequities in productive relations were overcome. The key indicators are (1) equity in organization, leadership, and decisionmaking; (2) equity in productive and reproductive labor; and (3) equity in access to and use of labor-saving equipment. Land was not an issue in either case, as the land for each cooperative had been abandoned or sold by former colonials and was appropriated for production by the state. The two cooperatives are the Seventh-of-April Cooperative in Dondo District (Sofala Province) in central Mozambique, and Cooperative A, a mixed-gender agricultural cooperative for former combatants in central Zimbabwe (see Smith 1985).[10] In both cooperatives women outnumbered men.

Seventh-of-April Cooperative

Cooperatives imply that the producers own the means of production and share equally in the benefits of production. Given this working definition, the Seventh-of-April Cooperative, named for the anniversary of the death of revolutionary heroine Josina Machel, fits the description. The first and most established of eight cooperatives in Dondo District, Seventh-of-April was formed in 1979. At that time some of its members were living on the land that was to be designated by the state for the cooperative. Most of the eighty-seven hectares in this agricultural cooperative were irrigated. Some peasant families who had lived there previously when the land was held by Portuguese owners still resided there. Others had their own family farms four to five hectares away. The cooperative had an established infrastructure with a small administrative building, a large concrete storage building, and a thatched "store" where cooperative members sold their produce. The cooperative also had a truck that transported its garden vegetables to the administrative center at Dondo. Therefore, in 1986 it was better off than other cooperatives in the region, which were just being initiated in the mid-1980s. In a region that experienced constant harassment from Renamo forces, the Seventh-of-April Cooperative also had managed to escape much of the destruction aimed at producer cooperatives as part of the Mozambican National Resistance's destabilization campaign against the FRELIMO government.

As of late 1986, the cooperative had 117 members, 89 women and 28 men. Many of the women's husbands had wage jobs in the town of Dondo and returned home only on weekends or holidays. The cooperative was run by a directorate composed of four men and three women who were elected by the cooperative's members. The directorate planned the work and production schedules, including what to plant, when to plant, and when to harvest.

The cooperative owned a diesel-operated pump that carried water during the dry season from a small lake adjacent to the cooperative's vegetable fields. The water ran through rubber hoses to large metal sprinklers situated at strategic points above several fields. Fuel to operate the pump came from the sale of the cooperative's garden vegetables, including onions, carrots, lettuce, eggplant, and red peppers. In addition, the cooperative had a large block of land planted in rice that it sold locally. In other blocks maize and cassava were grown for members' consumption.

Enough vegetables and grains were produced in 1986 to feed all members' families. The surplus of crops such as maize, rice, and beans were stored in a large covered concrete storage building containing huge, high-walled concrete bins at one end.

In 1986 the cooperative's members "paid" themselves in produce, planning to pay themselves small cash wages by 1988. Members formed two work brigades that operated four-day alternating shifts (Monday through Thursday, Wednesday through Saturday). The brigade took a midday two-hour break for literacy training and resumed work until 5:00 P.M. The four-day shifts allowed women, in particular, time to cultivate their own family gardens and carry out household maintenance tasks.

Members of both sexes, in individual and group interviews, agreed that their economic circumstances had improved since joining the cooperative. Testified one woman, "When we work together it makes life easier. If we are working alone as a family and the harvest fails, we have a problem. But here we work together and nobody suffers. We divide the harvest and if we want vegetables we can buy them from our store" (Davison 1987:11).

Though cooperative production had proved beneficial to both sexes, several younger women complained that Seventh-of-April had no crèche, or childcare center. Such centers exist in many workplaces in Mozambique, especially in urban areas, but had yet to be incorporated into agricultural cooperatives in the mid-1980s. As of 1986, the group's members had a total of 128 small children, and many younger females were observed carrying babies on their backs while working in the fields. Although males were willing to share productive tasks, reproductive tasks such as childcare remained largely the responsibility of female members. Their childcare needs, then, remained secondary to other needs directly related to agricultural production.

To what extent were gender inequities overcome by the cooperative scheme? In terms of leadership and decisionmaking, near parity was achieved in the gender composition of the directorate that made decisions for the group. Nonetheless, one female member admitted that the men were more likely to do the talking. In terms of access to literacy, which is often identified with leadership and has an empowering effect, both sexes had equal opportunity to learn reading, writing, and arithmetic. A male government assistant helped them to "keep their books."

Both qualitatively and quantitatively, women's productive roles were redefined by their participation in the cooperative with the result that they approached equality with men. Previously women had done the bulk of the labor with few incentives for improved production and little opportunity to make decisions about cash-crop production. Nor did they have much control over the benefits of production except from what they raised in their own gardens. In the cooperative both sexes shared equally the agricultural tasks related to clearing, planting, weeding, harvesting, and irrigation. However, men more often assumed tasks associated with the operation of mechanized equipment such as the irrigation pump, the tractor, and the truck. Consequently, men had more control over labor-saving equipment, including its maintenance. The directive established in state farms that women should have equal access to operating mechanized equipment had not "trickled out" to rural cooperatives in Dondo District.

Despite women's parallel roles in the cooperative and on their family farms, they continued to bear major responsibilities for cooking, childcare, and home maintenance. In the mid-1980s (and even in the early 1990s), Mozambican men showed little interest in taking over some of the reproductive tasks in order to lighten women's dual burden. We can conclude, then, that although parity had been gained in production, it had yet to be gained in reproduction.

Cooperative A in Zimbabwe

In Zimbabwe, producer cooperatives became a cornerstone of the state's "socialist development" in the early 1980s. By 1983, there were 119 agricultural cooperatives throughout Zimbabwe, with only those in resettlement schemes being government funded. The state-sponsored cooperatives in resettlement schemes catered to resource-poor, often landless, peasants. There were thirty such cooperatives by September 1983 occupying 66,775 hectares of land with 2,646 members (Smith 1985:7–8).

Cooperative A is a state-sponsored cooperative in one of the resettlement areas. It was initiated in 1981, one year after Zimbabwe's independence. Its primary purpose was to provide former combatants—those who had fought in the liberation struggle—with a livelihood. The cooperative encompasses 1,800 hectares of semiarid land. It largely served Shona-speaking men and women and their families, although ethnicity was not a criterion for membership.

Four criteria are used in Zimbabwe to distinguish cooperatives from other forms of production: (1) common ownership of productive resources; (2) voluntary membership; (3) democratic control; and (4) neutrality in race, gender, religion, and "political issues" (Smith 1985:5). Cooperative A began with 150 members—90 women and 60 men—who lived in communal housing on the cooperative. By 1985, its membership had dropped to 55—27 women and 28 men (8). The drop in membership was partly due to the communal living arrangements and partly to problems in decisionmaking.

Husbands and wives became separate members in the cooperative, each with his or her own vote in electing the committee that made major policy decisions concerning the cooperative. Over the first four years of the policy committee's existence (1981–1985) all offices with the exception of the deputy secretary and the treasurer were held by men. The treasurer's job was held by women between 1982 and 1985 (Smith 1985:42). Of the twenty-five administrative positions in the cooperative, only six were held by women. The farm manager and his deputy were both males, and of the five assistant managers, only one was a woman—the assistant manager responsible for the communal kitchen and health services. There also was a female welfare officer attached to the cooperative. When asked why more women were not in administrative positions, both sexes said that women were "less informed" (1985:38).

In Cooperative A, gender-neutral work teams were established for agricultural tasks. The teams were headed by men, but everyone, regardless of sex, carried out tasks related to cultivation and irrigation, and men were observed doing the weeding in the vegetable gardens, a task formerly considered to be a woman's job (Smith 1985:35). When men and women were asked about the gender division of labor, however, men were less apt to think of women doing the same jobs that men did and could not envisage women plowing, digging trenches, or working in a piggery; women had a much broader vision of what they could do.

Women with babies usually arrived late for their work shifts in the fields and left about thirty minutes early. They also took longer rest periods (Smith 1985:36). However, they were not penalized for their time spent in reproductive tasks. Often when children were weaned, members sent them to relatives. Childcare, as in the Mozambican cooperative, was a major addition to women's workload. Smith also observed that women with children spent more time on laundry and that women with husbands did their husbands' laundry without help from the men (1985:37).

Men and women gained equal access to most resources, and food and medical services were paid for by the state. In addition, each cooperative member was paid an allowance of Z$30 per month (in 1985 Zimdollars) on an equal basis (Smith 1985:39). Women got a three-month maternity leave with the allowance continuing during that time. Men, however, more often got access to managerial and technical training, whereas women received training in domestic crafts and secretarial skills—a gender stereotype that was not alleviated by the cooperative despite the intention to provide equal opportunities for both sexes.

Women's access to labor-saving equipment was more constrained than men's. They were found less often driving or maintaining tractors or handling plows, working on electrical equipment, or driving trucks. However, they did learn how to use a fuel-operated range and to operate a manual typewriter in the process of learning "office work." That women learned skills to operate labor-saving equipment identified with "women's work" is indicative of the persistence of Zimbabwe's gender division of labor despite attempts at restructuring through cooperative production.

In the two cooperatives just discussed, women and men became individual, independent members of the cooperative regardless of marital status. The ability to act as independent agents gave women as wives more autonomy than Zambia's maize schemes or Zimbabwe's resettlement schemes, which targeted individual male progressive farmers. Men and women participated in the governance of the cooperatives in Mozambique and Zimbabwe, but in the Mozambican case men spoke up more frequently in the decisionmaking process and in Zimbabwe they held most of the major leadership positions and were presumably vocal in those positions. Accordingly, although women were brought into the decisionmaking process, their participation was more symbolic than real because men continued to do most of the talking that led to decisions.

Gender roles in agricultural production were restructured through state intervention so that men and women performed the same tasks, including weeding and hauling water in both cooperatives. However, men were more apt to operate labor-saving farm equipment, especially if it was mechanized. In the cooperative in Mozambique, women rarely operated the irrigation pump, tractor, or truck. In Zimbabwe's Cooperative A the scenario was the same: Women less often drove or maintained the tractors, plows, trucks, and electrical equipment. At the same time women were encouraged to operate a range and a manual typewriter—equipment identified with female labor.

Even though some progress was made toward equalizing gender productive labor, women remained largely responsible for reproductive tasks, including laundry, cooking, and childcare. The dual burden associated with combining productive and reproductive roles was not addressed except to allow women with infants additional time to care for them. Consequently, the need to relieve women of some of their reproductive labor went unmet in both cooperatives. That Zimbabwean women's needs in this area were not being sufficiently addressed may in part account for the sharp drop in female cooperative members between 1981 and 1985—from 90 to 27 (60 percent).

Gender inequities in rural production schemes sponsored by the state and its apparatus remain remarkably persistent regardless of the mode of production. Contributing to this intransigence are legacies of male privilege and preference in the state and its bureaucracies that transcend both capitalist and socialist economic systems (Staudt 1990:5). The case studies of maize schemes in Zambia and Malawi and the producer cooperatives in Mozambique and Zimbabwe illustrate where productive and reproductive relations are most resistant to change. As long as the state at all levels— from the local development or cooperative committee to the planning officers in agriculture ministries—continues to be gendered male, equity in production and reproduction will lag, to the detriment of a nation's overall development.

When we look at the majority of southern African societies that subscribe to patrilineal ideology and practice virilocality in the late twentieth century, it is tempting to reach conclusions about gendered relations of production that then are applied to other societies in the region: Men control land and they control the labor that works that land. It is an assumption of male authority that persists in many state-sponsored agricultural development schemes. However, if one shifts to a predominantly matrilineal context where uxorilocality is the rule, as it is in much of Malawi and northern Mozambique, assumptions about gendered productive relations begin to fall away. Control over land and gender relations of production, as this chapter has demonstrated, are ordered differently in groups practicing matriliny and uxorilocality in the late twentieth century. Lineage and residence do make a difference (see also Arnfred 1988; Peters 1994; Crehan 1994; Pitcher 1995). As the matrilineal script is "foreign" to European and Western norms, it is discounted or given as a reason for holding back progress. It becomes a "problem" for agricultural development agents alarmed by Africa's lagging production, as Okoth-Ogendo (1993) astutely observes. In some cases it becomes equated with "traditionalism" or "false consciousness," as happened in postcolonial Mozambique (Pitcher 1995). Those subscribing to matriliny become the "other," juxtaposed in ideology and practice to the majority subscribing to patriliny. In a sense, subscribing to matriliny is similar to being left-handed in a right-handed world, but with economic consequences.

Watching from the wings, but very active in their pursuit of particular development agendas in each newly emerging southern African country, have been the multilateral and bilateral donor agencies. In Chapter 7, I take up the role of these agencies in shaping women's chances for gender empowerment in central southern Africa.

Notes

1. Moore and Vaughan (1994:210–211) make a similar point for upwardly mobile Bemba male farmers in Northern Province; land registration and entitlement provide a means for hybrid maize farmers, many of them migrant labor returnees, to ensure that an individual, usually a son or individual sons, will inherit their land rather than their matrikin.

2. The extent to which women may lose control over critical resources and decisionmaking in agricultural schemes has been documented for other matrilineal groups in Zambia. See Milimo (1986), Sharpe (1990), Moore and Vaughan (1994), Crehan (1994), and Jiggins et al. (1995). For Malawi see Spring (1983, 1995), Chipande (1987), Peters and Herrera (1989), and Kachapila (1992). For northern Mozambique see Arnfred (1988) and Pitcher (1995). And for the Mandinka in the Gambia see Dey (1982), Carney (1988), and Carney and Watts (1991).

3. Wives in the two areas Milimo surveyed most often removed stumps and burned and prepared land for maize cultivation with their husbands on the husbands' land (25.8 percent). In 20.6 percent of cases a wife carried out these tasks herself, usually on her own land (Milimo 1986:130). In only 6.4 percent of cases did husbands carry out such tasks themselves. A similar disparity emerged for other tasks related to maize production, including hoeing, plowing, planting, weeding, fertilizing, and harvesting. Taken together, they illustrate the critical role that wives played in hybrid maize production in these areas.

4. Pitcher (1995) demonstrates that in the late 1970s and 1980s the Mozambican state under FRELIMO undertook similar male-focused schemes for the production of cotton in Nampula, where matriliny predominates, with similar consequences for women. Most of these women "dropped out," preferring to work on their own farms.

5. A similar situation exists in Zambia, where female-headed households were 33 percent of the total households in 1980 (Geisler et al. 1985:7) and continue to be a significant proportion—as high as 60 percent of all households in some of the more remote, least advantaged districts (Jiggins et al. 1995:18).

6. The material in this section previously has been published in two articles and a book chapter (Davison 1992, 1993, 1995). I am grateful for permission to use this material.

7. Roughly 34 percent of Malawi's households are headed by females. The southern region has the highest percentage, followed by the central region.

8. It important to realize that the resources and labor needs of women in FHHs, MHHs (male-headed households), and JMHs (jointly managed households) differ. It is equally important to disaggregate the category of female-headed households not just by those who are single or widowed and those whose husbands are absent but within these categories, as suggested here. For a discussion of differentiating FHHs, see Peters (1995).

9. Over 50 percent of Zimbabwe's rural women belong to farmers' groups. One of the reasons given for joining is that women have an equal vote in decisions, more influence than they wield in their patrilineal households (Truscott 1989; Zwart 1990:12).

10. The data for the Mozambican case come from the author's research in 1986 (see Davison 1987, 1988b), and the data for Zimbabwe's Cooperative A comes from a study carried out by Zimbabwean Sheila Smith of four cooperatives in that country (Smith 1985).

7

Women's Empowerment: From Grassroots Organizations to International Policy Forums

In the few decades since achieving independence, the states of the Zambezi region have experienced increasing dependence on donor aid to achieve their postcolonial development goals. "Whether by choice or by default, states assume a lead role in aggregating the resources and hiring the technical expertise to help plan, regulate, or manage the development process. . . . Yet capital and technical resources are often in short supply," observes Kathleen Staudt (1990:5). To overcome the shortfall, these states have turned to the bilateral and multilateral agencies for assistance. In so doing, as Staudt points out, "they incur various costs or conditions, ranging from, most obviously, interest on loans to policy reform, expatriate personnel, external agency or PVO priorities, and other ideological baggage" (1990:5). That the international development community, including multilateral agencies, bilateral agencies, and nongovernmental organizations (NGOs), has had a hand in shaping the way development is envisaged and practiced in the four countries in this study is beyond question. The priorities, costs, and conditions of development as they affect gender relations are the subject of this chapter.

Development as a process historically has been gendered male; this is because men within development organizations and major donor agencies have dominated the thinking and knowledge disseminated about development, just as they have held the key decisionmaking positions in these organizations that influence the way development is conceived. This does not mean that all men have ignored the significance of gender to development, but it does mean that until the last decade of the twentieth century gender has been treated as a peripheral issue—and it still is in some donor agencies (Kardam 1990). The discourse on gender is muzzled partly because of the persisting belief that development is somehow "neutral" and partly because recognizing issues related to the gender distribution of power, wealth, and control of resources, including those within the agencies, would mean profound structural adjustments in the way donor agencies do business (Staudt 1990; Kardam 1990).

Approaches to Development in the 1980s

Two approaches to development characterized the activities of donor agencies in the 1980s. One was the efficiency/effectiveness approach and the other was an empowerment approach arising out of the work of Third World women (Moser 1989, 1993). Both have influenced development debates in the four states that include the Zambezi region.

Structural Adjustment
and the Efficiency Approach

The deterioration of African economies due to a number of factors that included escalating oil prices and declining foreign exchange earnings coupled with decreased revenue and shifting commodity prices led to changes in economic policies that affected development thinking. Stabilization and structural adjustment policies (SAPs) were initiated by the International Monetary Fund (IMF) and World Bank and adopted by African states in order not to lose their funding. The development donor community supported the new austerity measures, emphasizing efficiency and effectiveness in their programs and projects.

An infusion of foreign exchange and increased agricultural prices, along with improved marketing policies, enforced devaluation of currencies, and the imposition of constraints on state spending (usually at a cost to state-provided social services) were SAP measures taken to prevent the further decline of production that had characterized most African economies in the 1970s. However, the costs of structural adjustment affected some groups more than others in countries such as Malawi and Zambia. In particular, the urban poor, marginal smallholder farmers, and female-headed households in both urban and rural areas were adversely affected (Chisala and Mthindi 1989; Kandoole 1990; Due 1991).

In urban centers the often-working poor had to pay higher prices for food and increased fees for their children's education and health services

(Kandoole 1990; Roe and Chilowa 1990; Due 1991). For smallholder producers, increased prices for export-value crops such as tobacco, coffee, and cotton did not offset the increased costs of imported commodities such as fuel and fertilizer. In Malawi, fertilizer subsidies were removed to cut government costs in connection with the three structural adjustment programs initiated between 1981 and 1986 (Chisala and Mthindi 1989). Not only did the production of export crops decline as a result, but smallholders who had been growing hybrid maize for sale stopped growing it and switched to producing local maize, and marginal smallholders stopped using fertilizer on local maize, reducing their yields (Chisala and Mthindi 1989:7–8).

Female-headed households on average are more prone to labor shortages and have smaller parcels of land and fewer capital resources than jointly headed households (Chipande 1986; Ngwira 1989; Spring 1987; Due 1991). Structural adjustment forced them to pay higher prices for food when the food they had produced ran out. In addition, they could not afford the increased costs of services such as education and health care for their children (Due 1991). Finally, women's labor in these households increased because most could not afford to hire the seasonal workers they had previously depended on (Kaluwa 1990).

In alignment with structural adjustment and because of the resulting decline in social services, development policies were designed to meet women's practical needs over their strategic needs. The new efficiency approach relied on women's triple roles as producers, reproducers, and community organizers to meet the new state's demands (Moser 1989:1801). Peasant women were expected to extend their unpaid working day to underwrite the costs of development projects and the reproduction of labor. For instance, in many cases women were urged to contribute their unpaid labor to community development projects that otherwise would have been sponsored by government funding (Moser 1989; Kaufulu 1992).

The new drive for efficiency and effectiveness influenced women's development in other ways. For instance, women farmers received inputs only for crops that had a market surplus value; thus their need to improve their capacity for food production was neglected. Even though they began to gain access to credit in the 1980s, their control over capital was limited to funding for projects that had proved to be efficient—in other words, that already had a track record. Often women were able to get credit only on a group basis, whereas men continued to gain access to credit as individual farmers and entrepreneurs (Spring 1987, 1995; Kaunda 1989). Women made few gains in their ability to influence the shape of development in their respective countries. They made the most gains in small community projects funded by nongovernmental organizations (NGOs) in which they had a voice in planning and implementation. Peasant women, on the whole, remained skeptical of donor agency attempts to improve their lot.

The Empowerment Approach

The empowerment approach to development grew out of Third World women's experiences working in grassroots organizations and their written observations about the experiences of other women in their societies. Theirs was a response to the image of Third World women as victims, found in the earlier mainstream WID approaches (Moser 1989; Mohanty 1993b). The empowerment approach differs from the equity approach in its perceptions of the structural causes of women's inequalities and in the strategies proposed to reorder relations of power in nonindustrialized countries.[1]

Third World women's structural position in their countries and in the world economy results not only from men's control over resources and decisionmaking but from the history of colonialism and neocolonialism that exists in many of these countries (Sen and Grown 1987; Longwe 1988, 1990; Mohanty 1993a). In order to overcome these twin causes of oppression, women reasoned, they must mobilize and unite from the grassroots up in order to fulfill their practical and strategic needs as *they* define them. This alternative vision of development questions the relationship between power and development assumed in Western models. Rather than being viewed as domination by one party or group over another, power is conceived of as increased self-reliance and control over critical resources and decisionmaking, including personal life choices. Improving women's status per se is not the main objective. Redistribution of power within nations and between them is the real issue (Sen and Grown 1987; Moser 1989; Mohanty 1993b).

Longwe (1990) is very specific in analyzing what constitutes development for empowerment. She makes clear that the emphasis in Western models on fulfilling women's practical (basic) needs is at the low end of the empowerment scale because they treat women as passive recipients rather than active participants in development. According to her model, the highest level of empowerment is reached when women have complete control over the development process, including defining the priorities, establishing the means of implementation, and controlling the resources that are integral to development. *Access* to critical resources and decisionmaking arenas is not enough—what is critical for women's development is that they assume control of the process.

Longwe's Model of Empowered Development: From Welfare to Control

What makes Longwe's model of development (1988, 1990) especially useful is its attention to the needs of African women as practitioners and recipients of development. Her model comes out of her work with the Zambian Association for Research and Development (ZARD), which em-

TABLE 7.1   Empowerment for Development: Status Criteria

Levels of Empowerment	*Factors of Empowerment*
Highest	Control • Resources including land, labor, capital, labor-saving equipment, technology • Problem solving, decisionmaking, leadership • Training and education • Child spacing • Custody of children
Next highest	Participation (active, equal participants) • Priority setting • Policymaking • Planning • Implementation • Evaluation
Median	Conscientization • Awareness of gender differences • Awareness of gender biases and obstacles • Articulation of strategies for change • Action on change strategies
Lower	Access • Critical resources of production including land, labor, capital, credit, technology • Decisionmaking and leadership • Education and training • Medical and health resources
Lowest	Welfare (passive, unequal recipients) • Transfer of productive resources • Transfer of social services • Transfer of knowledge and advice • Transfer of technology

SOURCE: Adapted from Longwe 1990:7.

phasizes action research and participatory development. In a paper first presented at the NGO African Women's Task Force Meeting in Nairobi in April 1988, Longwe outlined various factors involved in women's transition from a position of passive recipients of development to one in which they have full empowerment and equal control with men over critical resources and decisionmaking.

In an analysis of a survey of development projects involving women in Zambia, Keller (1984) found that the projects addressed women's domestic or reproductive roles rather than their productive roles. In such cases, it was the welfare aspects of development that were being deployed. In assessing the quality of specific interventions in the Zambian projects, Longwe (1990:7) proposed, as a means of measuring women's development, a set of stratified criteria representing five aspects of development leading to increased empowerment. She sees women's empowerment as the ultimate goal. The five are, from lowest to highest, welfare, access, conscientization, participation, and control (of resources and decisionmaking). All five are interrelated and interdependent (see Table 7.1 for a modified version of Longwe's model).

The lowest order of development in Longwe's model is the *welfare* aspect because it addresses women's material well-being (including adequate nutrition, income, and medical care) relative to men's. It takes care of women's basic (practical) needs but does not involve women as active participants in determining or prioritizing these basic needs. Longwe argues that if women are not involved in the process, their welfare becomes "an act of charity by the male establishment" (1990:5). Also with the welfare aspect comes a transfer of advice, strategies, and, perhaps, technologies from the provider (either the state or a donor agency) to the welfare recipient. It is a unidirectional form of development.

Access to factors of production, as we have seen in Chapter 6, is vital to women's empowerment. Access means that women have equal access to scarce resources such as land and other forms of property, to labor, to skills training and education, to capital (including credit and marketing facilities), and to labor-saving equipment. By way of illustration, in Western Province, Zambia, land is not the greatest issue; women and men gain access to land through chiefs or community leaders. What is at issue is labor—women's labor—and women's access as farmers to training and extension services. A heavy workload and lack of cash to hire labor are among the women's constraints. In addition, they lack access to credit and financial services that might make it possible to hire labor and improve production. In response to their needs, a project was initiated by the Ministry of Agriculture in Western Province that targeted women rice farmers for extension services and assistance. With the assistance of a Dutch extension worker and several women in the Women's Extension Programme of the central ministry (the Ministry of Agriculture at the national level), women were formed into groups to better meet their needs (Jiggins et al. 1995:22–26). The group approach in this part of Zambia proved to be successful because, as one woman explained, "it fits our way of doing things here. . . . we learn to feel comfortable together" (Jiggins et al. 1995:23). Mobile training units geared to training in a single topic, such as fertilizer application, also helped women to gain access to knowledge that distance and their labor burdens had precluded them from achieving.

Gaining access to extension services that were a part of the regular extension program of the ministry was a beginning for these women but not an end. They also expressed interest in learning how to operate labor-saving equipment such as ox plows that previously only men in the area had operated. An ox-plowing training center had been set up in the province a decade earlier, in 1983, but only men were trained at the center. A few women who were interested began to train in the use of ox-drawn equipment, and at the 1990 agricultural show in the district, they gave a demonstration of their skills. Farmers of both sexes were impressed. This brings us to the next level of Longwe's development model—the need for conscientization. By being encouraged to learn how to use equipment previously identified as "men's," the women demonstrated to others of both sexes that ox plowing need not be gendered male.

Conscientization is critical for increased empowerment. It includes gender awareness and sensitivity to the needs and interests of both women and men. It means educating people to recognize women's issues through an examination of various forms of gender discrimination; for instance, in the use of certain equipment and in marriage and divorce laws, inheritance practices, child custody, and employment. The Women and Law in Southern Africa (WLSA) project is an example of an endeavor whose objective is empowerment through conscientization. Its purpose is to collect and disseminate information about women's legal rights in the SADC region and to educate women on how to use them. It also works to change laws that adversely affect women.[2]

As Longwe indicates, women's *participation* in the development process at all levels—from the grassroots to national policy forums—is a critical aspect of women's empowerment. Participation involves women's and men's equal involvement from the inception of a project to its implementation and evaluation. Women in the Zambian Ministry of Agriculture were involved in planning the training and extension service program in Western Province, and the women rice farmers were able to make their needs felt at this level. However, participation also demands that women be included equally with men in leadership and decisionmaking, a goal that has not been reached in most countries, including in the West.

As more farmers' groups sprang up in Western Province, men began to join them; it was critical that women develop their organizational and leadership skills so that they could retain control of the "people's participation groups" (PPGs). At first the Women's Extension Program (WEP) was responsible for the groups, but after a while, it was recognized that a person highly respected as an agricultural extension worker within the central ministry should be seconded to the province as provincial coordinator of the People's Participation Project. With funding from the FAO and the Dutch government, the woman selected was able to provide women with the leadership training needed to ensure their ongoing participation in the control of the groups. In this sense, then, they achieved the highest level of empowerment. They had achieved access to and control over the kind and venue of the training they received. They had achieved access to and control over labor-saving equipment that they had previously avoided for cultural reasons. And by the early 1990s, they were able to control the operation of the participatory groups of which they were a part.

The Zambian case is illustrative of how, even within a male-dominated state bureaucracy such as the Ministry of Agriculture, women's empowerment at the local level may be reached with the assistance of donor agencies. However, it is also true that the southern African states in this study are more likely to subscribe largely to the least controversial aspects of women's development. Measures designed to advance women's strategic needs, including their political needs, often meet with resistance.

Bureaucratic Obstacles to Women's Empowerment

Longwe outlines ten obstacles—what she terms "strategies of resistance"— that men, particularly in state bureaucracies, use to thwart women from achieving gender equality (1990:10). Like Susan Faludi, in her analysis of the state's and the media's resistance to feminism in the United States (1991), Longwe analyzes the resistance of African gendered states to implementing the 1985 U.N. Forward Looking Strategies (FLS). She concludes that in the 1980s, male members of African state bureaucracies devised a number of counterstrategies, both explicit and implicit, to resist implementing these strategies. Longwe's strategies of resistance fall into three categories: (1) strategies that involve rhetorical maneuvering, (2) strategies that "blame the victim," and (3) strategies that weaken the intent and force of policies designed to implement the FLS. Time and space do not permit a discussion of these obstacles, but it is important to recognize that rhetorical maneuvering, including denial of inequality, reverting to arguments of "tradition," and masking issues involved in women's need for empowerment are used by members of state bureaucracies in the region. In the next section I look at specific cases in Malawi and Zimbabwe where women are making progress toward empowerment despite the obstacles.

Advancing Women's Empowerment
in Malawi and Zimbabwe

If we assume, as Longwe has suggested, that southern African states and their male bureaucracies tend to be resistant to sharing power with women, what hope is there of women achieving empowerment? Has any real progress been made toward this goal since 1985? Malawi and Zimbabwe represent two different approaches to development. Malawi has emphasized a top-down approach with the state controlling most aspects of development; Zimbabwe allows for a mix of participatory, grassroots development (often sponsored by NGOs) and state-planned development.

In Malawi, efforts to advance women's development were largely state led until multiparty democracy was introduced in May 1994. In Zimbabwe, which has a longer history of women's organizations, advocacy for women's advancement and development comes more often from women's groups, NGOs, and labor union activists. The two states differ in their relationship to the international donor community as well. Malawi has largely depended on donor aid from U.N. agencies, the World Bank, and market-oriented bilateral aid agencies such as the British Overseas Development Agency, USAID, and the German bilateral agency GTZ. Few Scandinavian bilateral agencies were willing to support the oppressively authoritarian regime of Hastings Kamuzu Banda, and until the early 1990s, very few NGOs worked in Malawi because the state kept a tight rein on how development funds were distributed.

The political situations that existed in Malawi and Zimbabwe in the 1980s dramatically shifted in the mid-1990s. Whereas Malawi was a one-party state until 1994, in Zimbabwe more than one party participated in elections. Now the situation has nearly been reversed with Malawi embracing multiparty democracy as Zimbabwe leans toward a de facto one-party state given ZANU-PF's domination of Zimbabwe's 1995 elections. The shift in politics has implications for the donor community and its efforts on behalf of women.

Zimbabwe gained its independence at a time when international NGOs were beginning to proliferate and show demonstrated effectiveness in working with communities at the grassroots level. Moreover, an impressive number of NGOs catering to a variety of needs, including the needs of women, had already evolved in Zimbabwe. The presence of these NGOs working independently or in tandem with the state helped women to negotiate the process of development in Zimbabwe.

Malawi's basic resource is agriculture; Zimbabwe has a mixed economy with a firmly established industrial sector. As in the rest of central southern

Africa, in these two countries historical differences rooted in colonial occupation and differing ethnic formations based on contrasting lineage ideologies position women differently even though on the surface their circumstances may appear similar.

Malawi: Engineering Women's Development

From independence, Malawi's longtime president consistently talked about
development for "his" women. As titular leader of a matrilineal state committed to maintaining "traditions" while at the same time encouraging
"modernization" and capitalism, he oftentimes appeared to be operating at
cross purposes. This "avuncular state," as Hirschmann (1990) aptly referred to it, vacillated on the issue of women's advancement between
rhetorical gestures and tokenism on the one hand and solid action on the
other. The latter has been largely in response to donor agency pressure. In
the context of the U.N. Decade of Women conference in Nairobi, a fragile
movement for the improvement of women's economic and social status
began in the mid-1980s. It was led by urban educated women working in
the civil service sector and included ministry and governmental department
employees and university lecturers. The private sector employs few women,
and until the sea change in national politics in 1994, such women tended
not to be as involved in gender issues. Since the 1994 elections, a number
of women's business and professional groups have been forming that support the movement for women's advancement in Malawi.

Rural women constitute the vast majority of women in Malawi and have
relatively more authority in their "workplaces" (where they cultivate food
crops or work as seasonal hired laborers, traders, and beer brewers) than
women in urban settings. They control their households, with or without
husbands, and manage subsistence production and cash-crop production
on land that belongs to them. In areas where men have been encouraged to
produce cash-value crops for export either on estates or as smallholders
(often in conjunction with state-sponsored agrarian development schemes),
men tend to control more of the decisions related to cash-crop production
and are more likely to control household income. Before and after independence in Malawi, policymakers instituted and perpetuated the inequity
of "bringing men in" as primary players in agricultural development while
excluding women, who historically have managed much of Malawi's agricultural production at the household level.

In the next section I describe the state machinery that officially controls
the quantity and quality of women's development in Malawi. That section
is followed by one on the role of donor agencies in influencing the state's
commitment to women's development and on the changing role of women
in the first half of the 1990s.

The State and Women's Organizations

Three groups form the nucleus of the state's efforts to include women in Malawi's postindependence development: the League of Malawi Women (the women's political wing of the former ruling Malawi Congress Party, or MCP); the National Commission for Women in Development, an advisory body to the state; and Chitukuko cha Amai of Malawi (CCAM, or Development of Women), which is largely a charitable organization for helping impoverished women. It is a part of the League of Malawi Women but has its own secretariat.

The League of Malawi Women was the first to be organized. It was established during the transition to independence to help mobilize women (Government of Malawi/UNICEF 1987:31). It provides women with a limited avenue for political participation within the context of the MCP's activities. League leaders are responsible for mobilizing women's dance choruses for MCP candidates. These dance groups were recruited, on demand, to perform for the former president on all official occasions. Very few Malawians did not belong to MCP in the 1980s, as membership was required to enter local markets, ride buses, buy maize from ADMARC (the agricultural marketing parastatal), and vote in elections. The league's entertainment at official events acted as a visual reminder of women's "traditional" role in postindependent Malawian society. The women's uniformed presence also served to remind women that the state was responsible for women's development.

To address international concerns for women's development connected with the U.N. Women's Decade, the National Commission on Women in Development (NCWID) was set up in 1984 to assess Malawian women's status in various areas. A year later Chitukuko cha Amai of Malawi was established by the former president, Hastings Banda, with a secretariat in the Office of the President and Cabinet (OPC). Its chairperson and "national adviser" was the former president's "official hostess," Mama C. Tamanda Kadzamira. These two groups assumed official responsibility for women's development until 1994.

CCAM, which largely attracted elite urban women, was charged with improving the conditions of the country's most impoverished women. Income-generating activities, functional literacy, and child spacing were its primary concerns. When the MCP lost the 1994 elections to UDF (the United Democratic Front), CCAM was forced to give up its offices in the OPC and its official state-sponsored role. As CCAM is a class-based organization, its strategies for increasing rural women's opportunities were often out of step with the needs of the women it was designed to assist, and it was accused of being elitist. CCAM made the mistake of treating rural women as welfare recipients rather than as colleagues in its effort to initiate income-generating activities for rural women with marginal incomes. For instance, rural women drafted as labor in CCAM's rural restaurant schemes had little voice in the planning and management of these schemes and carried out most of the menial work; they soon dropped out because they found working on their own productive activities in agriculture to be more satisfying (Schellenberg and Nkunita 1988).

The National Commission for Women in Development has a broader base than CCAM because it acts as an umbrella organization for all groups working toward women's advancement in Malawi. It links the state, women's groups, and development agencies committed to assisting women's development. The commission's objectives are

- To promote and assist the establishment of institutions that innovate, implement, and monitor women's programs.
- To coordinate programs initiated by the state.
- To investigate various facets of women's status in Malawi, making recommendations to be implemented by the relevant ministries and departments. (National Commission on WID 1988)

The commission consists of representatives of various ministries. About half its membership is male. Under it are six topical investigative committees. Each committee has responsibility for a different aspect of women's overall development. The Legal Committee has attracted the most attention for its work on customary practices and statutes that affect women. Its work resulted in the publication of a book, *Women and the Law in Malawi* (NCWID 1993). It covers three major areas pertaining to women: land law, family law, and business law. The book clarifies women's rights regarding land tenure, movable property, inheritance, marriage, spousal mainte-nance, and child custody. Each of these sections includes recommendations for changes in laws that discriminate against women. The section on busi-ness law, though slim, informs women of laws related to trading and start-ing a business and explains laws pertaining to different types of business. The book is published in the national language, Chichewa, as well as in English. Legal education of Malawi's women is one of the NCWID Law Committee's goals.

Equally significant to Malawian women's advancement, NCWID also was active in coordinating women's groups' efforts to ensure that women's rights to political participation were included in the 1995 constitution. CCAM and the League of Malawi Women are narrowly focused on MCP issues; NCWID has a broader constituency than either of the other organi-zations. Therefore, it has continued to grow in significance with the transi-tion to multiparty democracy. It was instrumental, along with a newly formed NGO, the Society for Advancement of Women, in making sure that a senate designed to meet the needs of underrepresented groups such as women and chiefs is included in the new government structure. Through its coordination of a coalition of interested groups, it was successful in getting the parliament to approve inclusion of such a body in the constitution.

Supported by bilateral donor agencies, especially USAID, in 1993 the NCWID was instrumental in seeing that a women's desk officer was appointed in every government ministry so that gender issues relating to women's specific programs are addressed. Unfortunately, the NCWID has been handicapped by a very small staff (two women as of 1995) and has been limited to making recommendations rather than having the power to implement programs. It is also structurally handicapped by its placement in the Ministry of Women and Children's Affairs and Community Services (MOWCACS) rather than in the Finance Ministry, where most development decisions are made. The organization plans to change this situation when it becomes an NGO.

The Role of the Donor Agencies

Donor agencies have led development as much as they have assisted in development planning and implementation in Malawi. The most potent donor is the World Bank, which has supported infrastructure construction, agricultural projects, and education. I referred earlier to the World Bank's role in agrarian reforms in the 1970s and 1980s (see Chapter 6). More recently the bank has assisted the state with the design and implementation of its Structural Adjustment Program.

Of the U.N. agencies, UNICEF has a long-established program focused more on reducing infant and child mortality than on women's health needs. UNDP also has a strong presence in Malawi, but its projects for women have tended to target their reproductive roles rather than their productive roles. For example, in 1987 UNDP and FAO collaborated on the Family Life Education program for women instead of concentrating on their needs as food producers. However, in 1989, UNDP had two new projects for women, one of which was being executed by FAO. Both concentrate on income-generating activities for women farmers.

The most active bilateral agency until 1995, when it closed its national office in favor of a regional office in Harare, was the British ODA. It is followed by USAID, the German GTZ, Canada's CIDA (Canadian International Development Agency), and Taiwan's agricultural aid agency, which concentrates on agricultural demonstration projects. More recently the Japanese have become involved in agriculture and education projects. Of the bilateral agencies, USAID and GTZ have had the most influence in shaping women's inclusion in development.

The NGOs, other than church missionary groups, that worked in Malawi were limited to a few in the 1970s and 1980s, as most development initiatives had to go through the state. They included Save the Children Federation; Oxfam U.K.; Project Hope; the Christian Service Committee; World Vision; Action Aid; the Muslim Association of Malawi (MAM); and Development Enterprise, Management, and Technical Training (DEMATT), an NGO that began in 1988 and caters to the management-training needs of women who are operating or launching small and medium-sized businesses. However, as a result of Malawi's democratization in the early 1990s, by 1994 there were twenty-seven NGOs working in education alone (Chaturvedi 1994:11–16). Most of the agencies include programs that target women's needs.

Bilateral donor agencies have had a major hand in shaping gender-specific programs in Malawi. I limit my analysis of donor agencies' roles in shaping women's development to the frontrunners, USAID and GTZ—specifically, to USAID's role in education and agriculture in the late 1980s and 1990s and GTZ's role in implementing activities that benefit impoverished rural women.

USAID has been working in Malawi for three decades. Initially it was concerned with assisting the postcolonial state with increasing its export production and building infrastructure. In the 1980s, the agency became involved in shaping opportunities for women's development in two areas, agriculture and education. I first look at agricultural programs, then at education.

Women and Agriculture. In the early 1980s USAID encouraged and assisted the Ministry of Agriculture in setting up strategies for integrating women farmers into agricultural development programs aimed at improving production. These programs provided training and extension services, access to credit, and other inputs previously available to "progressive" Farmers' Club members. USAID's efforts coincided with the initiation of the Women's Programme in the ministry in 1982.

Part of USAID's mission was to evaluate the extent to which various divisions and departments within the ministry were amenable to the inclusion of women in their programs and agreed to provide WID training where needed (see Spring 1983, 1995). To its credit, the baseline survey that was initiated by the ministry in 1982, with USAID/Malawi assistance, included FHHs and wives of male farmers as targeted respondents. Based on the initial assessment of women farmers' needs, the ministry, with USAID input, was successful in initiating a number of programs that helped amplify the specific roles and needs of women in agriculture that could be addressed by the state. USAID assisted in training male extension workers to be more sensitive to the needs of female farmers (Spring 1983). Despite the ministry's commitment to training women in agricultural extension work, however, eight years later women still lagged far behind men in training and in having access to extension services (Schellenberg and Nkunita 1988). Part of the problem was that the training in gender sensitivity was designed largely to reach progressive farmers linked to Farmers' Clubs, and it had not "trickled out" to include those in the most remote areas.

One aspect of WIADP (Women in Agricultural Development Program), a stall-feeding program for cattle production, proved immensely successful. USAID assisted in seeing to it that rural women's needs for more control over productive resources were being addressed through the program. Equally important, their strategic needs were addressed by expanding their economic opportunities into an area that previously had been the exclusive terrain of men (Spring 1995). Had USAID not been involved, it is unlikely that the Ministry of Agriculture would have thought to include women in the stall-feeding program. Women's response to the program was positive, and those enrolled with their husbands or alone tended to spend income from cattle sales on their children's school fees, kitchen items, and payments on loans connected with the stall-feeding program (Spring 1995:264). Part of the success of the stall-feeding program derived from its focus on improving production rather than generating income; it was not identified as an IGA (income-generating activity) per se but was integrated with the rest of farmers' activities and was viewed "as a business" by them (Spring 1995:264). Although USAID has sponsored cooperative agricultural projects for women, it has experienced more success in efforts that address women farmers as individuals or family members rather than as groups.

In contrast to WIADP, FAO and the German development agency GTZ have taken a different approach to rural women's development. They have emphasized IGAs as a strategy for meeting rural women's need for increased income. In so doing, they have encouraged women in rural areas to form cooperatives so that these agencies could more easily provide them with services and credit (Laurel Rose, personal communication, 1991). But what has been the experience of rural Malawian women in these projects, who on the whole prefer individual production? Why have IGAs often failed to take hold?

FAO's program to encourage women to initiate their own income-generating projects was housed in the Ministry of Agriculture; GTZ's program was situated in what was formerly the Ministry of Community Services—now the Ministry of Women and Children's Affairs and Community Services (MOWCACS). The discussion here is limited to the GTZ joint program with MOWCACS, as it has been operating longer (since 1988) than the FAO-sponsored program, which began in 1991 and was not sustained beyond 1993.

Many of the women targeted by the GTZ-MOWCACS program were impoverished, with fewer than 0.5 hectares of land. They were unable to raise enough food to feed their families for an entire year and were forced to purchase basic staples such as maize, rice, and cassava by between the sixth and the ninth month after harvest (Government of Malawi/UNICEF 1987). As a result, these women often had to search for ways to increase their income to buy food and other necessities. Some worked for others as *ganyu* labor on a seasonal basis; others sold baked goods or brewed beer.

In its outreach to rural women, MOWCACS has used the approach of asking local chiefs to organize women in their areas. It uses community development assistants (CDAs) as facilitators to explain the purpose of the ministry's IGA program. The CDAs or the women themselves come up with the ideas. The activities suggested range from bakeries and poultry-keeping projects to groundnut oil processing and fish processing. What has limited the effectiveness of these projects is often the way they are set up. Women have been encouraged to collaborate on projects rather than to undertake them on an individual basis. Fish-processing IGAs serve as an example.

Women living along the shores of southern Lake Malawi were urged by MOWCACS to form fish-processing and -selling groups. Their membership ranged in 1991 between ten and twenty-one. Each group had two committees: one an executive committee made up of the group's leader, secretary, and treasurer and the other a loan committee responsible for securing loans for start-up funds and maintenance. MOWCACS provided skills training, and GTZ provided fuel-efficient kilns for smoking the fish. Women sold their fish on an individual basis.

Part of the problem in these collaborative ventures lies in their organization. The executive decisionmaking committee was dominated by the most educated women in a group, and the other women mistrusted these leaders; in one case a woman was accused of running off with the group's funds. But the more basic problem was that such a venture requires women to leave their own productive activities to provide labor for a venture that they do not fully control in terms of either management or finances. As women in matrilineal groups are accustomed to having relative authority over production, as we have seen previously, they are reluctant to give up this control for an enterprise that might prove risky. They would much prefer to launch their own ventures, on an individual basis or with their immediate families, as the 1990 survey of smallholder farmers undertaken by the Ministry of Agriculture confirmed (Culler, Patterson, and Matenje 1990).

In USAID's most recent efforts to involve women in smallholder households (those with less than 1.5 hectares and more than 0.8 hectares) in the production of a cash-value crop that formerly was dominated by men—burley tobacco—the Ministry of Agriculture and the agency have been careful to include women as individual producers, in the case of men with more than one wife, or as FHHs. Unfortunately, however, wives in monogamous marriages were not permitted to be burley club members (Hirschmann 1993a), demonstrating that agricultural development programs involving cash-crop production continue to be slanted toward men in MHHs even when a supposedly gender-sensitive donor agency is involved.

Part of the mandate of the program has been to reach women producers, as well as men, through burley farmers clubs (Joanne Hale, Agricultural Project Director, USAID/Malawi, personal communication, 1991; Hirschmann 1993a). In the first season (1991–1992), 10 percent of the burley club members were women; this figure increased slightly to 12.5 percent in 1992–1993 (Hirschmann 1993a:5). Hirschmann (1993b) found that more women had not become involved because of time constraints—an obstacle that also precludes women from joining IGAs (see Kaufulu 1992). Another constraint was the size of the credit package, which in 1992 was MK250 (US$73); women feared being overburdened in repaying the loan (Hirschmann 1993b). Female participants were also constrained by the timing of the credit advances, which did not always come when they were needed. FHHs in particular had greater financial needs. They also experienced labor shortages more often than their MHH counterparts, although this depended on the number and age of their children. We can conclude, then, that although the donor agencies have influenced the way that the gendered state views women producers—as the smallholder burley tobacco scheme illustrates—Malawian women producers still have a way to go before their strategic needs as individuals, separate from their husbands (in the case of MHHs or JMHs), are met.

Advancement Through Education.   Until the 1990s, the state of Malawi developed the tertiary sector of education to the neglect of the primary level. In 1972, the former president of Malawi took a significant step to improve girls' opportunities at the secondary level by requesting that one-third of the places in the nation's secondary schools be reserved for girls, a policy that was implemented yearly by the Ministry of Education and Culture (Government of Malawi 1988). But because only 3.5 percent of the relevant school age group have found a place in a secondary school, very few girls have benefited (Robinson, Davison, and Williams 1994:6). As a result, with the prodding of USAID, a program was initiated in 1991 to encourage more girls to enroll at the primary level and to stay in school so that they could progress to the secondary level. Referred to as GABLE (Girls' Attainment of Basic Literacy and Education), the program included an incentive whereby girls who were nonrepeaters at the primary level had their school fees paid through a USAID grant. The result was that girls' enrollment at the entry level increased from 48 percent in 1988–1989 to 51 percent in 1992–1993 and constituted 47 percent of the overall enrollment in that year (USAID/Malawi 1995:22).

To further encourage parents to send their children to school, the state, under the leadership of its new president, Baliki Muluzi, extended tuition-free education to all primary school students as of the 1995–1996 academic year. To increase the number of girls enrolled at the secondary level, USAID/Malawi is supporting scholarships for girls at this level. The state's role in promoting education has been supported by women's organizations and by NGOs, especially organizations with a religious affiliation.

At the university level, USAID encouraged the University of Malawi to set up a program designed to provide master's degree training for medium-level administrators in the theory and practice of WID. It is doubtful that the university administration would have implemented such a gender-focused program on its own without the incentive of funding and inputs, such as a computer and books, from a donor agency. As it was, a two-year master's degree program housed in the Sociology Department was launched in the 1990–1991 academic year. As part of their training, graduate students in the M.A. program are required to plan, coordinate, and evaluate gender-training workshops for their employing agencies, adding a multiplier effect to the program. The program was still in operation in 1993–1994 even though initial donor funding had been curtailed.

Zimbabwe: Women's Quest for Empowerment in a Patriarchal Society

When Zimbabwe achieved independence, ministries in the new state were reshuffled, and the need to address women's development was recognized in the creation of the Ministry of Community Development and Women's Affairs. This ministry was active in projects that met women's practical needs, often using a welfare approach, but did little to meet women's strategic needs. In the late 1980s Women's Affairs was removed from the ministry and put under the direct control of ZANU-PF, in essence becoming a program wing of the party. The shift meant that Women's Affairs was confined in its ability to make policy and act on it, becoming largely a recommending body for the party. Although the state lagged in its attention to women's issues, other groups outside the state apparatus were forming interest coalitions to push the state to improve Zimbabwean women's status.

What makes Zimbabwe's case strikingly different from Malawi's is the broad array of women's groups that existed at the time of independence. These groups represented women's varied interests—from family welfare to vocational training and business. Tangible issues in women's lives brought other groups into existence after independence. Class, ethnicity, occupation, and interest are the major factors distinguishing women's organizations in Zimbabwe.

Grassroots Organizations

Women's clubs (in some places referred to as homecraft clubs) grew out of grassroots organizing and the need for women's solidarity in the late colonial period. The members in these clubs are low-income peasant women and urban, often working, poor women. Nearly all are African. Included in such grassroots organizations are those that fall under the Federation of African Women's Clubs—an umbrella organization that coordinates the activities of three types of clubs: (1) smaller women's clubs; (2) church-based women's groups that fulfill women's needs for spiritual growth, family advice, and income generation; (3) the Women's Institute Clubs and township clubs formed prior to independence (Jorgensen 1982). The common interests that brought these women together were, first, African women's desire to be educated and, second, women's desire to improve their lives and the lives of their families. Family welfare, home management, and crafts were the activities most pursued by these groups in the late colonial period and through the early 1980s.

Since independence, grassroots groups have emerged around single issues confronting women and have then expanded to include other issues. An example is the Women's Action Group (WAG). It was formed in Harare in 1983 in response to the mass arrest of thousands of women accused of being prostitutes in a police-initiated campaign against urban women known as Operation Cleanup. Women put aside racial and ethnic differences to join forces in protesting the police's indiscriminate arrest of these women.

In the process of responding to Operation Cleanup, many questions were raised about women's position in Zimbabwean society. WAG's first activity was to organize a weekend workshop in May 1984 to discuss women's most crucial problems. The workshop was attended by 450 women from all parts of Zimbabwe. The major problems that came up were security of land rights, custody of and maintenance for children, inheritance rights, and *lobola* (bridewealth payments). WAG published the findings of the workshop and began planning for more focused workshops the following year. It has continued as a working group interested in advancing the rights and progress of women (Women's Action Group [WAG] 1985:16).

The Women's Action Group publishes a quarterly newsletter in Shona, Ndebele, and English, bringing to women's attention particular injustices and progress made toward eradicating them. It also provides useful information—tips on health, nutrition, first aid, and the like. WAG held two workshops in 1984, one on "baby dumping" and the other on women at work, the latter concerned with the problems women face in employment.

Although only 6.8 percent of Zimbabwe's women were employed in the nonagricultural sector at the time (WAG 1985:2), women were greatly interested in this issue. Problems discussed at the workshop related to discrimination in entry employment, low pay, inequality with men in training and promotion, lack of information on women's rights, equal participation in trade unions, unpaid maternity leave (changed in 1985), provision for breast-feeding in workplaces, health hazards, and sexual harassment in the workplace (WAG 1985:14).

WAG made use of a local theater group, Kodzero Yevashandi (Workers' Rights Theater Group), to dramatize some of the problems employed women face, providing humor and stimulating participants to think about the problems in their own work situations and to come up with strategies for solving them. Thus WAG was attending to women's strategic as well as practical needs. Moreover, members discussed ways to empower women in the workplace. In the mid-1990s, WAG implemented a primary health care program for women in Masvingo as a pilot project. It has proved to be successful in reaching previously unreached women in resettlement areas and acts as a communications forum, bringing together health providers and rural dwellers on policy issues (Davison 1996c). WAG represents an effort to bridge class, racial, and ethnic differences among Zimbabwean women in the interest of improving their empowerment and development.

Elite Organizations

Affiliates of international organizations (YWCA, Zimbabwe Association of University Women, Business and Professional Women) and nationally founded organizations such as Women for Peace and the Zimbabwe Women's Association (ZAWA) draw on urban, educated, elite women for their memberships. Teachers, nurses, social workers, and businesswomen support these groups.

As well as class differences, ethnic and racial differences characterize the organizations. ZAWA has an all African membership and leadership, whereas the YWCA's membership is predominantly African—mostly Shona women, but a handful of European-Zimbabwean women are active in the organization's leadership. The Zimbabwean Association of University Women formerly had few African members, but more recently its membership and that of Women for Peace have had equal numbers of Africans and Europeans; and an Asian and an African woman co-chaired Women for Peace in the early years after independence. In contrast, Business and Professional Women has a predominantly Euro-Zimbabwean membership with a few Asians and Africans.

The interests that motivate the elite groups are more focused than those of the grassroots groups, as their names imply. Women for Peace, for instance, was concerned before and after independence with establishing a lasting peace in Zimbabwe. The Zimbabwe Women's Association has as its main objective the promotion of African women's identity and legal rights. The YWCA covers a broad range of projects from general education and literacy to education on women's legal rights and family welfare issues.

Political Groups

Women's leagues existed in the two major political parties, ZANU-PF and PF-ZAPU, at the time of independence. Their membership drew from women at the grassroots level, but their leaders were elite women. Not surprisingly, Shona-speaking women predominated in ZANU-PF, and Ndebele were the majority in PF-ZAPU. These groups tended to support male politicians from their own ethnic groups rather than encouraging women to run for office. With the Unity Agreement in 1987, the leagues were merged. Women in party leagues do fund-raising for party activities and support candidates with performances similar to those described for the MCP League in Malawi. However, more recently women have been dissatisfied with their lack of opportunities for participation in the political process. In 1990, the ruling ZANU-PF planned to establish, legally, a one-party system—a move that was criticized by an educated electorate in which the business community and labor unions were the most vocal (see Mandaza and Sachikonye 1991). The transition to a single-party system was forestalled as a result. Women began to be aware of the potential for political abuse in Zimbabwe in an era of decreasing voter participation (Laasko 1995:11).[3]

In September 1994, in preparation for the national elections in 1995, a group of women from diverse groups—from the Presbyterian Women's Association and the Zimbabwe Teachers Association to WAG and the Women in Business and Indigenous Business Women's Organization—came together to devise a means of promoting greater political awareness and responsibility among the populace and to encourage more women to participate in the political process by voting and running for office. The meeting resulted in the founding of the Women Voters Association of Zimbabwe (WOVAZ), a nonprofit, nonpartisan NGO. Its mission is "to promote political responsibility through the informed and active participation of men and women in government" (Women Voters Association of Zimbabwe [hereafter WOVAZ] 1995:1). Voter education and registration, as well as the encouragement and support of women in political decisionmaking positions at all levels in and out of government, are two specific objectives of the group. In pursuing its objectives, WOVAZ joined a voter-education campaign in early 1995 that was being launched by a number of human rights organizations to prepare voters for the April-May general elections.[4] Specifically, WOVAZ's objective was a "women voter education" project that included supporting women's issues, publicizing and promoting women's political rights, sensitizing voters to the existence of qualified female candidates, and changing parties' political structures to eliminate practices that preclude women's full participation (WOVAZ 1995:4). WOVAZ was successful in that all the women who ran as ZANU-PF candidates in the primaries and later in the general elections were elected. The percentage of women elected to parliament increased slightly from the general elections held in 1990—from 12 percent, as pointed out earlier, to 13.3 percent (Laasko 1995:13). With more lead time, WOVAZ plans to have an even higher percentage of women participating in elections in the year 2000.

Women in Trade Unions

Most of the women in the formal labor sector are industrial workers in urban centers. These women, on average, end their formal education with primary education (to grade 7). As a result they are "locked into unskilled positions that offer no chance for promotion" (Made and Lagerstrom 1984:16). The skills that these women bring into industry often are extensions of skills they learned at home—sewing and tailoring in the garment industry, baking, food processing (including sorting and boxing), and cleaning. But there are women who are breaking barriers; some assemble radios and work on punch presses and other equipment identified with "men's work." These latter women, then, are meeting a strategic need that advances women's overall development.

Women become trade union members, but they rarely are involved in union work because, first, meetings are held at times when they are preoccupied with family maintenance tasks and, second, many women feel inadequate to contribute much because they feel their knowledge of the union's goals and labor laws is insufficient (Made and Lagerstrom 1984:22). Yet the unions have the potential to meet women workers' gender-specific needs.

Women's leagues in the unions have become a gender-specific mechanism for giving women a greater voice. But women who become involved in union activities find themselves with a triple labor burden because not only do they have their workload in the factory and at home but as organizers within the union, they must include a third type of labor. One woman who works as a receptionist for the Engineering and Metal Workers' Union became an activist and as part of her work tried to conscientize union members of both sexes to women's dual labor burden. The response she got from men took the form of resistance—she found that men always responded by saying that things couldn't be changed "because that's the way our ancestors did it" or they would argue that "it is our tradition [that women do the domestic labor]. Our forefathers started it" (Made and Lagerstrom 1984:42). Rhetorical maneuvering, drawing on "tradition" as a rationale, became the resistance strategy of these trade union men who were reluctant to give up their privileged position in the household to ease a woman's double labor burden. Until women have more of a critical mass and their voices are heard in trade unions, their workplace needs will continue to be shelved.

Coordinating Organizations

In addition to the various groups just outlined to which women have access, two women's organizations exist for the purpose of coordinating particular types of women's groups. These are the Women's Group Liaison and the Zimbabwe Women's Bureau (ZWB). The first group was established in 1968 to coordinate groups in the field of homecraft. In this respect it has been most concerned with women's reproductive roles. In contrast, the ZWB, founded in 1978, works to integrate African women into the development process by strengthening their productive roles through specific projects.

A nongovernmental agency, the ZWB has grown since independence. In 1992 it had 120 women's projects in operation from beekeeping to agricultural projects for increased food production (L. Chikwavaire, director of the ZWB, interview with the author, April 2, 1992). By May 1996, the number of groups had doubled (L. Chikwavaire, interview with the author, May 3, 1996). The bureau contributes to the sustainability of these projects by holding training courses in leadership, management, and accounting skills. In 1995, the organization provided training for 5,543 women and 1,297 men, demonstrating that it is not exclusively a women's organization (Mutimba and Maphosa 1995). In the process the bureau's work contributes to the empowerment of women who not only plan and implement these projects but control project resources. The bureau is addressing women's reproductive needs where there is a demand for childcare and the space to make it possible. For instance, at its center in a suburb of Harare, the bureau had a childcare center and preschool for working mothers in 1992. It has since moved to another location.

The ZWB's staff is entirely African, and Africans predominate on its governing board. The bureau depends heavily on external donor agencies and private foundations for financial support. As a gender-specific organization, ZWB has broadened its vision in the mid-1990s to include families as beneficiaries of training and inputs to sustainable agriculture. Families form corporate groups with women playing primary leadership roles in family management committees. Visits to several family groups assisted by ZWB in May 1996 confirmed that not only have women become empowered through leadership and management training but men in these groups have grown in their respect for their wives' and mothers' organizational skills and leadership capabilities (Davison 1996c).

In addition to women's groups and organizations, Zimbabwe has a host of other NGOs working in the fields of education, health, housing, and microenterprise generation that benefit women. Additionally, many international NGOs such as Save the Children Federation and Oxfam work with impoverished communities. Zimbabwe's approach to women's development has depended heavily on NGOs.

The empowerment of women at the grassroots level, however, has not "trickled up" to empower women at the national level, where Zimbabwe remains a male bastion. Few women are found in administrative positions in ministries and governmental departments. The lack of female participation at this level is a situation that WOVAZ, the Women Voters Association, would like to see change.

Donor Agencies in Zimbabwe: UNICEF and SIDA

The work of donor agencies in Zimbabwe supports the goals of local NGOs. The donors have taken the role of enabling agencies in the postcolonial period by providing baseline studies, initial funding for projects, and, in some cases, training for existing NGOs. In this respect, the role of the donor agencies is very different than it is in Malawi, where the multilateral and bilateral agencies have tended to lead development rather than follow the leads and needs of existing organizations in the country. My discussion here is limited to two organizations that have fulfilled these roles— one a multinational and the other a bilateral organization. In both cases, they have largely been concerned with meeting the needs of disadvantaged women and girls for equity and empowerment.

UNICEF and Women's and Girls' Development. UNICEF has operated in Zimbabwe since the country's independence in 1980. It assists NGOs by collecting, on a yearly basis, current data on the situation of children and women that can be used by other organizations. It also has collaborated with NGOs on a number of projects designed to improve rural women's and children's health care and education. One of these collaborative efforts involved a project that brought mobile health clinics within reach of mothers and children on large-scale commercial farms and in communal areas who previously had had little or no health care. Largely as a result of this collaborative effort, by 1990, immunization had been extended to 85 percent of all children, in comparison with only 25 percent at independence (UNICEF 1994b:1). The mobile clinics are similar to "under-five clinics," which are designed to monitor children's health care. Thus part of their function has been educative; they teach mothers how to care for infants and young children so that more survive to become adults. In 1980 the infant mortality rate was 88 per 1,000 live births in Zimbabwe. By 1990 it had dropped to 61 per 1,000. A similar drop occurred for children under five years of age. However, there was a rise in both mortality rates in the early 1990s, partly attributable to the severe drought in 1991 and 1992.

The maternal mortality rate during the 1980s was relatively stable at roughly 100 deaths per 100,000 live births (UNICEF 1994b:72). However, there was a sharp rise in maternal mortality rates at the tail end of the 1980s and into the 1990s with a range, in 1992, of 200–500 per 100,000 live births in Zimbabwe's two major urban centers (Harare and Bulawayo) and in four of the provinces. The government of Zimbabwe does not allow abortions except in specific cases of rape or endangerment to the mother's life, so abortions often are carried out through illegal means. Complications arising from abortions were the most frequently cited cause of maternal mortality in 1991 (Government of Zimbabwe 1992). Because abortion is a highly contested issue in Zimbabwe, as in other countries, UNICEF has not become involved in this particular issue but has concentrated on the health and education of disadvantaged children.

In 1994, UNICEF launched a program to advance the status of girls in Zimbabwe, partly in connection with the emphasis on the girl child at the Beijing conference on women in 1995 (UNICEF 1994a). The organization is concentrating on three populations—girls in rural areas; girls in urban areas; and girls on large-scale commercial farms, who are often the children of adult laborers—with the goal of decreasing their overall labor burden in the interests of their health and education.

In the rural areas, UNICEF, working with other groups in Zimbabwe, hopes to reduce the number of hours girls spend in fetching water and firewood, caring for younger members of the family, and working in marketplaces as assistants to their mothers or other women (UNICEF 1994a). Girls' ability to participate in education in rural areas is often constrained by the amount of work they have to do in connection with household maintenance and childcare. If their labor burden is reduced, they will have more time for school and schoolwork.

In the urban areas, UNICEF is concentrating on reducing the number of hours girls spend working as maids or minding children and in hawking and begging. As maids or childcare workers in urban homes, girls are often exploited. In most cases they receive no salary; they get room and board, and some may get some vocational training. They work long hours and may be subject to both sexual and psychological harassment. In some cases they are sexually abused by male members of a household. Those who hawk goods or beg on urban streets face other dangers. They may be robbed, beaten, and sexually abused. They may be forced to work without adequate protection against the weather. They often go hungry, and some are forced to sleep in doorways or on the streets.

On commercial farms, girls often work alongside their mothers in performing the most labor intensive tasks connected with cash-crop production. They also assist with household maintenance and childcare. UNICEF would like to see the labor of girls in commercial production, including cultivation, weeding, harvesting, and hauling, curtailed. Furthermore, girls working on large-scale commercial farms are the most disadvantaged in terms of education. Few commercial farms provide adequate schooling for the children of their laborers and some do not provide it at all. Some commercial farmers are reluctant to do so, as it means forgoing the labor of these children. Others do not want to spend scarce resources on educating laborers' children or feel that it should not be their responsibility (Nyagura and Mupawaenda 1994). As a result, the large commercial farm areas have lagged behind other areas in the provision of education.

The UNICEF 1994 Situation Analysis profiles four girls between the ages of ten and thirteen who represent different types of socioeconomic settings in Zimbabwe (UNICEF 1994b:3–8). The following profile of Neria, the thirteen-year-old daughter of a farm laborer in a large-scale commercial farm area, is drawn from that publication.

Neria's family of eight shares a two-room house with a separate outdoor kitchen and a grass-thatched bathing room. The more than 100 families who work on this large-scale tobacco farm live in a cleared compound and share a single communal pit toilet.[5] The nearest clinic is about twenty kilometers away, but there is a trained health worker on the farm. Neria's father earns Z$180 (roughly US$23 at 1994 rates) per month. Neria's mother engages in seasonal work as a tobacco grader; she is not paid a fixed wage. She may work for six months earning Z$150 (US$22 at 1994 rates) per month (UNICEF 1994b:37). When she is working, her day begins at 5:30 A.M., so Neria prepares breakfast for the smaller children. The family has a small plot of land (fourteen yards by fourteen yards), allotted to them by the farm owner, on which to grow maize. In a drought year, such as 1992, it yields nothing. Then the family has to depend on securing a bag of maize from the owner, which must be paid for at a later date. The family has no livestock to supplement income (UNICEF 1994b:4).

Neria has a sixth-grade education but little hope of advancing to the secondary level because the nearest secondary school is located twenty kilometers away and its tuition fees are likely to be unaffordable. Her older brothers attended only three years of secondary school in a communal area forty kilometers away from the farm. Neria would like to complete secondary school and become a teacher, but she stands little chance of achieving her goal. Like other commercial farm workers in Zimbabwe, she is disenfranchised (UNICEF 1994b:8); as an adult, she will have little political power unless she leaves the farm. Neria, like other women laborers on commercial farms, will probably marry early.

The case study of Neria is important because, until the latter part of the 1980s, very little was known about the conditions of laborers on large-scale commercial farms, although they account for 15 percent of Zimbabwe's total population (Government of Zimbabwe [hereafter GOZ] 1991:Appendix 3, 3). What has emerged from baseline studies is that these laborers are among the most disadvantaged in Zimbabwe (GOZ 1987; Swedish International Development Agency [hereafter SIDA] n.d.; Nyagura and Mupawaenda 1994).

SIDA: Meeting the Needs of Women and Children in Commercial Farming Areas.   Commercial farms are the single largest employer of labor in Zimbabwe. The permanent labor force in 1986 was estimated to be 168,000 with an additional 180,000 employed seasonally on a part-time basis (Fahlen 1987:20). The average monthly income on commercial farms in 1985 was Z$72 (roughly US$20 at the 1985 rate) (GOZ 1991:Annex 3, 3); in 1994 it was Z$115 (roughly US$21). School enrollment rates at the primary and secondary levels are the lowest in Zimbabwe with 61 percent of children between the ages of five and seventeen enrolled in primary schools in comparison to 63 percent in urban areas, 67 percent in the communal areas, and 72 percent in the resettlement–small-scale commercial farm areas (World Bank 1995:12). Only 4 percent are enrolled in secondary schools in comparison to 10 percent in the communal areas, 12 percent in the resettlement areas, and 24 percent in urban areas (World Bank 1995:12). Because commercial farm workers and their families are among the most impoverished in Zimbabwe, SIDA, the Swedish International Development Agency, in the mid-1980s began a series of dialogues with the government to determine how to best meet the needs of this group. In contrast to UNICEF, SIDA works directly with the government of Zimbabwe on projects that will benefit a single sector—large-scale commercial farming. However, it also assists the government periodically in assessments of specific programs in the education sector. For instance, in 1994, SIDA carried out an assessment of an NGO, the Zimbabwe Foundation for Education with Production (ZIMFED), to identify its significance as an educational institution and decide whether it should continue to receive donor support. SIDA's projects and assessments are sensitive to the needs of women and girls in Zimbabwe.

SIDA's sector review of education in 1985 revealed a paucity of education and educational infrastructure in the commercial farming areas, and as a result it agreed to construct a cluster of district education offices and staff housing in two disadvantaged districts in order to assist teachers, who were largely untrained (SIDA n.d.:15). The project was extended in 1986 to include two more clusters of houses.

In 1987, SIDA met with the Ministry of Finance, Economic Planning and Development (MFEPD) and agreed to expand its initial assistance to commercial farming areas by identifying other projects that might be initiated by the government with the benefit of SIDA funding (Fahlen 1987:2). Six projects were proposed. The first was an extension of the Farm Health Workers (FHWs) scheme to include adult functional literacy. This program targeted women in that most FHWs in the commercial farm areas are women. The FHWs had been successful not only in reaching disadvantaged communities but in setting up preschool programs and Women's Club activities for women in communal farm compounds.

A second project was a pilot scheme for a farm rural services center to coordinate government services in health, education, and community outreach for commercial farm laborers who live on farm compounds. In particular, the project would assist women and their children. Part of the problem of reaching this population was that they were often isolated from towns or government centers where government services are provided. Other projects related to improving household water supplies and sanitation on remote estates and to providing GAPUZ (General Agricultural and Plantation Workers Union of Zimbabwe) members and staff with training in labor relations, negotiation, occupational health measures, and institution building.

As education continued to be a priority, SIDA decided to put most of its funding into assisting education in the commercial farm areas. In 1990 the government, with the assistance of SIDA, launched a project to improve children's education in these areas by assisting commercial farm owners who wished to start or expand primary schools and by directly assisting students.

The aim of assistance to farm owners was to construct the requisite physical structure to become registered with the Ministry of Education and Culture and thus to qualify for government-paid teachers and other support (SIDA 1994:18). Construction included two-classroom blocks with adequate toilet facilities and a borehole with a pump or a tap to ensure the availability of water. Table 7.2 shows the results. In 1991–1992, 32 schools were built or upgraded, and by 1994–1995, the number had risen to 40 schools. In total, 153 commercial farm schools were constructed.

The second part of the project was to assist children in commercial farm areas directly, with a ratio of seven girls to three boys in each of the nine regions (SIDA 1994:18). A total of ninety capable but marginalized children were chosen for the program in 1991. They received tuition, boarding, uniforms, and bedding fees through a direct grant. A total of 353 children were awarded grants between 1991 and 1992 and 1994 and 1995 (see Table 7.2). Those selected on merit to go on to secondary school were doing very well at the beginning of 1995, and the girls especially had become gender role models (SIDA 1994:19). As of this writing, it was too early for SIDA to assess the long-term impact on the students' lives, but it is known that educated women have a better understanding of children's

TABLE 7.2   SIDA's Assistance to Children in Commercial Farming Areas in
Zimbabwe, 1991–1995

Year	Number of Schools Assisted	Number of Children Assisted
1991–1992	32	90
1992–1993	41	88
1993–1994	40	88
1994–1995	40	87
Total	153	353

SOURCE: Swedish International Development Agency 1994:19.

health care needs, are apt to have fewer children, and are likely to see that
their children are educated (Floro and Wolf 1990; King and Hill 1991).

A 1994 assessment of educational attitudes and conditions affecting the
education of women and girls in the commercial farming areas (Nyagura
and Mupawaenda 1994) determined that 70 percent of the forty-three
farmers responding felt that literacy is important for farmworkers in order
for them "to perform their duties as required" (Nyagura and Mupawaenda
1994:21), but women's and girls' education was not regarded as important
by either the farmers or the workers. Girls' education was viewed as "dis-
pensable" (Nyagura and Mupawaenda 1994:37). The reasons most often
cited were that girls get pregnant or married; they get involved in sexual activities; they become "uncontrollable," "too proud," or "foolish"; and
once they have their education, they leave their families to get married and
the investment is lost (Nyagura and Mupawaenda 1994:37–39). Consequently, SIDA's project to support three times the number of girls as boys
in the commercial farm areas may have a multiplier effect in the long run
if these girls are successful in demonstrating that an investment in a girl's
education is valuable and contributes to the larger society.

Some Conclusions About the Role of the State
and Donor Agencies in Advancing Women's
Empowerment in Malawi and Zimbabwe

At the level of the state, Malawi has made more progress since indepen-
dence in integrating women in critical decisionmaking positions than
Zimbabwe. Women have been principal secretaries in three ministries—the
Ministry of Community Services, the Ministry of Education, and the
Ministry of Labor. Women are also being brought into other administrative

positions, for example, the women's desk officers in each ministry. NCWID has been at the forefront of a movement to ensure that more rights for Malawian women are included in the new constitution and that women achieve equity in at least one body of the national legislation by 1999.

The donor agencies working in Malawi, especially USAID and GTZ, have targeted women's and girls' advancement as crucial for this country's overall development. There is no question but that USAID's own increasing interest in advancing women's development in agriculture and education led to its funding and support of gendered programs in Malawi. In the late 1980s, the Malawian state, in its constant quest for scarce development funds and because of its concern about implementing the U.N. Forward Looking Strategies, responded to USAID's program interests by setting in motion the institutional mechanisms for increasing women's and girls' visibility and for meeting women's productive needs. In the process, some of women's strategic needs also were met through women's participation in agricultural projects, such as stall-fed cattle production, that previously had largely involved men. Women's potential for advancement was also enhanced by the GABLE program for girls' education and by the university graduate program in WID.

In the agriculture and education projects in Malawi, the involved women experienced increased empowerment, gaining equal access with men to scarce development resources: training, education, and credit. They experienced conscientization, a high-level aspect of empowerment according to Longwe's model (1990), and were able to participate in some aspects of the development process. For example, staff of the Women's Program in the Ministry of Agriculture participated in planning a manual for addressing women's needs in agricultural extension work. Similarly, women in various ministries and lecturers in the university participated in planning the courses to be taught in the master's degree program. What the women involved in these programs failed to achieve, however, was control over the resources and the decisionmaking process at all levels. At the highest administrative levels, in particular, men remain in control in Malawi and are reluctant to share that control with women. Malawian women are not alone in meeting major obstacles to achieving this highest level of development, nor can they be treated as an aggregate category. It is crucial to realize that not all Malawian women have common interests. Women in uxorilocal, matrilineal situations have a different set of needs and priorities from those in virilocal situations. Their security in land and individual *banja* production shape their priorities.

In Zimbabwe, women in the 1980s also experienced men's reluctance to share control over resources and decisionmaking even though women played an active part in the liberation struggle. Most of Zimbabwean women's gains have been outside the confines of the gendered state.

In large part, the efforts of the NGOs in Zimbabwe have been successful because they work at the grassroots level and increasingly involve the recipients of development in the planning, implementation, and evaluation of such projects. This participatory approach is in sharp contrast to Malawi's top-down approach, and as a result it has had more appeal for women because they are involved in shaping their own development rather than having it shaped for them. As Zimbabwe is a country with a long history of patriarchy, women's opportunity to participate in development becomes an incentive for them to examine other facets of their lives that need changing if they are to achieve equality with men.

Whereas in Malawi the state, led by the former president and prodded by donor agencies, has engineered the construction of women's development, in Zimbabwe, women at the grassroots level have led the way for women's development, forming pressure groups in some cases that have influenced the state to make changes that increase women's opportunities and rights, especially rights linked to their reproductive roles as daughters, wives, and mothers. The two countries, then, represent different scenarios with respect to gendered development. Chapter 8 looks more generally at gendered development.

Notes

1. The theoretical groundwork for this new approach came out of the DAWN (Development Alternatives with Women for a New Era) group in New Delhi. Composed of members from Third World countries who are grassroots organizers and women's advocates, DAWN's major tenets are found in Sen and Grown (1987).

2. The WLSA project, based in Harare, Zimbabwe, includes Botswana, Lesotho, Swaziland, Mozambique, Zambia, and Zimbabwe. Namibia also has recently been included. Unfortunately, Malawi is not a participant. The project is primarily funded by the Danish bilateral aid agency DANIDA (Danish Agency for International Development) but has also received grants from the Ford Foundation. It compiles country reports based on the work of research teams in each country and holds workshops focused on aspects of women's legal rights in the region.

3. Voter participation was below 20 percent in several by-elections preceding the general election in 1995 (Laasko 1995:11), and increasing democratization elsewhere in southern Africa could not be ignored.

4. The voter-education campaign was moderately successful in that 54 percent of the registered electorate in the constituencies where there was a contest voted (Laasko 1995:18). However, efforts to democratize the primaries that preceded the general election were less successful, which meant that opposition candidates stood less chance of standing in the national elections.

5. The situation described by this UNICEF case study is not unusual for Zimbabwe; the situation is much worse on most large-scale commercial farms

(UNICEF 1994b:4). Moreover, these conditions are repeated in the other three countries in this study. For example, in Malawi, Kaufulu and Davison (1992) found that laborers' families on tea estates in Thyolo District were often crowded into compounds with little land made available for subsistence production. In one case, only one pit latrine was provided for over 100 households. On other tea estates, conditions were slightly better with a row of cement-block pit latrines. However, few estates provided adequate schooling; if a school existed, it rarely included more than four grades. Health care was rarely provided.

8

Advancing Gender Equity
in the Future

Does gender equity, as a critical aspect of development, stand a chance in southern Africa? In order to analyze the process of gendered development, including the way it is constantly restructured and changed, it is necessary to critically review the way development approaches birthed in the north have impacted women's development in the states of the Zambezi region. In this final chapter I take up this task in order to answer the initial question.

Until the 1980s, most approaches had a negative effect on southern African women by bringing men into the development process to the virtual exclusion of women. If women were seen at all, it was in their roles as reproducers and not as producers. Moreover, the type of development that "trickled down" to women treated rural and impoverished urban women as victims; such programs used a "charitable" welfare approach rather than an enabling approach that focused on the women's interests and strengths, with their increased empowerment being the objective.

The end of the U.N. Decade of Women in 1985 and the resulting U.N. Convention to End All Forms of Discrimination Against Women framed the gender work to be carried out over the next decade. Equality, development, and peace became the new *relational* paradigm linking women's development to other needs. Gender equity was a central aspect of this new vision, one that was reinforced and extended at the Beijing conference in 1995. Of crucial importance, gender equity involves redistribution—of critical productive resources; of decisionmaking power, which in turn may affect the way decisions are reached; and of authority to act on decisions at all levels. At a subliminal level, the prospects of such a gender shift may threaten those who have become entrenched in state-legitimated bureaucracies. Likewise, the gendered redistribution of development resources, decisionmaking, and authority can pose a threat to individuals whose ideas have become entrenched in male-dominated development agencies and lending institutions. A change in the way gender is structured in any institution is bound to bring a certain amount of dissonance and struggle. Yet as the case of the Ministry of Agriculture's Peoples' Participation Project in western Zambia illustrates, restructuring is possible. In some cases, as in Malawi, it may come from the national level. In others, it may have to begin at the provincial or local level and then "trickle up" to be effective.

The U.N. Women's Decade brought equity issues to the surface but did not alleviate the tensions in gender relations or prompt new redistributive policies for the states in the region. Marginalized women in the south began to observe that women who championed gender equity in the north were retrenching; they were falling back on older, male-generated models symbolized in "growth with efficiency and effectiveness" (GEE) rather than working toward "global gender equity" (GGE).

Reassessing their own needs within the historical contexts of their specific countries, women in southern African countries and other Third World states began to envisage a new model of development—one based on equality with men in each culturally specific, national context. This alternative view of development has reminded elite First World women that historically, the experiences of these women are at variance with theirs and that gender subordination is embedded in a specific history of colonial occupation, exploitative class relations, and racism.

Sara Longwe suggests that for African women the development process has become derailed. Women are treated by states and development agencies as a "disadvantaged minority" rather than as a productive majority. Women in the four countries in this study are the numerical majority, but they continue to be the political and economic minorities. As male leaders in these countries like to tell us, "They are the backbone of agricultural production." Yet they do not share equally with men in the fruits of agrarian change. Through conscientization and active participation in the development process, however, as Longwe suggests, empowerment *with* men can be achieved.

Unique among the four countries that are central to this inquiry, Mozambique made a conscious effort to address gender inequalities in its experiment with socialist transformation in the late 1970s and 1980s. In the ten-year period when redistributive policies were integrated into Mozambique's state development plans, women's productive needs were partly met through the redistribution of productive relations on state farms and in producer cooperatives and through the provision of childcare in many, but not all, workplaces. In addition, a redistribution of organizational decisionmaking roles took place with women assuming responsibility for organizing work brigades and managing production. However, very little progress was made in restructuring gender roles at the household level, and women's share of national positions was more symbolic than real.

Within Mozambique's diverse regions, a schism exists between matrilineal groups in the north and in the patrilineal south that poses a tension for this state and its women. The patrilineal south, centered at Maputo, has led development so far. Little has been known about the matrilineal north, which largely escaped the exploitation of male emigrant labor that plagued Zambezia and the south. The north has tended to be viewed by the state as "traditional" and "backward," partly because its population refuses to give up matrilineal succession rights and communal land-tenure practices and partly because the chiefs and traditional leaders in these matrilineal areas were viewed as reactionary by FRELIMO, which took away their powers at independence. Agriculture in the north is based on individualized family farming, as it is in southern Malawi. And family farming continues to be the predominant mode of production, although a history of schemes to increase production through state farming and cooperatives has been tried. Most recently, the state has engaged in joint ventures in cotton production with private companies. But women continue to give the bulk of their time and labor to family production (Pitcher 1995).

Despite the gains made by women in Mozambique's postindependence decade, the increasing attention given to privatization and production for a global market by the state under the leadership of Joaquim Chissano has precipitated a loss in the equity gains that Mozambican women realized between 1983 and 1985.[1] Even though women hold a higher proportion of legislative seats in their national assembly than women in the other three states in this study, they hold few of the appointed positions in the cabinet. Mozambican women look to women's appointment to cabinet positions as a true test of the state's commitment to gender equity at the highest level. Given the nature of party elections in Mozambique, the cabinet is where women's empowerment at the national level will be realized.

In Malawi, women's development at the national level has been engineered by the gendered, avuncular state. Under such conditions, only a few women have risen to achieve measurable empowerment. Women are most empowered in the rural areas, where women peasant producers in matrilineal hearthholds have managed to sustain a certain self-sufficiency and distance from the state, however elusive. For women closer to the state apparatus, the authority of the gendered state recently has come under scrutiny and a new coalition of women's groups is pushing to ensure that women's legal and political rights are protected and their political participation is ensured. With a new political structure, the potential for empowerment is real.

Zimbabwe's women have a more strident voice than Malawian women. Their struggle for liberation and equality mirrors their nation's liberation struggle. Working at the grassroots, largely outside the state apparatus, many women have become aware of their practical and strategic needs and have formulated strategies for achieving them. At times progress appears slow—especially in implementing reforms for improving women's status that have been agreed on through new policies. But a politically aware critical mass of women exists in Zimbabwe. These women are in the process of conscientizing other women. Although the task of achieving empowerment is formidable in this country of entrenched patriarchy, Zimbabwean women have found strength in their solidarity.

Zimbabwean women have had more legal and social obstacles to face than Malawian women, partly because of Zimbabwe's past history of patrilineal and patriarchal relations of production and reproduction and partly because of the particular type of settler colonization that Zimbabwe experienced. Thus history and lineage ideology have figured prominently in the way gender relations have evolved.

Zambia is at a crossroads. In this former settler colony with a history of missionization, or "evangelical imperialism" as Comaroff and Comaroff (1992:37) refer to it, many of the characteristics of matriliny that gave women a central place—such as succession rights to land and uxorilocality, associated with ethnic groups in the eastern and northern parts of the country—have been altered. Patriarchal capitalism became entrenched despite Kaunda's humanist platform. Mining helped to set the agenda. A western-educated male state bureaucracy extended the culture of colonial paternalism to Zambia's women regardless of their circumstances. It is not insignificant that until the mid-1990s, Zambia was one of the few states in the region that had not made a concerted effort to reform the system of Roman-Dutch law inherited from its former colonizers.

Many observers thought that democratization of the political system in 1991 would bring positive changes for Zambia's women. However, that has not been the case. Democracy, as we know, is not a sufficient condition for gender equity and women's overall empowerment. It takes women and men working together to change attitudes and age-old behavioral patterns to achieve real equality. To date, neither the leaders of the UNIP nor those of the MMD have shown any real commitment to sharing power and redistributing resources to enable women's advancement at the national level in Zambia. At the same time, women at the grassroots level are making notable headway in the 1990s in gaining access to scarce development resources such as training, extension services, and labor-saving technologies. They also are learning how to control resources such as capital and its investment in farm resources, oxen, and plows and the allocation of their labor to various crops. In addition, they are learning how to manage and lead producer groups. Consequently, whereas well-educated urban women may experience a sense of frustration in their efforts to become empowered, peasant women in specific cases such as that described earlier for Western Province may be experiencing a greater sense of control and empowerment. Their battleground is the rice fields rather than parliament. And whatever empowerment they achieve will be gained within this local context. However, if the battle of the rice fields is multiplied in other provinces, it is just possible that those in power will be forced to shift their vision from what one woman wears in parliament to the many women who have the power to increase or decrease Zambia's overall agricultural production.

Development Strategies and Rural Women: Must We Work Together?

International development agencies eager to enhance the economic viability of rural women began devising various strategies and projects to improve the material quality of their lives in the 1980s. Agricultural projects and income-generating activities that required women's *cooperative* production were central among the strategies tried in 1985–1995. In some places these efforts have taken hold, as in some parts of Zambia and, to some extent, in Zimbabwe, but in other areas such as southern Malawi and northern Mozambique, they have been far less successful.

In communities where patriliny and virilocality are practiced, women who out-marry often find it desirable and even necessary to form productive alliances with other women in a community to maximize their productive capacity, especially if they do not have lineage rights to land. The situation of women in the minority of groups that are matrilineal, as has been suggested, is different because women have more direct access to land through their lineages. And where they marry uxorilocally, they live in close proximity to their land with access to and relative control over family labor. This relative control over land and labor gives these women a sense of autonomy, an autonomy that their counterparts in patrilineal groups do not share (Geisler et al. 1985; Rocha 1988). Also, women in matrilineal, uxorilocal contexts are hesitant to participate in collaborative forms of production with other women in their villages because they may have conflicting claims to land and their commodity crops may compete with other women's in the local market, as in the case of women farmers in southern Malawi and in Mozambique (Pitcher 1995).

Lineage ideology certainly is not the only factor influencing women's decisions about joining a cooperative enterprise; certainly mismanagement of funds, lack of leadership and motivation, and lack of adequate transportation or markets are other determining factors. Nonetheless, the tenacity with which women cling to individual family production in Malawi, some parts of northern Zambia, and northern Mozambique is an indication that development for them does not include cooperative production.

Max-Neff, Elizalde, and Hopenhayn (1986) argue persuasively that an effective approach to development is one that goes beyond quantifying labor's effects on the quality of life to an inclusion of its role in the satisfaction of human needs as a catalyst for improving society (1986:67). Such a broadened vision fits well with the practical and strategic needs of peasant women who prefer individualized development. Women in predominantly matrilineal groups where uxorilocality is practiced prefer to increase their access to scarce resources such as credit on an individual rather than a group basis. Control over the economic aspects of their lives means increasing their individual income—their financial empowerment—while retaining their relative authority in farm-level production.

Development theorists must recognize that rural women, as a category, are not powerless. Some women feel more or less powerful than others, and these perceptions of self matter in women's abilities to act (Kariuki 1985; Davison 1989). Programs designed to improve women's chances for increased empowerment must at the same time sustain existing forms of power at the grassroots level. Connecting women in matrilineal households to credit and extension services that enable them as *individual* producers to increase production is a more culturally appropriate form of development than cooperative production. This was the case for women rice farmers in western Zambia (Jiggins et al. 1995) and is the case for individual women burley tobacco and maize farmers in Malawi (Hirschmann 1993a; Davison 1992, 1995). Making cooperative production a prerequisite for obtaining inputs—including credit—will only discourage women in uxorilocal, matrilineal households.

The inequalities experienced by various types of female-headed households—regardless of lineage ideology—which constitute between 30 and 40 percent of the total Zambian population (Zambian Association for Research and Development 1985:5), 33 percent of Malawi's population, and roughly similar proportions in Mozambique (WLSA 1992) and Zimbabwe (Armstrong 1992) must be attended to. Women whose husbands are absent due to the pull of migrant labor but who receive regular remittances must be treated differently from women whose husbands have virtually abandoned them. Young single mothers with children have a set of needs different from that of older widows. Each category of FHHs must be provided with specific inputs that meet its particular needs. Like male-headed households and jointly headed households (JHHs), FHHs cannot be treated as a single aggregate category.

The case studies of development projects in this volume demonstrate that planning development for women's economic and social empowerment cannot take place in a vacuum. Development occurs within a particular ethnic, regional, and historical context. Lineage is a factor to be addressed in this context.

Development priorities are changing in central southern Africa. If donor agencies' efforts are to be effective, they must attend to the needs of women as well as men for empowerment at all levels—from the individual hearth-hold to the state bureaucracy.

Common Concerns of Women and Men in the Region

The majority of women and men in the region have three concerns in common: (1) growing land scarcity, (2) lack of scarce resources to improve production and reduced labor, and (3) lack of control over market forces that determine the prices for crops. Each is briefly discussed in terms of gender, lineage, and ethnicity.

Growing Land Scarcity

Without land to grow food, production ceases. Men in patrilineal groups see their patrimony disappearing into smaller and smaller pieces just as women (and men) in matrilineal groups do. Struggles over land erupt more frequently than in the past between fathers and sons, between maternal uncles and their sisters' sons, among brothers, and among sisters. Some brothers and sisters, especially with education, give up their immediate interest in land to take up wage work. Others struggle with leaner, less fertile parcels to eke out a living. Some men in patrilineal and matrilineal-virilocal groups accumulate and consolidate holdings at the expense of other men who find themselves landless. Women in matrilineal groups have fewer resources than men in patrilineal groups and therefore less opportunity to accumulate land. Wives in patrilineal groups and matrilineal-virilocal groups have a dependency relationship with their husband-landholders that is problematic unless they have managed to purchase or acquire land of their own.

For men in matrilineal groups there are two options with regard to land and its control. One is to manipulate the practice of matriliny so that with the payment of bridewealth, a man retains control over his matrilineal land and his wife becomes dependent on him, an option that women in patrilineal groups do not have. The other option is to "drop out" of the system, heading for an urban area and wage employment. For women the options are more complex. Where a woman has relative autonomy through uxorilocality, she may continue to cultivate her matrilineal land with increased inputs on less land than her mother tilled. If she is successful, she may increase production to the point where she is able to acquire additional land, thus expanding production. In other cases she has the option of following her husband to an urban area, leaving her land in a relative's hands. If she is single, she may select this option on her own depending on the fertility of her land and her interests.

Whereas gendered states and development agencies have studied the patrilineal options related to land in some detail, not much thought has been given to creative options that sustain rather than delete matrilineally held land from development schemes. If women control particular parcels of land, why should they not be given the option of either retaining their parcels within legally recognized communal holdings or transferring their land to individual title to protect their rights in individual ownership? Why does land registration most often come down to individualized male entitlement?

Scarce Resources and Labor-Saving Technology

Among the scarce resources related to agricultural production are technological inputs, including improved seed, fertilizer, and composting technology; labor-saving equipment; and credit. By "bringing men in" and focusing on their needs as producers, women's equal needs as producers have been ignored to an alarming extent. It is time to put an end to this lopsided development. Women farmers are as entitled as men to technological, extension, and credit resources that will make a difference in their production. The support groups for individual women rice growers in western Zambia provide a model.

The need to access and control inputs cuts across lineage ideology and gender except when collateral in land is required for credit. In such cases, women in matrilineal groups with land are in a favored position over women in patrilineal groups who do not control their land. Just as crucial, dividing households into MHHs and FHHs does not help illuminate wives' productive roles and labor needs in either patrilineal or matrilineal households. In matrilineal groups that practice uxorilocality, a study of the ways that jointly managed households make decisions about production, allocate labor, and make investments might better serve the needs of the women in these households.

Equally significant to development are strategies for resource sharing between genders that come from African innovations. For example, in

Lesotho, where state elites and patrilineal peasants alike support the continuation of Lesotho's customary land-tenure system, "borrowing" forms the basis of resource sharing between men and women with different sets of resources. Steven Lawry (1993) illustrates how holders of land without access to plows (mainly single women) collaborate with land-poor owners of plows (mostly men) to the advantage of both. The land-poor male household head borrows land from the female landowner and in turn, uses his plow to till his borrowed land and the other land she holds. In the case of the crop raised on the borrowed land, the female landholder and the male plow owner share proceeds from crop sales equally. Such an arrangement demonstrates local ingenuity and willingness to share resources on an individual basis in a way that is beneficial to both women and men.

Control of Market Forces

Women and men in smallholder households are tied to national and international economies the complexity of which they rarely understand. The price they get for what they produce is the bottom line. If this price is fixed at a minimal level to meet the demands of urban dwellers for low food prices, the producer suffers regardless of gender. Inequities in pricing and market structures are recognized, but short of work stoppages (agrarian strikes) the peasant producer has little power to influence the decisions of marketing boards and international market structures—for instance, GATT (General Agreement on Tariffs and Trade).

Having acknowledged these constraints, I should note that at the household level, differences that are shaped by lineage lead to different perceptions of fluctuations in market pricing. Male producers in patrilineal households and men in virilocal, matrilineal households are more apt to have a vested interest in global and local market fluctuations because they often are the ones in the household to control income from cash-value crop production. Where men and women share household decisionmaking, as they often do in jointly headed households, both are affected. Similarly, the incomes of women who grow cash-value crops in matrilineal-uxorilocal situations where a man is absent much of the time or no adult male producer exists will be affected by market prices. The majority of FHHs headed by single women, who are more apt to have limited resources, will be little affected because they sell their produce locally. This is also the case for MHHs where a man is single and does not have access to the labor of a wife or children; these households have been ignored in agrarian schemes. Differences in marital status and, relatedly, in economic status distinguish men and women within a single ethnic group and community. Such differences matter in planning and implementing projects.

Women's Access to and Control
of the Decisionmaking Process

Longwe (1990) challenges us to think about development not just in terms of access to resources, training, education, and the like but in terms of the importance of *participation* in decisions that affect people's control of these resources. Participation is not always efficient. It can be cumbersome and laborious—in a word, messy. At the same time, it ensures more effective development. People who participate have a vested interest in solutions. Just as important, they are likely to become empowered along the way.

From increased empowerment in a negotiated process, the potential for *control sharing* emerges. Gaining control does not necessarily mean wresting control by manipulation or force from someone else or another group. It can arise when a wedge has been opened or a space created for the less powerful to enter and share in making critical decisions. This kind of space has been created by some gender-sensitive men working with gender-sensitive women in state bureaucracies and development agencies. It is this vision of control sharing rather than control domination that motivates many Third World women to hold out for an alternative vision of development that breaks down structural socioeconomic differences between nation-states, between classes, and between ethnic groups and genders while at the same time recognizing that class, nationalism, ethnicity, and, yes, lineage differences are salient forces shaping the way women (and men) perceive their gender needs and priorities (Bryceson 1995; Basu 1995).

Conclusions on
Gender, Lineage, and Ethnicity

Gender, as I initially pointed out, is at the heart of lineage ideology. In southern Africa, lineage and descent were traced through the male or the female line. Historically, the direction in which lineage was gendered ordered the options and obligations of women and men in a specifically self-defined group. It also shaped their control over productive and reproductive resources. Where a group was matrilineal, women had more direct access to land and they maintained authority over their children. If, in addition, uxorilocality was practiced, a woman also had access to the labor of a husband in constructing a house, in some places a granary, and for agricultural chores. Equally important, he had to provide her with children through his reproductive labor, though he had no rights in these children. She had access to the labor and support of matrikin, as needed. When she grew older, she also had rights to the labor of her daughters' husbands when these daughters married. Gifted, articulate women; those with a penchant for leadership or women who came from a significant lineage; rainmakers and shamans—any of these might become empowered as a political leader in her own right. That a woman could head a clan, make decisions about the land, raid or trade, was beyond dispute. That she was given the option of ruling was more complicated and depended, in large part, on her relationships with her male siblings.

For women in patrilineal groups, the situation, historically and currently, is more ambiguous. As she usually marries out, she is a stranger in her husband's village. Her children belong to his clan or lineage rather than to hers. Her parents lose a daughter, although they are likely to gain some bridewealth in compensation. A woman in a patrilocal or virilocal situation has no recognized rights in land. She gains access to land through her husband. If she is unmarried, her father or mother may assign a piece of land to her. In the past, if she was widowed she was expected to marry the deceased husband's brother so that the children would remain in the care of the patrilineage, and in some areas, this expectation still applies. A husband usually builds the house and a granary. He is expected to provide his wife with children. However, should there be no children, he will take a second wife. Assuming that infertility is the wife's fault, he may even return a childless wife to her home. Historically, if a woman was a member of a ruling lineage, her chances of controlling resources (land and labor) were far greater than those for a peasant woman. Slaves, in either matrilineal or patrilineal groups, had no rights except to food and shelter.

During the period prior to British colonization, when an ethnic group was successful in conquering and subjugating another group, the latter was often forced to adopt the dominant group's lineage ideology and marital practices. Where the patrilineal Ngoni and Kololo came into contact with matrilineal groups, the latter tended to adopt the patrilineal succession and virilocal residence practices of the dominant group. However, this was not always the case. Where matrilineal groups dominated, they might subsume a less powerful patrilineal group. We cannot assume that because patriliny was widespread in southern African by the time the first colonial observers arrived, it predominated throughout the precolonial period. Matrilineal groups existed throughout Zambia, Malawi, and northern Mozambique. And contrary to popular opinion, matriliny did not give way to patriliny but was sustained throughout the region even though some matrilineal groups adopted virilocal residence patterns during the period of British or Portuguese conquest.

When land was fully available and free, as it was for centuries, labor was the quintessential issue that made a difference in production. Leaders were measured by the number of people they could bring under their control so that land could be tilled, cattle herded, and yet more people fed. Wealth in people is not an idle concept. In communities that measure wealth in this way, the members have a mutual responsibility through networks of obligations.

The ideology that empowered and provided the glue for this network of relations was descent—acknowledged according to connections to a known and recognized ancestor or to a mythical ancestor, usually the "first person to settle on the land." That this first settler could be a woman or a sister and brother rather than "a man and his wife," as in the Christian epic, was discounted by Westerners. Matrilineal ideology not withstanding, power and the authority to control land and labor became gendered male under colonial occupation and by extension through African states.

I discussed in Chapters 3 and 4 how the colonial state attempted to extract male labor along with land at the turn of the century and the strategies employed by various groups and individual households to resist that demand. But the ever-escalating hut tax and the incessant demand for labor put an indefatigable squeeze on patrilineal and matrilineal households in Southern Rhodesia in the 1920s and in Northern Rhodesia and Nyasaland by the early 1930s. Large numbers of men were coerced or forced to sell their labor, especially in Mozambique. Yet in other cases the draw of cash wages encouraged men to sell their labor away from home. Some women migrated as well to seek income-producing activities. Even though the dynamics of labor lost to rural communities differed in form and intensity by country and locality, the net effect was that rural women (and their children) were burdened with a broader range of agricultural tasks to be accomplished with less labor available for recruitment. In groups where agricultural tasks previously were shared between spouses, women became the primary producers and often the providers in their families, joining their counterparts in female-headed households.

The women left behind, especially those in "native reserves," found themselves plagued by not only a labor shortage but a dwindling land base and soil that was less fertile. Meanwhile, colonial agricultural researchers and extension workers determined that agricultural production was indeed slipping in these so-called reserves and began to foster countermeasures aimed at soil conservation and increased production. They targeted women for the implementation of conservation measures and men for agrarian reform projects to stimulate cash-crop production, especially of maize, cotton, and tobacco. I have discussed the effects on female farmers—whose major concerns were with food production—of these colonial agrarian reform policies. But that they were perpetuated and extended by donor agencies and African states in the 1960s and 1970s only added to the agrarian crisis that emerged in the 1980s. Significantly, it took that crisis to prod agrarian reformers into investigating the role of women in Africa's farming systems. For four decades, women had been largely ignored except for isolated assessments carried out with minimal resources. Only in the latter part of the 1980s did policymakers begin to acknowledge women's *economic value* to African agriculture and to development generally and to put forward measures to redress their long neglect. However, these measures have not given much recognition to the differences among women by lineage, marital status, or ethnicity.

In the 1990s, women who head their own households experience the loss of male labor differently in matrilineal and patrilineal groups. Women in matrilineal groups whose husbands are deceased or have abandoned their families to work elsewhere continue to retain access to land and often to control income they earn from production. Just as important, where they marry uxorilocally they have the support of matrikin living in close proximity. In contrast, for women in patrilineal groups, once a husband emigrates, the risk of losing income intensifies. Moreover, as a "stranger" in her husband's village, a woman must reach out and seek support from other virilocally married women who, like herself, may be far from kin. The networks these women create sustain them when their husbands leave to seek wage work far away.[2] Women in matrilineal groups, though adversely affected by male emigration, have the advantage of stable links with land and control over family labor.

In this study of gender, lineage ideology, and ethnicity in central southern Africa, I have stressed that unless we historically conceptualize the development process, any discussion of the variables that currently influence African development is meaningless. Historians acknowledge the value of time frames and historical specificity in evaluating current social formations. Social scientists, though Johnny-come-latelies, have begun incorporating historical processes in their analyses of current phenomena. At the same time, social scientists of various hues provide entry into the particularities of sociocultural, economic, and demographic factors in the process of change that at times become broadly painted with the stroke of a historian's pen. The need for a synergy between the two approaches exists, as this volume illustrates.

By tracing the historical roots of gender biases and their perpetuation through time concurrently with the social formation of lineage ideologies and ethnicities in one specific area, this study has served to clarify how these three interrelate throughout periods of underdevelopment and development particular to the region. At the same time, the use of a comparative approach that transcends national boundaries artificially created by colonial powers a century ago helps in examining how social formations based on lineage became part of the cultural framework of many ethnic groups.

Analyses of lineage ideologies, however, suffer unless these ideologies are linked to practices—including the contradictions and ambiguities of everyday living. Critical in examining how lineage ideology is signaled and practiced in various contexts have been the voices and opinions of Africans that permeate this study. These voices are not a uniform lot; they vary, as I have noted, by class, ethnicity, and gender.

A study of lineage differences in Africa serves no purpose unless it is linked to an understanding of how development as a process can be made to better serve the needs of the majority of people who live and often work in rural areas. Because most of the rural dwellers in the region I have examined are women, their needs and interests as members of specific cultural groups demand our attention. Too often in the past we have investigated women's practical and strategic needs in patrilineally organized societies and have dismissed matrilineality or treated it as problematic. It is time to give commensurate attention to matrilineal formations not just because they persist in southern Africa but because matriliny has implications for the way we define development and conceptualize empowerment. Empowerment that is mutually beneficial to both sexes is what women in the Zambezi region would like to achieve in the next decade.

Notes

1. Mozambican women are not alone in losing productive status when socialist production is replaced by capitalist production. Ample evidence now exists that women in the East German Republic, many of whom held managerial positions in state-run industries and farms, lost their positions after unification with West Germany (Freitag, personal communication 1993).

2. Deutsch (1987) demonstrates how Mexican women in northern New Mexico have similarly used networks with other women to sustain their villages when their husbands have migrated north to Colorado as migrant workers. Because the women had married away from their own villages, they depended on these networks.

References

Aberle, D. F. 1962. "Matrilineal Descent in Cross-Cultural Perspective." In *Matrilineal Kinship*, edited by D. Schneider and K. Gough. Berkeley: University of California Press.

Abraham, D. P. 1962. "The Early Political History of the Kingdom of Mwana Mutapa." In *Historians in Tropical Africa*. Salisbury: International African Institute.

Adams, J. M. 1991. "Female Wage Labor in Rural Zimbabwe." *World Development* 19(2/3):163–176.

Afonja, S. 1986. "Changing Modes of Production and the Sexual Division of Labor Among the Yoruba." In *Women's Work*, edited by E. Leacock and H. Safa. South Hadley, MA: Bergin & Garvey.

Ajayi, A.J.F. 1965. *Christian Missions in Nigeria: 1841–1891*. London: Longman.

Akpamgbo, C. 1977. "A 'Woman to Woman Marriage' and the Repugnancy Clause: A Case of Putting New Wine in Old Bottles." *African Law Studies* 14:87–95.

Allen, C. 1991. "Gender, Participation and Radicalism in African Nationalism: Its Contemporary Significance." In *Democracy and Socialism in Africa*, edited by R. Cohen and H. Goulbourne. Boulder and London: Westview Press.

al-Mas'udi, M. 1962. "The Ivory Trade." In *East African Coast: Select Documents*, edited by G.S.P. Freeman-Greenville. Oxford: Oxford University Press.

Alpers, E. 1968. "The Mutapa and Malawi Political Systems to the Time of the Ngoni Invasions." In *Aspects of Central African History*, edited by T. O. Ranger. Evanston, IL: Northwestern University Press.

Amadiume, I. 1987. *Male Daughters, Female Husbands*. London: Zed Press.

Anderson, W. H. 1919. *On the Trail of Livingston*. Mountain View: n.p.

Arhin, Kwame. 1983. "The Political and Military Roles of Akan Women." In *Female and Male in West Africa*, edited by C. Oppong. London: George Allen & Unwin.

Armstrong, A. 1992. *Struggling over Scarce Resources: Women and Maintenance in Southern Africa*. Harare: University of Zimbabwe.

Armstrong, A., et al. 1993. "Uncovering Reality: Excavating Women's Rights in African Family Law." Working paper no. 7, Women and Law in Southern Africa (WLSA), Harare.

Arnfred, S. 1988. "Women in Mozambique: Gender Struggle and Gender Politics." *Review of African Political Economy* 41:5–12.

Arrighi, G. 1973. "Labour Supplies in Historical Perspective." In *Essays in the Political Economy of Africa*, edited by G. Arrighi and J. Saul. New York: Monthly Review Press.

Awe, Bolanle. 1977. "The Yalode in the Traditional Yoruba Political System." In *Sexual Stratification: A Cross-Cultural View,* edited by A. Schlegel. New York: Columbia University Press.

Axelson, E. 1980. *Portuguese in South-East Africa, 1600–1700.* Johannesburg: Witwatersrand University Press.

Banda, R. J. 1984. "Western Education: A Corroding Factor on African Traditional Life." Unpublished master's thesis, Chancellor College, University of Malawi, Zomba.

Barnes, T. A. 1987. "African Female Labour and the Urban Economy of Colonial Zimbabwe, with Special Reference to Harare, 1920–1939." Unpublished master's thesis, University of Zimbabwe, Harare.

_____. 1992. "The Fight for Control of African Women's Mobility in Colonial Zimbabwe, 1900–1939." *Signs* 17(3):586–608.

_____. 1995. "Am I a Man? Gender and the Pass Laws in Urban Colonial Zimababwe." Johannesburg: University of Witswatersrand. Mimeographed.

Barnett, S., and M. Silverman. 1979. *Ideology in Everyday Life.* Ann Arbor: University of Michigan Press.

Basehart, H. 1962. "Ashanti." In *Matrilineal Kinship,* edited by D. Schneider and K. Gough. Berkeley: University of California Press.

Basu, A., ed. 1995. *The Challenge of Local Feminisms.* Boulder and London: Westview Press.

Batezat, E., and M. Mwalo. 1989. *Women in Zimbabwe.* Harare: SAPES.

Beach, D. N. 1976. "Historiography of the People of Zimbabwe in the 1960's." *Rhodesian History* 4:21–30.

_____. 1977. "The Shona Economy: Branches of Production." In *The Roots of Rural Poverty in Central and Southern Africa,* edited by R. Palmer and N. Parsons. London: Heinemann.

_____. 1980. *The Shona and Zimbabwe, 900–1850.* Gweru: Mambo Press.

_____. 1984. *Zimbabwe Before 1900.* Gweru: Mambo Press.

_____. 1994. *The Shona and Their Neighbors.* Oxford and Cambridge: Blackwell.

Beneria, L. 1983. "Accounting for Women's Work." In *Women and Development: The Sexual Division of Labor in Rural Economies.* Geneva: ILO.

Berg, N., and A. Gundersen. 1992. "Legal Reform in Mozambique: Equality and Emancipation for Women Through Popular Justice?" In *Women and the Law in Mozambique.* Harare: WLSA.

Berry, S. 1975. *Cocoa, Custom and Socio-Economic Change in Rural Western Nigeria.* Oxford: Clarendon Press.

_____. 1993. *No Condition Is Permanent: The Social Dynamics of Agrarian Change in Sub-Saharan Africa.* Madison: University of Wisconsin Press.

Bloch, Maurice. 1987. "Descent and Sources of Contradiction in the Representations of Women and Kinship." In *Gender and Kinship: Essays Toward a Unified Analysis,* edited by J. Collier and S. Yanagisako. Stanford: Stanford University Press.

Bocarro, A. [1899] 1964. "Extracts from the Decade Written by Antonio Bocarro, His Majesty's Chronicler for the State of India, of the Performance of the Portuguese in the East." In *Records of South-Eastern Africa* 3, edited by G. M. Theal. Johannesburg: University of Witswatersrand.

Boserup, E. 1970. *Woman's Role in Economic Development*. New York: St. Martin's Press.

Bourdillon, M.F.C. 1976. *The Shona Peoples: An Ethnographic Study of the Contemporary Shona with Special Reference to the Religion*. Gweru: Mambo Press.

Bowen, M. L. 1993. "Socialist Transitions: Policy Reforms in Mozambique." In *Land in African Agrarian Systems*, edited by T. J. Bassett and D. E. Crummey. Madison: University of Wisconsin.

Bratton, M. 1980. *The Local Politics of Rural Development: Peasant and Party-States in Zambia*. Hanover, NH: University Press of New England.

Bruce, J. W. 1993. "Do Indigenous Tenure Systems Constrain Agricultural Development?" In *Land in African Agrarian Systems*, edited by T. J. Bassett and D. E. Crummey. Madison: University of Wisconsin Press.

Bryceson, J. F., ed. 1995. *Women Wielding the Hoe: Lessons from Rural Africa for Feminist Theory and Development Practice*. Oxford: Berg.

Bryson, J. C. 1981. "Women and Agriculture in Sub-Saharan Africa: Implications for Development (an exploratory study)." In *African Women in the Development Process*, edited by N. Nelson. London: Frank Cass.

Bullock, C. 1913. *Mashona Laws and Customs*. Salisbury: Argus.

Burdette, M. C. 1984. *Zambia: Between Two Worlds*. Boulder and London: Westview Press.

Burke, E. E., ed. 1969. *The Journals of Carl Mauch: His Travels in the Transvaal and Rhodesia, 1869–1872*. Salisbury: National Archives of Rhodesia.

Butler, J. 1989. "Afrikaner Women and the Creation of Ethnicity in a Small South African Town, 1902–1950." In *The Creation of Tribalism in Southern Africa*, edited by L. Vail. London: James Currey; and Berkeley: University of California Press.

Butler, Judith. 1990. *Gender Trouble*. New York: Routledge Press.

Callaway, B. 1987. *Muslim Hausa Women in Nigeria*. Rochester: New York University Press.

Carney, J. A. 1988. "Struggles over Land and Crops in an Irrigated Rice Scheme: The Gambia." In *Agriculture, Women, and Land: The African Experience*, edited by J. Davison. Boulder and London: Westview Press.

Carney, J. A., and M. Watts. 1991. "Disciplining Women?" *Signs* 16(4):651–681.

Chanaiwa, D. 1973. *The Zimbabwe Controversy: A Case of Colonial Historiography*. Syracuse: Syracuse University Press.

Chanock, M. 1977. "Agricultural Change and Continuity in Malawi." In *The Roots of Rural Poverty in Central and Southern Africa*, edited by R. Palmer and N. Parsons. London: Heinemann.

_____. 1985. *Law, Custom and Social Order: The Colonial Experience in Malawi and Zambia*. Cambridge: Cambridge University Press.

Chaturvedi, S. 1994. *Non-Governmental Organisations (NGOs) in the Education Sector*. Lilongwe: USAID.

Chauncey, G. 1981. "The Locus of Reproduction: Women's Labour in the Zambian Copperbelt." *Journal of Southern African Studies* 7(2):135–164.

Chavunduka, G. L. 1970. "Social Change in a Shona Ward." Occasional paper no. 4, Department of Sociology, University of Zimbabwe, Salisbury.

Cheater, A. P. 1983. "Formal and Informal Rights to Land in Zimbabwe's Black Freehold Areas: A Case Study from Msengezi." In *Past and Present in Zimbabwe*, edited by J.D.Y. Peel and T. O. Ranger. Manchester: Manchester University Press.

Chieza, M. 1983. "Participation of Women in National Development: A Case Study of Nyachuru Women's Group." Unpublished master's thesis, University of Zimbabwe, Harare.

Chimombo, S. 1994. *Napolo and the Python*. London: Heinemann.

Chipande, G. 1986. "Households and Rural Development Efforts with Special Reference to Phalombe Area of Southern Malawi." Paper presented at Workshop on Rural Development Strategies and Programmes, Lilongwe, December 30–January 5.

_____. 1987. "Innovation Adoption Among Female-Headed Households: The Case of Malawi." *Development and Change* 18:315–327.

Chisala, E. A., and G. B. Mthindi. 1989. "Structural Adjustment and the Smallholder Agricultural Growth in Malawi." Paper presented at the workshop The Effect of Structural Adjustment Programmes, Blantyre, November 26–30.

Cliffe, Lionel. 1978. "Labour Migration and Peasant Differences: Zambian Experiences." *Journal of Peasant Studies* 5(3):326–346.

Collier, J. F., and S. J. Yanagisako. 1987. "Introduction." In *Gender and Kinship: Essays Toward a Unified Analysis*. Stanford: Stanford University Press.

Collins, P. H. 1993. "Toward an Afrocentric Feminist Epistomology." In *Feminist Frameworks* (3rd ed.), edited by A. M. Jaggar and P. S. Rotenberg. New York: McGraw Hill.

Colson, E. 1950. "The Tonga Social System." In *African Systems of Kinship and Marriage*, edited by A. R. Radcliffe-Brown and D. Forde. London: Oxford University Press for the International African Institute.

_____. 1951. "The Plateau Tonga." In *Seven Tribes of British Central Africa*, edited by E. Colson and M. Gluckman. Manchester: Manchester University Press.

_____. 1962. "Plateau Tonga." In *Matrilineal Kinship*, edited by D. Schneider and K. Gough. Berkeley: University of California Press.

_____. 1970. "Family Change in Contemporary Africa." In *Black Africa*, edited by J. Middleton. New York: Macmillan.

Colson, E., and M. Gluckman. 1951. *Seven Tribes of British Central Africa*. Manchester: Manchester University Press.

Colson, E., and T. Scudder. 1988. *For Prayer and Profit: The Ritual, Economic and Social Importance of Beer in Gwembe District, Zambia, 1950–1982*. Stanford: Stanford University Press.

Comaroff, J. L. 1987a. "Of Totemism and Ethnicity: Consciousness, Practice and the Signs of Inequality." *Ethnos* 52(3–4):301–322.

_____. 1987b. "Sulgenderis: Feminism, Kinship Theory, and Structural 'Domains.'" In *Gender and Kinship: Essays Toward a Unified Analysis*, edited by J. Collier and S. Yanagisako. Stanford: Stanford University Press.

Comaroff, J. L., and J. Comaroff. 1992. *Ethnography and the Historical Imagination*. Boulder and London: Westview Press.

Coontz, S., and P. Henderson, eds. 1986. *Women's Work, Men's Property: The Origins of Gender and Class.* London: Verson.

Crehan, K. 1994. "Land, Labour and Gender: Matriliny in 1980s Rural Zambia." Paper presented at the annual African Studies Association meetings, Toronto, November 3–6.

Culler, C., H. Patterson, and I. C. Matenje. 1990. *A Survey of Women in Agriculture in Malawi.* Lilongwe: Ministry of Agriculture.

Cutrufelli, M. R. 1983. *Women of Africa: Roots of Oppression.* London: Zed Press.

Davies, M., ed. 1983. *Third World—Second Sex.* London: Zed Press.

Davison, J. 1987. "Gender Relations in Collective Production in Sofala Province, Mozambique." Working paper, Women in Development Series, Michigan State University, Ann Arbor.

Davison, J., ed. 1988a. "Introduction." *Agriculture, Women, and Land: The African Experience,* edited by J. Davison. Boulder and London: Westview Press.

_____. 1988b. "Gender Structuring in Collective Production in Sofala Province, Mozambique." In *Agriculture, Women, and Land: The African Experience,* edited by J. Davison. Boulder and London: Westview Press.

_____. 1989. *Voices from Mutira: Lives of Rural Gikuyu Women.* Boulder: Lynne Rienner.

_____. 1992. "Changing Relations of Production in Southern Malawi's Households: Implications for Involving Rural Women in Development." *Journal of Contemporary African Studies* 11(1):72–84.

_____. 1993. "Tenacious Women: Clinging to Banja Household Production in the Face of Changing Gender Relations in Malawi." *Journal of Southern African Studies* 19(3):405–421.

_____. 1995. "Must Women Work Together? Development Agency Assumptions Versus Changing Production in Southern Malawi Households." In *Women Wielding the Hoe: Lessons from Rural Africa for Feminist Theory and Development Practice,* edited by J. F. Bryceson. Oxford: Berg.

_____. 1996a. *Voices from Mutira: Change in Lives of Rural Gikuyu Women, 1910–1995.* Boulder: Lynne Rienner.

_____. 1996b. "Women in Southern Africa." In *Encyclopedia of Third World Women,* edited by N. Stromquist. New York: Garland.

_____. 1996c. *Kellogg Foundation's Initiative in Southern Africa: Planning for the Future.* Washington, DC: Academy for Educational Development.

Davison, J., and M. Kanyuka. 1990. *An Ethnographic Study of Factors Affecting the Education of Girls in Southern Malawi.* Lilongwe: Academy for Educational Development for the Ministry of Education and Culture and USAID/Malawi.

de Silva, T. 1992. Interview with the author, Maputo, April 10.

Deutsch, S. 1987. "Women and Intercultural Relations: The Case of Hispanic New Mexico and Colorado." *Signs* 12(4):719–739.

Dey, J. 1982. "Development Planning in the Gambia: The Gap Between Planners' and Farmers' Perceptions, Expectations and Objectives." *World Development* 10(5):377–396.

Dias, J., and M. Dias. [1962] 1970. *Os Maçondes de Moçambique,* 3 vols. Lisboa: University of Lisboa. Vol. III: 1718.

Dobert, M. 1979. "Government and Politics." In *Zambia: A Country Study*, edited by I. Kaplan. Washington, DC: American University.

Dolny, H. 1985. "The Challenge of Agriculture." In *The Difficult Road to Socialism in Mozambique*, edited by J. Saul. New York: Monthly Review Press.

Dorward, H. n.d. "The History of Livingstonia." Ekwendeni: Ekwendeni Mission. Mimeographed..

Dos Santos, J. R. [1552] 1972. "Ethiopia Oriental." In *Records of South Eastern Africa*, vol. 7, edited by G. M. Theal. Cape Town: University Printers.

_____. 1940. *Missão Antropologia de Moçambique*. Lisbon: Agencia General das Colonias.

Douglas, M. 1969. "Is Matriliny Doomed in Africa?" In *Man in Africa,* edited by M. Douglas and P. Kaberry. London: Tavistock.

Drinkwater, M. J. 1987. *Exhausted Messages: Training and Groups. A Comparative Evaluation of Zimbabwe's Training and Visiting System.* Harare: Department of Agricultural Economics and Extension, University of Zimbabwe.

Due, J. 1991. "Policies to Overcome the Negative Effects of Structural Adjustment Programs on African Female-Headed Households." In *Structural Adjustment Programs and African Women Farmers,* edited by C. Gladwin. Gainesville: University of Florida Press.

Duly, A.R.W. 1946. "The Lower Shire District: Notes on Land Tenure and Individual Rights." *Nyasaland Journal* 17:11–14.

Edemikpong, C. 1988. "Letter to Concerned Organizations on Female Circumcision in Nigeria." March 12.

Edgerton, R. 1971. *The Individual in Cultural Adaptation: A Study of Four East African Peoples.* Berkeley: University of California Press.

Egmose, R. K. 1981. *Aspirations of Kenyan School Girls in Regard to Educational Training and Choice of Occupation and Career.* Nairobi: Bureau of Educational Research, Kenyatta University.

Ekejiuba, F. I. 1995. "Down to Fundamentals: Women-Centred Hearth-holds in Rural West Africa." In *Women Wielding the Hoe: Lessons from Rural Africa for Feminist Theory and Practice,* edited by J. F. Bryceson. Oxford: Berg.

Elkiss, T. H. 1981. *The Quest for an African Eldorado: Sofala, Southern Zambia and the Portuguese, 1500–1865.* Waltham, MA: Crossroads Press.

Epstein, A. L. 1975. "Military Organisation and the Pre-Colonial Polity of the Bemba of Zambia." *Man* 10:199–217.

_____. 1981. *Urbanization and Kinship: The Domestic Domain on the Copperbelt of Zambia, 1950–1956.* London: Academic Press.

Esterhuysen, E. C. 1974. "Lobola in Biblical Perspective." In *Proceedings of the Rhodesia Christian Conference.* Morgenster: Morgenster Mission Press.

European Parliamentarians for Southern Africa (EPSA). 1995. *Mozambican Peace Process Bulletin,* April 1995:2.

Evans, A., and K. Young. 1988. *Gender Issues in Household Labour Allocation: The Transformation of a Farming System in Northern Province.* Zambia and London: ODA.

Evans, J., and J. Kydd. 1990. *Phlombe Women's Agricultural Development Programme.* Lilongwe: ODA/Malawi.

Fahlen, M. 1987. *Support to Farm Workers on Commercial Farms in Zimbabwe.* Harare: Swedish International Development Agency (SIDA).

Faludi, S. 1991. *Backlash: The Undeclared War Against American Women.* New York and London: Anchor/Doubleday.

Feierman, S. 1990. *Peasant Intellectuals, Anthropology and History in Northern Tanzania.* Madison: University of Wisconsin Press.

Ferguson, A., with B. Liatto-Katundu. 1994. "Women in Politics in Zambia: What Difference Has Democracy Made?" *African Rural and Urban Studies* 1(2):11–30.

Ferguson, A., and K. Ludwig with B. Liatto-Katundu and I. Manda. 1995. "Zambian Women in Politics: An Assessment of Changes Resulting from the 1991 Political Transition." Working paper, Political Reform in Africa, Michigan State University, Lansing.

Ferreira, R. A. 1975. *Pequeña: Historia de Moçambique Pre-colonia.* Maputo: Fundo de Turismo.

Floro, M., and J. Wolf. 1990. *The Economic and Social Impacts of Girls' Primary Education in Developing Countries.* Washington, DC: USAID.

Foucault, M. 1980. *The History of Sexuality,* vol. 1, translated by R. Hurley. New York: Vintage Press.

Fox, R. G. 1990. "Introduction." In *Nationalist Ideologies and the Production of National Cultures,* edited by R. G. Fox. Washington, DC: American Ethnological Society.

Fuller, C. E. 1955. *An Ethnohistoric Study of Continuity and Change in Gwambe Culture.* Unpublished Ph.D. dissertation, Northwestern University, Evanston, IL.

Funk, S. 1988. "Women's Land Rights in Zimbabwe: An Overview." Occasional paper no. 13, Department of Rural and Urban Planning, University of Zimbabwe, Harare.

_____. 1992. "Bourgeois Theories of Gender and Feminism and Their Shortcomings with Reference to Southern African Countries." In *Gender in Southern Africa,* edited by R. Meena. Harare: SAPES Books.

_____. 1995. "USAID Gender and Democracy Project." Paper presented to the Workshop on Gender and Democracy in Africa, Lilongwe, July.

Gaidzanwa, R. B. 1985. *Images of Women in Zimbabwean Literature.* Harare: College Press.

Gamitto, A.C.P. [1831] 1960. *King Kazembe and the Marave, Chva, Bisa, Bemba, Lunda and Other Peoples of Southern Africa,* translated by I. Cunnison. Lisbon: Agencia General da Colonias.

Garlake, P. S. 1983. "Prehistory and Ideology in Zimbabwe." In *Past and Present in Zimbabwe,* edited by J.D.Y. Peel and T. O. Ranger. Manchester: Manchester University Press.

Geisler, G. G. 1987. "Sisters Under the Skin: Women and the Women's League in Zambia." *Journal of Modern African Studies* 25(1):43–66.

_____. 1992. "Who Is Losing Out: Structural Adjustment, Gender and the Agricultural Sector in Zambia." *Journal of Modern African Studies* 30(1):113–139.

Geisler, G. G., B. Keller, and P. Chuzu. 1985. *The Needs of Rural Women in Northern Province: Analysis and Recommendations.* Lusaka: NCDP and NORAD.

Gelfand, M. 1971. *Diet and Tradition in an African Culture.* Edinburgh: University of Edinburgh.

Gerard, E. 1941. "Costumes dos Maçua do Medo," *Moçambique* 27:5–23.

Gilomee, H. 1989. "The Beginnings of Afrikaner Ethnic Consciousness, 1850–1915." In *The Creation of Tribalism in Southern Africa*, edited by L. Vail. London: James Currey; and Berkeley: University of California Press.

Gluckman, M. 1950. "Kinship and Marriage Among the Lozi of Northern Rhodesia and the Zulu of Natal." *African Systems of Kinship and Marriage*, edited by A. Radcliffe-Brown and D. Forde. London: Oxford University Press.

Gough, K. 1962. "Variation in Residence." In *Matrilineal Kinship*, edited by D. Schneider and K. Gough. Berkeley: University of California Press.

Gouldsbury, C. 1915–1916. "Notes on the Customary Law of the Awemba of Northern Rhodesia and Kindred Tribes: Part II—The Law of Personal Relations and the Law of Contract." *Journal of the African Society* 15:157–178.

Government of Malawi, National Statistics Office. 1984. *Malawi Family Formation Survey, 1984.* Zomba: Government Printers.

_____. 1988. *Education Statistics: 1988.* Lilongwe: Ministry of Education and Culture (MOEC).

Government of Malawi/UNICEF. 1987. *The Situation of Children and Women in Malawi.* Lilongwe: GOM/UNICEF.

Government of Zambia, Central Statistics Office. 1981. *Preliminary Report: 1980. Census of Population and Households.* Lusaka: CSO.

Government of Zimbabwe (GOZ). 1987. *A Study of Educational Needs of Children in the Commercial Farming Areas of Zimbabwe: A Proposal.* Harare: MOEC.

_____. 1991. *Zimbabwe: Framework for Economic Reform (1991–1995).* Harare: Government of Zimbabwe Printers.

_____. Ministry of Health and Child Welfare. 1992. *Epidemiology Annual Reports for 1989–92.* Harare: MOHCW (Epidemiology).

Guimaraes, A. 1986. Interview with the author, Maputo, July 26.

Guyer, J. 1984. *Family and Farm in Southern Cameroon.* Boston: Boston University African Studies Center.

Gwaunza, E., and E. Zana. 1990. "Maintenance in Zimbabwe." In *Working Paper on Maintenance Law in Southern Africa.* Harare:WLSA.

Hafkin, N. 1973. "Trade, Society and Politics in Northern Mozambique, c. 1753–1913." Unpublished Ph.D. dissertation, Boston University.

Hall, R. 1966. "Missionaries and Explorers." In *A Short History of Zambia,* edited by B. M. Fagan. Nairobi and Lusaka: Oxford University Press.

Haney, W. G., and J. B. Knowles. 1987. "Women and Farming: Changing Roles, Changing Structures." *Signs* 12(4):797–800.

Hara, Rev. L.S.N. 1991. Interview with the author, Ekwendeni Mission, July 11.

Harries, P. 1989. "Exclusion, Classification and Internal Colonialism: The Emergence of Ethnicity Among the Tsonga-Speakers of South Africa." In *The Creation of Tribalism in Southern Africa,* edited by L. Vail. London: James Currey.

_____. 1994. *Work, Culture and Identity: Migrant Laborers in Mozambique and South Africa, 1860–1910.* Portsmouth: Heinemann.

Heisler, H. 1984. *Urbanization and the Government of Migration: The Inter-relation of Urban and Rural Life in Zambia.* New York: St. Martin's Press.

Hennessy, R. 1993. *Materialist Feminism and the Politics of Discourse.* New York: Routledge Press.

Henriksen, T. 1978. *Mozambique: A History.* London: Oxford University Press.

Himmelstrand, K. 1990. "Can an AID Bureaucracy Empower Women?" In *Women, International Development, and Politics: The Bureaucratic Mire,* edited by K. Staudt. Philadelphia: Temple University Press.

Hirschmann, D. 1986. "Women's Participation in Malawi's Local Councils and District Development Committees." *Planning and Administration* 13(1):43–51.

_____. 1990. "The Malawi Case: Enclave Politics, Core Resistance, and 'Nkhoswe No. 1.'" In *Women, International Development and Politics: The Bureaucratic Mire,* edited by K. Staudt. Philadelphia: Temple University Press.

_____. 1993a. *Equity and Gender.* Report prepared for USAID/Malawi. Washington, DC: International Development Program, School of International Service, American University.

_____. 1993b. *Interviews with Women Burley Farmers in Phlombe and Zomba Districts.* Lilongwe: USAID/Malawi.

Hirschmann, D., and M. Vaughan. 1984. *Women Farmers in Malawi: Food Production in Zomba District.* Berkeley: Institute for International Studies (IIS), University of California Press.

Hobley, C. W. 1910. "Kikuyu Customs and Beliefs." *Journal of the Royal Anthropological Institute* 40:428–445.

Hogan, N. 1980. "The Posthumous Vindication of Zachariah Gqishela." In *Economy and Society in Pre-industrial South Africa,* edited by S. Marks and A. Atmore. London: Tavistock.

Holleman, J. F. 1951. "Some 'Shona' Tribes of Southern Rhodesia." In *Seven Tribes of British Central Africa.* Manchester: Manchester University Press.

Hoover, J. J. 1979. "Society and Its Environment." In *Zambia: A Country Study.* Washington, DC: American University.

Iliffe, J. 1990. *Famine in Zimbabwe, 1890–1960.* Harare and Gweru: Mambo Press.

Isaacman, A. 1972. *Mozambique: The Africanization of a European Institution.* Madison: University of Wisconsin Press.

_____. 1996. *Cotton Is the Mother of Poverty: Peasants, Work, and Rural Struggle in Colonial Mozambique, 1932–1961.* Portsmouth: Heinemann.

Isaacman, A., and B. Isaacman. 1983. *Mozambique: From Colonialism to Revolution, 1900–1982.* Boulder: Westview Press.

Jeater, D. 1993. *Marriage, Perversion and Power: The Construction of Moral Discourse in Southern Rhodesia, 1980–1930.* Cambridge: Cambridge University Press.

Jiggins, J. 1980. "Female-Headed Households: Mpika Sample, Northern Province." Occasional paper no. 5, Rural Development Studies Bureau, Lusaka.

Jiggins, J., with P. Maimbo and M. Masona. 1995. "Breaking New Ground: Reaching Out to Women Farmers in Western Zambia." In *SEEDS 2: Supporting Women's Work Around the World,* edited by A. Leonard. New York: Feminist Press.

Joekes, S. 1985. "Working for Lipstick? Male and Female Labour in the Clothing Industry in Morocco." In *Women, Work and Ideology in the Third World,* edited by H. Afshar. London: Tavistock.

Jorgensen, K. 1982. *Women's Programs in Zimbabwe.* Harare: Women's Bureau.

Junod, H. A. 1927. *The Life of a South African Tribe, Vol. 1, Social Life.* London: Macmillan.

_____. [1912] 1962. *The Life of a South African Tribe, Vol. 1, Social Life.* New Hyde Park, NY: University Books.

Kaberry, Phyllis. 1952. *Women of the Grassfields: A Study of the Economic Position of Women in Bamenda, British Cameroons.* London: Her Majesty's Stationary Office.

Kachapila, H. A. 1992. "Role of Women in Cash Crop Production in Central Malawi During the Colonial Period, 1920–1964: An Agenda for Research." Paper presented at the History Seminar Series, Chancellor College, University of Malawi, Zomba.

Kaluwa, E. 1990. "Structural Adjustment and Smallholders in Malawi." Paper presented at the Workshop on the Effects of Structural Adjustment in Malawi, Lilongwe, April.

Kandawire, J.A.R. 1979. *Thangata: Forced Labour or Reciprocal Assistance?* Unpublished Ph.D. dissertation, University of Malawi, Zomba.

Kandoole, B. S. 1990. "Economic Constraints of Structural Adjustment in Malawi." Paper presented at the Workshop on the Effects of Structural Adjustment in Malawi, Lilongwe, April.

Kapakasa, A. M. 1990. "The Economics of Initiations and the Impact of Schooling." Washington, DC: George Washington University. Mimeographed.

Kaplan, I., ed. 1979. *Zambia: A Country Study.* Washington, DC: American University.

Kardam, N. 1990. "The Adaptability of International Development Agencies: The Response of the World Bank to WID." In *Women, International Development, and Politics,* edited by K. Staudt. Philadelphia: Temple University Press.

Kariuki, P. 1985. "Women's Aspirations and Self-Perceptions of Their Own Situation in Society." In *Women and Development in Africa,* edited by G. S. Were. Nairobi: Gideon Were for the Journal of Eastern African Research and Development.

Kaufulu, F. 1992. *A Comparison of Women's Use-Value and Exchange-Value Labour in Three Areas in Zomba District.* Unpublished master's thesis, University of Malawi, Zomba.

Kaufulu, F., and J. Davison. 1992. *Child Spacing Attitudes, Nutrition Practices, and Treatment of Children's Illnesses in the Thyolo Tea Estate Compounds.* Thyolo: Project Hope, Child Survival Project.

Kaunda, J. M. 1989. *Agricultural Credit Policy, Bureaucracy and the Subordination of Rural Women in the Development Process.* Norwich: School of Development Studies, University of East Anglia.

Kay, G. 1965. *Changing Patterns of Settlement and Land Use in the Eastern Province of Northern Rhodesia.* Yorkshire: University of Hull.

Kayongo, K. 1987. *Reciprocity and Interdependence: The Rise and Fall of the Kololo Empire in Southern Africa in the 19th Century.* Lund, Sweden: Almquist and Wiksell.

Keefe, S. E. 1989. "Measuring Ethnicity and Its Political Consequences in a Southern Appalachian High School." In *Negotiating Ethnicity: The Impact of Anthropological Theory and Practice,* edited by S. E. Keefe. Washington, DC: American Anthropological Association.

Keller, B. B. 1984. *The Integration of Zambian Women in Development.* Lusaka: Norwegian Agency for Development (NORAD).

Kenyatta, Jomo. [1938] 1968. *Facing Mount Kenya.* London: Secker and Warburg.

Kettlewell, R. W. 1965. *Agricultural Change in Nyasaland: 1945–1960.* Stanford: Food Research Institute, Stanford University.

King, E., and M. Hill, eds. 1991. *Women's Education in Developing Countries: Barriers, Benefits and Policy.* Washington, DC: World Bank.

Konzakapanzi, R. 1992. Interview with the author, Lilongwe, February.

Krige, E. 1974. "Woman-Marriage with Special Reference to the Lovedu—Its Significance for the Definition of Marriage." *Africa* 44:11–37.

Kriger, N. 1988. "The Zimbabwean War of Liberation: Struggles Within the Struggle." *Journal of Southern African Studies* 14(2):305–322.

_____. 1992. *Zimbabwe's Guerrilla War: Peasant Voices.* Cambridge and New York: Cambridge University Press.

Krishnamurty, B. S. 1964. *Land and Labour in Nyasaland: 1891–1914.* London: University of London.

Kruks, S., and B. Wisner. 1981. *The State, the Party and the Female Peasantry in Mozambique.* Maputo: Eduardo Mondlane University Press.

Kubheka, N. 1994. "Theatre-in-Education: Empowerment of Girls and Women Through Theatre." Paper presented at the Brainstorming Workshop between SIDA and MoEC, Harare, December 7–9.

Kydd, J., and R. Christiansen. 1982. "Structural Change in Malawi Since Independence." *World Development* 10(5):355–77.

Laasko, L. 1995. "Relationship Between the State and Civil Society in the Zimbabwean Elections, 1995." Working paper 1/95, Institute of Development Studies, University of Helsinki.

La Fontaine, J. S. 1977. "Ritualization of Women's Life in Crises in Bugisu." In *The Interpretation of Ritual,* edited by J. S. La Fontaine. London: Tavistock.

Lan, David. 1985. *Guns and Rain: Guerillas and Spirit Mediums in Zimbabwe.* Berkeley: University of California Press.

Lancaster, C. S. 1981. *The Goba of the Zambezi: Sex Roles, Economics and Change.* Norman: University of Oklahoma Press.

Langworthy, H. W. 1972. *Zambia Before 1980: Aspects of Pre-colonial History.* London: Longman.

Lawry, S. W. 1993. "Transactions in Cropland Held Under Customary Tenure in Lesotho." In *Land in African Agrarian Systems,* edited by T. J. Bassett and D. E. Crummey. Madison: University of Wisconsin Press.

Lewis, B. 1990. "Farming Women, Public Policy, and the Women's Ministry: A Case Study from Cameroon." In *Women, International Development and Politics,* edited by K. Staudt. Philadelphia: Temple University Press.

Liatto-Katundu, B. 1993. "The Women's Lobby and Gender Relations in Zambia." *Review of African Political Economy,* no. 56:97–125.

Linden, Ian. 1974. *Catholics, Peasants, and Chewa Resistance in Nyasaland, 1889–1939.* Berkeley: University of California Press.

Liwimbi. 1992. "Girls' Perceptions, Aspirations and Options for Education and Careers in Dedza District." Unpublished master's thesis, Chancellor College, University of Malawi, Zomba.

Lobato, A. 1957. *Evolução Administrativa e Economica de Moçambique, 1752–63.* Lisbon: Government of Portugal.

Longwe, S. H. 1988. "From Welfare to Empowerment." Paper presented at the NGO African Women's Task Force Meeting, Nairobi, April 11–15.

_____. 1990. "From Welfare to Empowerment: The Situation of Women in Development in Africa: A Post UN Women's Decade Update and Future Directions." WID Series working paper no. 204, Michigan State University, Ann Arbor.

Lovett, M. 1989. "Gender Relations, Class Formation, and the Colonial State in Africa." In *Women and the State in Africa,* edited by J. Parpart and S. Stichter. Boulder and London: Lynne Rienner.

MacCormack, C. 1977. "Biological Events and Cultural Control." *Signs* 3(2):31–48.

Made, P., and B. Lagerstrom. 1984. *Zimbabwean Women in Industry.* Harare: Zimbabwe Publishing House.

Mainga, M. 1973. *Bulozi Under the Luyana Kings.* London: Longman.

Makambera, M. 1992. "Interviews with Nankungwes in Thyolo and Blantyre Districts" (fieldnotes). Blantyre: Johns Hopkins Medical Center AIDS Project.

Mandala, E. C. 1990. *Work and Control in a Peasant Economy: A History of the Lower Tchiri Valley in Malawi.* Madison: University of Wisconsin Press.

Mandaza, I., and L. M. Sachikonye, eds. 1991. *The One-Party State and Democracy: The Zimbabwe Debate.* Harare: SAPES Books.

Mannathoko, C. 1992. "Feminist Theories and the Study of Gender in Southern Africa." In *Gender in Southern Africa,* edited by R. Meena. Harare: SAPES Books.

Marks, S. 1986. *The Ambiguities of Dependence in South Africa: Class, Nationalism and the State in Twentieth Century Natal.* Johannesburg: Ravan Press.

Marks, S., and R. Rathbone. 1983. "Introduction." *Journal of African History* 24(2):150–155.

Marshall, J. 1985. "Literacy, Labour Process and State Formation: Experiences of Popular Education in Mozambique." Paper presented at the Joint Meeting of the Canadian Association of Latin American and Caribbean Studies and the Canadian Association of African Studies, Montreal, May.

Mashumba, S. 1988. "The Changing Roles of Women: A Comparative Study of Women in Resettlement and Communal Areas in Wedza." Unpublished master's thesis, University of Zimbabwe, Harare.

Max-Neff, M., R. Elizalde, and M. Hopenhayn. 1986. *Desarrollo a Escala Humana: Una Opcion para el Futuro.* Upsala: Dag Hammarskjold Foundation, CEPAUR.

May, J. 1983. *Zimbabwean Women in Colonial and Customary Law.* Gweru: Mambo Press.

Mazur, R. E. 1985. "Reversal in the Labor Reserves of Zimbabwe? Prospects for Change." Paper presented at the annual meetings of the African Studies Association, New Orleans, November 23–26.

Mbulo, M. P. 1980. *The Effects of Cash Crop Production on Men's and Women's and Children's Participation in Agricultural Production.* Lusaka: University of Zambia.

McCracken, K. J. 1967. *Livingstonia Mission and the Evolution of Malawi: 1873–1939.* Cambridge: Cambridge University Press.

_____. 1983. "Planters, Peasants and the Colonial State: The Impact of the Native Tobacco Board in the Central Province of Malawi." *Journal of Southern African Studies* 9, no. 2:172–192.

Meena, R. 1992. "Gender Research/Studies in Southern Africa: An Overview." In *Gender in Southern Africa: Conceptual and Theoretical Issues,* edited by R. Meena. Harare: SAPES Books.

Meillassoux, C. 1981. *Maidens, Meal and Money: Capitalism and the Domestic Community.* Cambridge: Cambridge University Press.

Mernissi, F. 1987. *Beyond the Veil: Male-Female Dynamics in Modern Muslim Society.* Bloomington and Indianapolis: Indiana University Press.

Milimo, M. C. 1986. "Women, Population and Food in Africa: The Zambian Case." *African Development* 11(4):95–133.

Minh-ha, T. T. 1989. *Woman, Native, Other.* Bloomington: Indiana University Press.

Mitchell, C. J. 1952. "Preliminary Notes on Land Tenure and Agriculture Among the Machinga." *Nyasaland Journal* 5, no. 2:18–30.

_____. 1956. *The Yao Village.* Manchester: Manchester University Press.

Mlambo, E. 1972. *Rhodesia: The Struggle for a Birthright.* London: C. Hurst.

Mohanty, C. T. 1992. "Feminist Encounter: Locating the Politics of Experience." In *Destabilizing Theory: Contemporary Feminist Debates,* edited by M. Barrett and A. Phillips. Stanford: Stanford University Press.

_____. 1993a. "Introduction: Cartographies of Struggle." In *Third World Women and the Politics of Feminism.* Bloomington: Indiana University Press.

_____. 1993b. "Under Western Eyes: Feminist Scholarship and Colonial Discourses." In *Third World Women and the Politics of Feminism.* Bloomington: Indiana University Press.

Mondlane, E. [1969] 1983. *The Struggle for Mozambique.* London: Zed Press.

Moore, H. 1988. *Feminism and Anthropology.* Minneapolis: University of Minnesota Press.

Moore, H., and M. Vaughan. 1994. *Cutting Down Trees: Gender, Nutrition and Agricultural Change in the Northern Province of Zambia: 1890–1990.* Portsmouth: Heinemann; London: James Curry; Lusaka: University of Zambia.

Moser, C. 1989. "Practical Gender Needs and Strategic Needs in Development." *World Development* 17(2):1799–1825.

_____. 1993. *Gender Planning and Development: Theory, Practice and Training.* New York and London: Routledge.

Moss, B. A. 1990. *Holding Body and Soul Together: The History of the Zimbabwean Women's Ruwadsano Manyano in Methodist Churches, 1890–1980.* Bloomington: Indiana University Press.

Mozambiquefile. 1995. "New Government Appointed." *Mozambiquefile.* January.

Msora, B. 1992. Interview with the author, Harare, April 12.

Mtetwa, R.M.C. 1974. "A Dynamic Pre-Colonial Economy: The Dumas Case, 1720–1900." Salisbury: University of Rhodesia. Mimeographed.

Muchena, O. 1979. "The Changing Position of African Women in Rural Zimbabwe." *Zimbabwe Journal of Economics* 1(1):50–63.

_____. 1982. *Women's Participation in the Rural Labour Force in Zimbabwe.* Lusaka: International Labor Organization (ILO).

Mudenge, S.I.G. 1988. *A Political History of the Munhumutapa, c. 1400–1902.* Harare: Zimbabwe Publishing House.

Mukwita, A. 1995. "Nawakwi Chased." *Post* (Lusaka), no. 352, November 24:1.

Munalula, M. M., and W. S. Mwenda. 1995. "Case Study: Women and Inheritance Law in Zambia." In *African Women South of the Sahara,* edited by M. J. Hay and S. Strichter. London: Longman.

Munslow, B. 1983. *Mozambique: The Revolution and Its Origin.* New York and Lagos: Longman.

Muriuki, Godfrey. 1974. *A History of the Kikuyu: 1500–1900.* Nairobi: Oxford University Press.

Murphree, W. M. 1969. *Christianity and the Shona.* London: S.C.M. Press.

Mushore, L. 1990. "Loice Mushore." In *Mothers of the Revolution,* edited by I. Staunton. Harare: Baobab Books.

Mutambirwa, J.A.C. 1980. *The Rise of Settler Power in Southern Rhodesia (Zimbabwe), 1898–1923.* Rutherford: Fairleigh Dickinson University Press.

Mutemba, M. 1977. "Thwarted Development: A Case Study of Economic Change in the Kabwe Rural District of Zambia, 1902–70." In *The Roots of Rural Poverty in Central and Southern Africa*, edited by R. Palmer and N. Parsons. London: Heinemann.

_____. 1982. "Women and Agricultural Change in the Railway Region of Zambia: Dispossession and Counterstrategies, 1930–1970." In *Women and Work in Africa*, edited by E. G. Bay. Boulder: Westview Press.

Mutimba, J., and P. Maphosa. 1995. *An Evaluation of Zimbabwe Women's Bureau.* Harare: ZWB.

Mvunga, M. P. 1978. "Land, Law and Policy in Zambia: Kabwe Rural District, 1850–1970." Unpublished master's thesis, University of London.

Mvusi, T.R.M. 1995. "Gender, Kinship and Power Among the Bemba of Zambia: A Critique." Paper presented at the annual meetings of the African Studies Association, Orlando, Florida, November 22–26.

Mwamula-Lubandi, E. D. 1992. *Clan Theory in African Development Studies Analysis: Reconsidering African Development Promotive Bases.* Lantham, MD: University Press of America.

Nankumba, J. S. 1989. "Land Ownership and Household Food Security: An Overview of the Dynamics of Land Tenure and Agrarian Systems in Malawi." Lilongwe: Bunda College, University of Malawi. Mimeographed.

Narayan, U. 1989. "The Project of Feminist Epistemology: Perspectives from a Non-Western Feminist." In *Gender/Body/Knowledge,* edited by A. M. Jaggar and S. R. Bordo. New Brunswick: Rutgers University Press.

National Commission on WID (NCWID). 1988. *Statement of Purpose of the Commission.* Lilongwe: NCWID.

_____. 1993. *Women and the Law in Malawi.* Lilongwe: NCWID.

Ncube, Welshman. 1986. "The Matrimonial Property Rights of Women During and After Marriage in Zimbabwe: A Study of Property Relations, Domestic Labour and Power Relations Within the Family." Unpublished master's thesis, University of Zimbabwe, Harare.

Ndlovu, C. P. 1974. "Missionaries and Traders in the Ndebele Kingdom, 1859–1890: An African Response to Colonialism." Unpublished Ph.D. dissertation, State University of New York, Stony Brook.

Newberry, David. 1991. *Kings and Clans: Ijwi Island and the Lake Kivu Rift, 1780–1840.* Madison: University of Wisconsin Press.

_____. 1995. "The Invention of Rwanda: The Alchemy of Ethnicity." Paper presented at the annual meetings of the African Studies Association, Orlando, Florida, November 22-26.

Newitt, M.D.D. 1973. *Portuguese Settlement on the Zambesi: Exploitation, Land Tenure and Colonial Rule in East Africa.* London: Longman.

Ngwenya, J. 1983. "Women and Liberation in Zimbabwe." In *Third World— Second Sex,* edited by M. Davies. London: Zed Press.

Ngwira, N. 1989. "Sectoral Analysis of the Programmes and Policies Affecting the Status of Women in Malawi." Paper presented at the National Seminar on Population and Development, Zomba, June 5–9.

Ntara, S. J. [1944] 1973. *The History of the Chewa. (Mbiiri ya Chewa).* Wiesbaden: Franz Steiner Verlag GMBH.

Nyagura, L. M., and A. C. Mupawaenda. 1994. *A Study of the Factors Affecting the Education of Women and Girls in the Commercial Farming Areas of Zimbabwe.* Harare: Ministry of Education and Culture.

Nyasha, N. 1983. "Four Years of Armed Struggle in Zimbabwe." *In Third World— Second Sex,* edited by M. Davies. London: Zed Press.

Nyirenda, S. 1931. *History of the Tumbuka People,* translated by T. Cullin Young. Johannesburg: University of Witwatersrand.

Obbo, C. 1980. *African Women: Their Struggle for Economic Independence.* London: Zed Press.

Oboler, R. S. 1985. *Women, Power and Economic Change: The Nandi of Kenya.* Stanford: Stanford University Press.

Okali, C. 1983. *Cocoa and Kinship in Ghana.* London: KPI.

Okonjo, Kamene. 1976. "The Dual Political Sex System in Operation: Igbo Women and Community Politics in Midwestern Nigeria." In *Women in Africa,* edited by N. Hafkin and E. Bay. Stanford: Stanford University Press.

Okoth-Ogendo, H.W.O. 1993. "Agrarian Reform in Sub-Saharan Africa: An Assessment of State Responses to the African Agrarian Crisis and Their Implications for Agricultural Development." In *Land in African Agrarian Systems,* edited by T. J. Bassett and D. E. Crummey. Madison: University of Wisconsin Press.

O'Laughlin, B. 1995. "Myth of the African Family in the World of Development." In *Women Wielding the Hoe: Lessons from Rural Africa for Feminist Theory and Development Practice,* edited by D. F. Bryceson. Oxford: Berg.

Oppong, C., ed. 1983. *Female and Male in West Africa.* London: George Allen and Unwin.

Pachai, B., ed. 1972. *The Early History of Malawi.* London: Longman.

Palmer, R. 1977a. "The Agricultural History of Rhodesia." In *The Roots of Rural Poverty in Central and Southern Africa,* edited by R. Palmer and N. Parsons. London: Heinemann.

_____. 1977b. *Land and Racial Domination in Rhodesia.* London: Heinemann.

Palmer, R., and N. Parsons, eds. 1977. *The Roots of Rural Poverty in Central and Southern Africa.* London: Heinemann.

Pankhurst, D. 1988. "The Dynamics of the Social Relations of Production and Reproduction in Zimbabwean Communal Areas." Unpublished Ph.D. dissertation, University of Liverpool.

Pankhurst, D., and S. Jacobs. 1988. "Land Tenure, Gender Relations, and Agricultural Production: The Case of Zimbabwe's Peasantry." In *Agriculture, Women, and Land: The African Experience*, edited by J. Davison. Boulder: Westview Press.

Papstein, R. 1989. "From Ethnic Identity to Tribalism: The Upper Zambezi Region of Zambia, 1830–1981." In *The Creation of Tribalism in Southern Africa*, edited by L. Vail. London: James Currey; and Berkeley: University of California Press.

Parpart, J. L. 1986. "Class and Gender on the Copperbelt: Women in Northern Rhodesian Copper Mining Communities, 1926–1964." In *Women and Class in Africa*, edited by C. Robertson and Iris Berger. New York: Holmes and Meier.

_____. 1993. "Who Is the 'Other'?: A Postmodern Feminist Critique of Women and Development Theory and Practice." *Development and Change* 24:439-464.

Parpart, J. L., and K. Staudt, eds. 1989. *Women and the State in Africa.* Boulder and London: Lynne Rienner.

Parsons, N., and R. Palmer. 1977. "Introduction: Historical Background." In *The Roots of Rural Poverty in Central and Southern Africa*, edited by R. Palmer and N. Parsons. London: Heinemann.

Peel, J.D.Y., and T. O. Ranger, eds. 1983. *Past and Present in Zimbabwe.* Manchester: Manchester University Press.

Penvenne, J. 1989. "'We Are All Portuguese!' Challenging the Political Economy of Assimilation: Lourenço Marques, 1870–1933." In *The Creation of Tribalism in Southern Africa*, edited by L. Vail. London: James Currey; and Berkeley: University of California Press.

Peters, P. 1991. Personal communication with the author (raw data from Zomba District Survey).

_____. 1994. "Matriliny, Land and Gender in Southern Malawi." Paper presented at the annual meetings of the African Studies Association, Toronto, November 3–6.

_____. 1995. "Uses and Abuses of the Concept of 'Female-headed Households' in Research on Agrarian Transformation and Policy." In *Women Wielding the Hoe: Lessons from Rural Africa for Feminist Theory and Practice,* edited by D. F. Bryceson. Oxford: Berg.

Peters, P., and G. Herrera. 1989. *Cash Cropping, Food Scarcity and Nutrition.* Cambridge, MA: Harvard Institute of International Research (HIID).

Phimister, I. R. 1976. "Pre-Colonial Gold Mining in Southern Zambezia: A Reassessment." *African Social Research* 21:3–25.

_____. 1988. *An Economic and Social History of Zimbabwe: Capital Accumulation and Class Struggle, 1890–1948.* London: Longman.

Phiri, K. M. 1977. "Cultural and Political Change in Pre-Colonial History of Malawi." *Society of Malawi Journal* 30(2):6–9.

_____. 1984. "Production and Exchange in Pre-Colonial Malawi." In *Malawi: An Alternative Pattern of Development.* Edinburgh: University of Edinburgh.

Phiri, K. M., M. Vaughan, and I. Makuluni. 1977. *Amachinga Yao Tradition: II. Oral History Project.* Zomba: Chancellor College, University of Malawi.

Pinto, A. P., and I. Chicalia. 1990. "Maintenance Law in Mozambique." In *Working Papers on Maintenance Law in Southern Africa.* Harare: WLSA.

Pitcher, A. 1993. "Lineage, Gender and Cash: Women and Cotton in Northern Mozambique." Paper presented at the annual meetings of the African Studies Association, Boston, December 4–7.

_____. 1995. "Conflict and Cooperation: Gendered Roles and Responsibilities Amongst Cotton Households in Northern Mozambique." Ithaca: Cornell University. Mimeographed..

Poewe, K. O. 1981. *Matrilineal Ideology.* New York: Academic Press.

Pryor, F. L. 1990. *The Political Economy of Poverty, Equity and Growth: Malawi and Madagascar.* New York: Oxford University Press for the World Bank.

Radcliffe-Brown, A. R., and D. Fortes, eds. 1950. *African Systems of Kinship and Marriage.* London: Oxford University Press for International African Institute.

Rangeley, W.H.J. 1952. "Two Nyasaland Rain Shrines: Makewana the Mother of a People." *Nyasaland Journal* 5(2):31–50.

_____. 1963. "The Ayao." *Nyasaland Journal* 16(1):10–22.

Ranger, T. O. 1967. *Revolt in Southern Rhodesia, 1896–7.* London: Heinemann.

_____. 1970. *The African Voice in Southern Rhodesia, 1898–1930.* London: Heinemann.

_____. 1983. "Tradition and Travesty: Chiefs and the Administration in Makonda District, 1960–1980." In *Past and Present in Zimbabwe.* Manchester: Manchester University Press.

_____. 1984. *Peasant Consciousness and Guerrilla War in Zimbabwe.* London: James Currey.

_____. 1989a. "Missionaries, Migrants and the Manyika: The Invention of Ethnicity in Zimbabwe." In *The Creation of Tribalism in Southern Africa,* edited by L. Vail. London: James Currey; and Berkeley: University of California Press.

_____. 1989b. "The Politics of Prophecy in Matabeleland." Paper presented at the Fifth Satherthweite Seminar, Cape Town, South Africa.

Rattray, R. S. 1929. *Ashanti Law and Constitution.* Oxford: Oxford University Press.

Reynolds, P. 1991. *Dance, Civet Cat: Child Labour in the Zambezi Valley.* Athens: Ohio University Press; and Harare: Baobab Books.

Rich, T. 1983. "Legacies of the Past? The Results of the 1980 Election in Midland Province, Zimbabwe." In *Past and Present in Zimbabwe,* edited by J.D.Y. Peel and T. O. Ranger. Manchester: Manchester University Press.

Richards, A. 1939. *Land, Labor and Diet in Northern Rhodesia.* Oxford: Oxford University Press.

_____. 1940. "The Political System of the Bemba Tribe in North-Eastern Rhodesia." In *African Political Systems.* London: Oxford University Press.

_____. 1950. "Some Types of Family Structures Amongst the Central Bantu." In *African Systems of Kinship and Marriage,* edited by R. Radcliffe-Brown and D. Forde. Oxford: Oxford University Press.

_____. 1958. "A Changing Pattern of Agriculture in East Africa: The Bemba of Northern Rhodesia." *Geographical Journal* 124(3):302–314.

_____. [1957] 1982. *Chisungu: A Girl's Initiation Ceremony Among the Bemba of Zambia.* London and New York: Tavistock.

Richartz, F. J. 1896. *Information About the Mission Farm.* Chishawasha. Chishawasha: Jesuit Archives.

_____. 1905. "Habits and Customs of the Mashonas." Part 3 of *Zambesi Mission Record* 2. N.p.: n.p.

Rigby, I.C.C. 1954. *Nyasaland Protectorate Law Reports.* Zomba: Government Printers.

Roberts, A. D. 1973. *A History of the Bemba: Political Growth and Change in North Eastern Zambia Before 1990.* London: Longman.

Roberts, A. F. 1989. "History, Ethnicity and Change in the 'Christian Kingdom' of Southeastern Zaire." In *The Creation of Tribalism in Southern Africa,* edited by L. Vail. London: James Currey; and Berkeley: University of California Press.

Roberts, S. 1964. "A Comparison of the Family Law and Custom of Two Matrilineal Systems in Nyasaland." *Nyasaland Journal* 17(1):24–41.

Robinson, B., J. Davison, and J. Williams. 1994. *Malawi Education Policy Sector Analysis.* Lilongwe: USAID.

Rocha, I. 1988. "Un exemplo de resistencia cultural—os Chope da Moçambique." In *Moçambique: Cultura e Historia de um Pais.* Coimbra: Instituto de Antropologia, Universidade de Coimbra.

Roe, G., and W. Chilowa. 1990. "The Effects of Structural Adjustment on Urban Poor Households." Paper presented at the Workshop on the Effects of Structural Adjustment in Malawi, Lilongwe, April.

Rogers, C. A., and C. Franz. 1962. *Racial Themes in Southern Rhodesia.* New Haven: Yale University Press.

Rosaldo, M. Z. 1974. "Women, Culture and Society: A Theoretical Overview." In *Culture and Society,* edited by M. Rosaldo and L. Lamphere. Stanford: Stanford University Press.

Sacks, K. 1979. *Sisters and Wives.* Westport: Greenwood Press.

Sanday, P. R. 1974. "Female Status in the Public Domain." In *Women, Culture and Society,* edited by M. Rosaldo and L. Lamphere. Stanford: Stanford University Press.

Sanderson, F. E. 1966. "Nyasaland Migrant Labour in British Central Africa, 1890–1939." Unpublished master's thesis, University of London.

Sangambo, M. K. 1979. *The History of the Luvale People and the Chieftainship.* Zambesi: Mize Palace.

Saul, J. 1985. "Introduction." In *The Difficult Road to Socialism in Mozambique,* edited by J. Saul. New York: Monthly Review Press.

Schellenberg, M., and A. Nkunita. 1988. *Women's Programmes in Malawi: A Survey on Governmental and Non-Governmental Women's Programmes.* Lilongwe: Ministry of Community Services.

Schildkrout, E. 1982. "Dependence and Autonomy: The Economic Activities of Secluded Hausa Women in Kano, Nigeria." In *Women and Work in Africa,* edited by E. Bay. Boulder: Westview Press.

Schlegel, A. 1972. *Male Dominance and Female Autonomy: Domestic Authority in Matrilineal Societies.* Washington, DC: Human Relations, A. F. Press.

Schmidt, E. 1991. "Patriarchy, Capitalism and a Colonial State in Zimbabwe." *Signs* 16:731–756.

_____. 1992. *Peasants, Traders and Wives: Shona Women in the History of Zimbabwe, 1870–1939.* Portsmouth: Heinemann.

Schneider, J. 1962. "The Distinctive Features of Matrilineal Descent Groups." In *Matrilineal Kinship,* edited by J. Schneider and K. Gough. Berkeley: University of California Press.

Schoffeleers, M. 1968. *The Lower Shire Valley of Malawi: Its Ecology, Population Distribution, Ethnic Divisions and Systems of Marriage.* Limbe: Gweru Press.

_____. 1980. "Trade, Warfare and Social Inequality: The Case of the Lower Shire Valley of Malawi, 1590–1622 A.D." *Society of Malawi Journal* 33(2):6–23.

_____. 1984. "Economic Change and Religious Polarization in an African Rural District." In *Malawi: An Alternative Pattern of Development.* Edinburgh: University of Edinburgh, Centre of African Studies.

Schuster, I. 1979. *New Women of Lusaka.* Palo Alto, CA: Mayfield.

_____. 1983. "Constraints and Opportunities in Political Participation: The Case of Zambian Women." *Africa* 21(2):8–27.

_____. 1985. "Political Women: The Zambian Experience." In *Women's Worlds,* edited by M. Safir, M. Mednick, D. Israeli, and J. Bernard. New York: Praeger.

Scudder, Thayer. [1962] 1975. *The Ecology of the Gwembe Tonga.* Manchester: University of Manchester.

Sen, G., and C. Grown. 1987. *Development, Crises, and Alternative Visions: Third World Women's Perspectives.* New York: Monthly Review Press.

Sharpe, B. 1990. "Nutrition and the Commercialization of Agriculture in Northern Zambia." In *The Dynamics of Agricultural Policy and Reform in Zambia,* edited by A. Woods. Ames: Iowa State University Press.

Sheldon, K. 1994. "Women and Revolution in Mozambique: A Luta Continua." In *Women in Revolution in Africa, Asia and the New World,* edited by M. A. Tetreault. Columbia: University of South Carolina Press.

Siegel, Brian. 1989. "The 'Wild' and 'Lazy' Lamba: Ethnic Stereotypes on the Central African Copperbelt." In *The Creation of Tribalism in Southern Africa,* edited by L. Vail. London: James Currey; and Berkeley: University of California Press.

Skjønsberg, Else. 1989. *Change in an African Village: Kefa Speaks*. West Hartford, CT: Kumarian Press.

Smaldone, J. P. 1979. "Historical Setting." In *Zambia: A Country Study*. Washington, DC: American University.

Smith, S. 1985. "An Investigation into the Extent of Participation of Women Within Four Mixed-Sex Producer Cooperatives." Unpublished master's thesis, University of Zimbabwe, Harare.

Spring, A. 1983. *Priorities for Women's Programmes: Women in Agricultural Development Projects*. Lilongwe: Chiteze Agricultural Research Station.

_____. 1987. "Women Farmers and Food Issues in Africa: Some Considerations and Suggested Solutions." Working paper no. 139, Women in Development, Michigan State University, Ann Arbor.

_____. 1995. *Agricultural Development and Gender Issues in Malawi*. Latham, MD: University Press of America.

Stamp, Patricia. 1991. "Burying Otieno: The Politics of Gender and Ethnicity in Kenya." *Signs* 16(4):808–848.

Staudt, K. 1990. "Introduction." In *Women, International Development, and Politics: The Bureaucratic Mire*, edited by K. Staudt. Philadelphia: Temple University Press.

Staunton, I., ed. 1990. *Mothers of the Revolution*. Harare: Baobab Books.

Stoneman, C. 1976. "Foreign Capital and the Prospects for Zimbabwe." *World Development* 4(1):25–58.

Stromgaard, P. 1985. "A Subsistence Society Under Pressure: The Bemba of Northern Zambia." *Africa* 55(1):39–58.

Swedish International Development Agency (SIDA). n.d. "Schools for Children in the Commercial Farming Areas." Harare: SIDA/Zimbabwe. Mimeographed.

_____. 1987. *A Study of the Educational Needs of Children in the Communal Farming Areas of Zimbabwe*. Harare: SIDA/Zimbabwe.

_____. 1994. "Assistance to Children in the Commercial Farming Areas." Harare: SIDA/Zimbabwe. Mimeographed.

Tracy, P. 1965. *The Lost Valley*. Cape Town and Pretoria: Human and Rousseau.

Trivedy, R. 1987. *Investigating Poverty: Action Research in Southern Malawi*. Blantyre: Oxfam UK.

Truscott, K. 1989. *Women and Tillage: Strategic Issues Posed by Farmers' Groups*. Harare: Institute for Agricultural Economics (IAE).

Turner, V. W. 1962. "Three Symbols of Passage in Ndembu Circumcision Ritual." In *Essays on the Ritual of Social Relations*, edited by M. Gluckman. Manchester: Manchester University Press.

_____. 1969. *The Ritual Process*. Ithaca: Cornell University Press.

United Nations Children's Fund (UNICEF). 1994a. "The Girl Child in the Family and Wider Society." Paper presented at the celebration of the Day of the African Child, Harare, June 16.

_____. 1994b. *Children and Women in Zimbabwe: A Situation Update—1994*. Harare: UNICEF/Zimbabwe.

United Nations Development Programme (UNDP). 1993. *Human Development Index—1993*. New York: UNDP.

Urdang, S. 1984. "The Last Transition? Women and Development in Mozambique." *Review of African Political Economy* 27-28:8–32.

_____. 1989. *And Still They Dance: Women, War and the Struggle for Change in Mozambique.* New York: Monthly Review Press.

U.S. Agency for International Development (USAID)/Malawi. 1995. *Girls' Attainment of Basic Literacy and Education Program—PAAD.* Lilongwe: USAID/Malawi.

Vail, H. L. 1972. "Suggestions Towards a Reinterpreted Tumbuka History." In *The Early History of Malawi,* edited by B. Pachai. London: Longman.

_____. 1989. "Introduction: Ethnicity in Southern African History." In *The Creation of Tribalism in Southern Africa,* edited by L. Vail. London: James Currey; and Berkeley: University of California Press.

Vail, L., and L. White. 1980. *Capitalism and Colonialism in Mozambique: A Study of Quelimane District.* London: Heinemann.

_____. 1989. "Tribalism in Political History." In *The Creation of Tribalism in Southern Africa,* edited by L. Vail. London: James Currey; and Berkeley: University of California Press.

Vambe, L. 1972. *An Ill-Fated People.* London: Heinemann.

Van Allen, Judith. 1976. "'Aba Riots' of Igbo 'Women's War'? Ideology, Stratification and the Invisibility of Women." In *Women in Africa,* edited by N. Hafkin and E. Bay. Stanford: Stanford University Press.

Van Horn, L. 1977. "The Agricultural History of Barotseland, 1840–1964." In *The Roots of Rural Poverty in Central and Southern Africa,* edited by R. Palmer and N. Parsons. London: Heinemann.

van Onselen, C. 1976. *Chibaro: African Mine Labour in Southern Rhodesia, 1900–1933.* London: Pluto Press.

van Velsen, R. 1964. *The Politics of Kinship: A Study in Social Manipulation Among the Lakeside Tonga of Malawi.* Manchester: Manchester University Press.

Vaughan, M. 1987. *The Story of an African Famine: Gender and Famine in Twentieth-Century Malawi.* Cambridge: Cambridge University Press.

Weinrich, A.K.H. 1975. *African Farmers in Rhodesia.* Oxford: Oxford University Press.

_____. 1979. *Women and Racial Discrimination in Rhodesia.* Paris: UNESCO.

_____. 1982. *African Marriage in Zimbabwe.* Gweru and Harare: Mambo Press.

Weiss, R. 1994. *Zimbabwe and the New Elite.* London: I.B. Tauris.

Weissling, L. E. 1980. *Rural Development from Zambian Villagers' Perspectives.* Edmonton: University of Alberta.

Welch, G. H., F. Dagnino, and A. Sachs. 1985. "Transforming the Foundation of Family Law in the Mozambique Revolution." *Journal of Southern African Studies* 12(1):60–73.

Wells, J. 1995. "From Bondage to Breadwinner: The Evolution of Zimbabwean Women's Social Status over Three Generations." Paper presented at the annual meetings of the African Studies Association, Orlando, Florida, November 22–26.

Werbner, R. 1967. "Federal Administration, Rank and Civil Strife Among Bemba Royals and Nobles." *Africa* 37:22–49.

_____. 1991. *The Tears of the Dead: The Social Biography of an African Family.* Washington, DC: Smithsonian Institution Press.

Weyl, U., and D. Stilz. 1989. *CARD: An Analysis of Its Results, Strategy and Sustainability.* Masvingo: Belmont Press.

White, Landeg. 1987. *Magomero: Portrait of an African Village.* Cambridge: Cambridge University Press.

Wilson, G. 1951. "The Nyakyusa of South-Western Tanganyika." In *Seven Tribes of British Central Africa*, edited by E. Colson and M. Gluckman. London: Oxford University Press.

Wilson, M. 1957. *Rituals of Kinship Among the Nyakyusa.* London: Oxford University Press.

Women in Law in South Africa (WLSA). 1992. *Inheritance Law in Southern Africa.* Harare: WLSA.

Women's Action Group (WAG). 1985. *Women at Work: Report of the WAG Workshop.* Harare: WAG.

Women Voters Association of Zimbabwe (WOVAZ). 1995. "Objectives of the Association." In *Constitution.* Harare: WOVAZ.

Woods, T. 1992. "Nyau and the Construction of Gender in Nineteenth Century Malawi." Paper presented at the History Seminar Series, Chancellor College, University of Malawi, April.

World Bank. 1995. *The Public Sector and Poverty Reduction Options.* Harare: World Bank Mission.

Wright, M. 1983. "Technology, Marriage and Women's Work in the History of Maize-Growers in Mazabuka, Zambia: A Reconnaissance." *Journal of Southern African Studies* 10(1):71–85.

_____. 1993. *Strategies of Slaves and Women.* New York: L Barber Press.

Young, C. 1993. "The Dialectics of Cultural Pluralism: Concept and Reality." In *The Rising Tide of Cultural Pluralism: The Nation-State at Bay?* Madison: University of Wisconsin Press.

Young, S. 1977. "Fertility and Famine: Women's Agricultural History in Southern Mozambique." In *The Roots of Rural Poverty in Central and Southern Africa*, edited by R. Palmer and N. Parsons. London: Heinemann.

Zachrisson, P. 1978. "An African Area of Change: Belingme 1894–1946." *Bulletin of History* no. 17. Gothenburg: University of Gothenburg.

Zambian Association for Research and Development (ZARD). 1985. *Importance of Research in Developmental Issues Concerning Rural Women in Zambia.* Lusaka: ZARD.

Zwart, G. 1990. *Women's Issues in Agriculture.* Harare: World Bank Mission.

About the Book and Author

Based on extensive fieldwork, this study telescopes how lineage ideologies are constructed and change over time in the Zambezi River region, where matriliny and patriliny coexist. The author challenges the notion that patrilineality has subsumed matrilineal formations and demonstrates that despite colonial policies that privileged patrilineal gender relations of production—a preference that was extended by the postcolonial states—matrilineal relations of production have been adroitly sustained and even dominate in large parts of Malawi, northern Mozambique, and parts of Zambia and Zimbabwe. Looking specifically at the linkages between gender and ethnicity in the construction of lineage ideologies, the author offers a comparative study of women's changing status in the region and explores the implications for development policies at both the local and state levels.

Jean Davison is an independent consultant and president of the International Development and Education Association. She is the editor and author of *Agriculture, Women, and Land: The African Experience* (Westview 1988) and author of *Voices from Mutira: Change in the Lives of Rural Gikuyu Women, 1910–1995* (1996).

Index